Representative Essays,
English and American

Representative Essays, English and American

EDITED BY

JOHN ROBERT MOORE

Essay Index Reprint Series

BOOKS FOR LIBRARIES PRESS

FREEPORT, NEW YORK

First Published 1930
Reprinted 1972

Library of Congress Cataloging in Publication Data

Moore, John Robert, 1890-   ed.
    Representative essays, English and American.

    (Essay index reprint series)
    Reprint of the 1930 ed.
    Bibliography: p.
    1. English essays. 2. American essays. I. Title.
PR1362.M6 1972   824'.008   72-284
ISBN 0-8369-2808-3

PRINTED IN THE UNITED STATES OF AMERICA
BY
NEW WORLD BOOK MANUFACTURING CO., INC.
HALLANDALE, FLORIDA 33009

Preface

This volume is one of a group intended for a survey course in English literature. The selections included illustrate all the more important types of essays, so that the volume is adapted for use (1) in a study of literature by types or (2) in a course in the essay.

In this volume the introduction and the critical sketches are meant to afford enough background for an intelligent reading of the essays, and the bibliography has been planned to encourage a more extensive acquaintance with literature of this type. No attempt has been made to furnish new critical texts of most of the essays, but care has been exercised to avoid corrupt and unintelligible readings. In the older essays punctuation and spelling have been normalized wherever a change seemed desirable for the sake of clearness. In the footnotes it has been my purpose to answer such questions as those which have come up in my own classes — questions which editors too often pass over entirely or bury under a monument of details. I have endeavored throughout to enable the student to understand the essays in order that he may enjoy them.

A considerable number of the essays have not previously appeared in any present-day collection, and Professor Babbitt's fine essay is here reprinted for the first time from the magazine in which it appeared. But although I have sought for freshness in the selections, I have preferred significant and representative examples to the odd or the unfamiliar. In very few cases have I offered incomplete selections from longer works, and then only when the passages seemed entirely separable and independent.

The arrangement of essays by types not only emphasizes the historical development of the essay and the different character-

Preface

istics which it has acquired; it makes easy the study of contrasting examples of each type. The recent editorial essay by White is paralleled by an eighteenth-century editorial essay by Defoe; the sympathetic character essay on "A Child" by Earle is set off against the sarcastic humor of Butler's character of "A Romance Writer." It has not seemed practical to include in this volume such parallels for every individual type; but in each instance where parallel readings are not given they are suggested in the notes or in the bibliography.

The inclusion of American essays as well as English is due in part to the relative excellence of American writers of this literary form, and in part to the artificiality of national barriers in a study of the essay. Of our earlier essayists one was an elderly Pennsylvanian residing in France, another was a young Frenchman residing in New York, a third was a Scotchman traveling throughout the Northern, Eastern, and Southern states on horseback, by water, or on foot. Today the intermingling of national influences is even more marked. An essayist may be born in the United States and educated at Oxford, and he may be publishing his work in London and in New York.

J. R. M.

BLOOMINGTON, INDIANA

[iv]

Contents

Contents

Contents

[vii]

Contents

Introduction

1. *The Essay as an Intimate Expression.* Quite unlike the drama, which owes its existence and much of its character to public presentation and to the attitude of a social group, the essay is an intimate form of expression. It is primarily a personal communication from the author to his reader, or even from the author to the pages of his own notebook. Many of Addison's essays, although intended for use in a daily periodical, were written down privately in a commonplace book months in advance of actual publication; many of the essays of Montaigne and of Bacon were years in reaching the light of print; and the entry from the diary of Pepys which is included here, in essential respects a perfect little essay, was written down in a secret manuscript which only one or two other people ever saw during the author's lifetime, in a difficult shorthand code that was not deciphered and published until one hundred and fifty-eight years after this entry was made.

This intimacy of expression is perhaps the chief quality of essay style. The writer seems to be thinking aloud or to be talking over his inkstand at a single listener. No other modern writers have had personal followings quite like those of such essayists as Lamb or Stevenson. A large group of readers love not the books alone but the man who wrote them, and they regard the essays not as mere literary documents but as communications from a friend.

2. *Influence of the Method of Publication.* Intimate as it is, the essay is greatly affected by the conditions of its publication. The essays of Bacon, written at intervals for final appearance in book form and intended for aristocratic readers, made no effort to secure a wide contemporary circulation. They had a

Introduction

very real appeal to the readers for whom they were meant; but their great expansion and the development of a freer literary style in the third edition (1625) were due not to the demands of Bacon's readers but rather to a development in his own ideas and in his method. But even here the conscious desire for literary fame is evident: the third edition was soon afterwards issued (1628) in a Latin translation, to make sure, as the author said, "that the Latin volume of them (being in the universal language) may last as long as books last."

Quite different were the periodical essays of the eighteenth century. These were unsigned, and they were usually written in a certain tone or fashion, as if from the pen of an imaginary editor — Isaac Bickerstaff or Mr. Spectator or Nestor Ironside or the Rambler. Often a periodical would enlist the aid of several writers, but little or no effort was made to vary from the style adopted for the periodical. The best known of all these periodical essays appeared daily in the *Spectator* (1711–1712). Their length was limited by the single sheet on which each number was printed; their Puritan readers called for religious or moral discourses in many of the Saturday issues; their popular appeal among middle-class readers required a less aristocratic point of view than that of Bacon, an interest in such daily concerns as manners and morals rather than in the preparation of young noblemen for public affairs or for directing great estates; and when the heavy stamp tax reduced the circulation, it caused the eventual discontinuance of the periodical.

The literary magazines of the nineteenth century, with their greater space, gave an opportunity for longer articles; and these were usually signed, or, even if signed with a fictitious name, they were written in the author's own distinctive style and character. Their less frequent appearance gave the writers time for more careful thinking and more finished writing. In the reviews there was a certain uniformity of tone, so that one might speak of a "Quarterly" or an "Edinburgh" review. But the age of the personal essayist had arrived; literary styles and

[x]

Introduction

personalities as unlike each other as Lamb, Hazlitt, Hunt, and De Quincey were all admirably successful in different kinds of essays, and style and personality are a main feature of the work of each. In our own generation there is the increased importance of the daily newspaper (with its essayist's column) and of the volumes of essays by a single author (each volume often developing a fairly consistent view of life).

3. *The Essay not a Form, but a Point of View.* A distinguished critic has said of one type of poetry that "the ballad is form." Much the same thing might be said for the sonnet, the dramatic monologue, or the short story. But the essay has no fixed form. It is usually brief, it is written in prose, but it has almost no other restriction in regard to its manner. It may be written in the first person or in the third, or it may be addressed throughout to the reader in the second person. It may be in dialogue or in letter form; it may be narrative or expository in method; it may express a dream or an Oriental fantasy or an observation from a kitchen window; it may be strictly logical in substance, or it may consist of random musings with no attempt at organization.

The essential feature of the essay is *not its form but its point of view.* Its main characteristic is its observation and consideration of life. This is what one writer has called "its interpretative function," "its contemplative observation." There are all possible degrees of serious thought or of light fancy in the essay: one man's essays may, like Bacon's, "come home to men's business and bosoms," and another's may be a defense of nonsense, an apology for idlers, or a description of observed trifles.

It is probably true, however, that the essay, more than most forms of literature, tends to express the author's reflections on life. However light and whimsical may be the subject or the method, the writer is very likely to "moral on the time." As an intimate expression of the author's own thinking, the essay is likely to be peculiarly contemporary in its point of view. It is

[xi]

Introduction

quite characteristic that the essays of our own time are given to examining the tendencies of the age and are seeking a more perfect adjustment in human life.

4. *Definition of the Essay.* In modern usage a long and detailed dissertation on an abstract or a very difficult subject, such as Locke's "Essay concerning Human Understanding," is not regarded as a true essay of any sort. Nor can a critical or a philosophical poem, such as Pope's "Essay on Criticism" and his "Essay on Man," be justly considered in the modern sense of the word as an essay. If these were included in the class, we should have to regard a very large part of all didactic writings in prose or in verse as essays, and the term would be so general as to have no practical significance.

The essay originally implied something "essayed," or tried, a tentative study, stray jottings on a subject rather than a coherent composition, "certain brief notes," "grains of salt," or "an irregular, undigested piece." More and more has the term come to suggest exquisite finish of literary form, although even yet the essay is likely to leave its subject undecided — to stimulate interest rather than to settle an argument. It may be defined somewhat in this fashion: *An essay is a composition, usually brief and chiefly or altogether in prose, on any particular subject or branch of a subject, in which the purpose is interpretative and the style and the point of view are more or less adapted to the subject and to the author.* It has much in common with the short story: it can be read at a sitting, it deals with a single idea, and it makes a single impression or series of impressions.

5. *Forms of the Essay.* For more than a century past, since the decline of the experimental and specialized forms of the seventeenth and eighteenth centuries, essays have tended to divide fairly sharply into two main classes: the familiar and the formal, each with its own various subdivisions and kinds. The exact line of separation is not always easy to draw; some of the most characteristic familiar essays are written with a high seriousness, and some of the formal essays (such as those

Introduction

of Mencken) are enlivened throughout by the jingling bells of a jester. The difference between the formal and the familiar essay is as much a matter of artistic purpose and of the author's personality as of literary form or thought.

The scientific essay is often considered as a special type of the formal essay, but it is not so represented here. When a scientific essay is primarily a formal discussion of scientific principles, it may be fairly regarded as a philosophical or didactic essay; but when it is primarily an intimate record of man's observation of nature, it may be properly considered as a descriptive essay. The exact nomenclature is of little importance; the value of any such classification depends entirely on its practical usefulness — on the assistance it gives in understanding the spirit, the literary method, and the purpose of the writer.

6. *History of the Essay.* A brief historical sketch of the essay is peculiarly unsatisfactory for three reasons: general statements are likely to prove unsound because of the wide variations among individual writers; a detailed survey of the subject is likely to lead to a bewildering maze of names and dates; and it is impossible to deal at the same time with such unlike things as the extreme opposites to be found in familiar and formal essays.

For the careful student the bibliography contains references to the most useful histories of the different forms of the essay. For a less minute study the critical sketches prefixed to the sections of this volume will be found sufficient.

7. *Purpose of the Essay.* More than of any other form of literature, it may be said of the essay (as Sebastian Bach said of music) that "it is for the glory of God — and a very pleasant recreation."

There is a levity, a spirit of banter, running through the essay, from Montaigne to Morley. Such titles as "A Chapter on Ears," "On the Graces and Anxieties of Pig-Driving," "On Chasing One's Hat," and "Pigs as Pets" indicate that, however serious life may be, the essayist is not disposed to cry about it.

Introduction

I can recall no important essays with the lugubrious titles so familiar in a certain type of even the best poetry: "Stanzas Written in Dejection near Naples" or "Despondency, an Ode" or "Man was Made to Mourn."

It is true that a considerable number of essays deal with such subjects as "Youth and Old Age," "Death," or "Deaths of Little Children." But here the solemn reflections of the essayist are not the language of despair, and the sympathy of the essayist is not the sympathy of self-pity. Personal as it often is, the essay is too objective to be sentimental; too full of sunlight and the outer air to lend itself to the romantic man of feeling who looks sadly at human existence and exclaims,

> "For God's sake, let us sit upon the ground
> And tell sad stories of the death of kings."

The essay tends rather, like tragic drama, to purify the human heart by a contemplation of life — to

> Cleanse the stuff'd bosom of that perilous stuff
> Which weighs upon the heart.

But the essay rarely sounds the depths of human misery. Sometimes there is a sense of the littleness of men, as in Hazlitt's "Travelling Abroad"; sometimes pathos, as in Goldsmith's "A City Night Piece"; sometimes the onrush of a threatened doom, as in De Quincey's "The English Mail-Coach"; sometimes a deep emotion which is fraught with "the tears of things," as in Lamb's "Dream-Children." Still, the essayist is more disposed to smile than to weep, to exult than to despair. And often his observation of life is most clear from the loneliness of Walden, and often his joy of life is most keen from his death-awaiting refuge in the southern seas.

Representative Essays
English and American

The Aphoristic Essay

It is sometimes said that the essay is one of the newest of literary forms, not receiving its name or its essential character until the publication of Montaigne's "Essais" in France (1580) and of Bacon's thin first volume of "Essayes" in England (1597).

However, the essays of Montaigne and of Bacon are the result of a long development from the "wisdom" books of the Bible and from the dialogues, letters, maxims, and other reflective writings among the Greeks and the Romans. In the Middle Ages almost no progress toward the essay was made. Men of literary training were theological in their outlook on life; there was little individualism of expression, little interest in secular learning, and little of that gentle questioning about life which is the source of the essay.

With Montaigne, in France, we come upon a man steeped in the Renaissance love of learning and disposed to connect his readings with his own interpretation of things. Most of all, he was possessed of the qualities which have given rise to the familiar essay: a highly readable but somewhat rambling style, a fondness for observation and for the use of illustrations, a strong personality with a keen sense of the humor of life, and a rationalistic mind, which was disposed to weigh things instead of accepting surface values. Montaigne is still the greatest single influence in the familiar essay; wherever he is widely read, as in England at the beginning of the nineteenth century, the personal essay is likely to burst again into full flower.

In England the first man to use the name "essay" was Francis Bacon. Other seventeenth-century writers, such as Cornwallis and Cowley, owed far more to Montaigne than

The Aphoristic Essay

Bacon did. His work remained less personal than that of Montaigne, and it is less related to the familiar essay than to the "wisdom" books of the ancients. In his first volume (1597) his style is extremely terse and epigrammatic; and although his later volumes (1612 and 1625) were more freely written and more carefully elaborated, with most of his early essays completely rewritten in a fuller form, he remains best known as a writer of single sentences or aphorisms. He wrote for the young aristocrat anxious to prepare for success in "the great world" of public affairs; and his essays are largely made up of the learning of the Renaissance, with many quotations from great men and examples from the past. It is curiously instructive to compare the worldly aphorisms of Bacon with the glowing idealism in Emerson's essays; or to compare the appeal which Bacon made to the aristocratic young man with the homely proverbial philosophy which Benjamin Franklin wrote for young tradesmen, and with the broadly humorous but often very shrewd maxims of "Josh Billings" and other Americans who have entertained and instructed the masses.

Bacon has been pictured as a man who married for money and not for love, who sacrificed his friend and patron for his own advancement, who held the highest legal office and yet accepted bribes. He has also been pictured as the first modern mind, the philosopher and investigator who broke with the Middle Ages and founded modern science. It is not easy to understand human character; perhaps Bacon was something of most of these. His greatest fault was in his coldness, in his insensibility to human impulses of affection or loyalty or honor as opposed to self-interest and worldly prudence. His strength was in his calm observation, his ability to deal justly with facts and with himself. His contemporaries seem to have had this in mind when they erected as his monument a statue of judicial serenity, with the motto *Sic sedebat* ("So he sat"). He accepted bribes, as did other judges of his day; but even in his disgrace not one of his decisions was ever reversed.

[4]

The Aphoristic Essay

Bacon was the greatest English essayist of the seventeenth century, but he does not represent the main forward development in the familiar essay. Rather he is the greatest of the English writers of aphorisms, of wise and penetrating thoughts. The bulk of his essays is slight in comparison with that of his voluminous scientific writings; but in their terse and luminous flashes of insight, in their picture of the false ideals an' the virtues of his own age, they will be interesting to general readers who will never venture upon such volumes as "Novum Organum" and "De Augmentis Scientiarum."

SIR FRANCIS BACON

[1561–1626]

OF REVENGE

Revenge is a kind of wild justice; which the more man's nature runs to, the more ought law to weed it out. For as for the first wrong, it doth but offend the law; but the revenge of that wrong putteth the law out of office. Certainly, in taking revenge, a man is but even with his enemy; but in passing it over, he is superior, for it is a prince's part to pardon. And Solomon, I am sure, saith, "It is the glory of a man to pass by an offense."[1] That which is past is gone, and irrevocable; and wise men have enough to do with things present and to come; therefore they do but trifle with themselves, that labor in past matters. There is no man doth a wrong for the wrong's sake; but thereby to purchase himself profit, or pleasure, or honor, or the like. Therefore why should I be angry with a man for loving himself better than me? And if any man should do wrong merely out of ill-nature, why, yet it is but like the thorn or brier, which prick and scratch, because they can do no other. The most tolerable sort of revenge is for those wrongs which there is no law to remedy; but then let a man take heed the revenge be such as there is no law to punish, else a man's enemy is still beforehand, and it is two for one. Some, when they take revenge, are desirous the party should know whence it cometh. This is the more generous. For the delight seemeth to be not so much in doing the hurt as in making the party repent. But base and crafty cowards are like the arrow that flieth in the

[1] The discretion of a man deferreth his anger; and it is his glory to pass over a transgression. — Proverbs xix, 11

Sir Francis Bacon

dark. Cosmus,[1] duke of Florence, had a desperate saying against perfidious or neglecting friends, as if those wrongs were unpardonable: "You shall read," saith he, "that we are commanded to forgive our enemies; but you never read that we are commanded to forgive our friends." But yet the spirit of Job was in a better tune: "Shall we," saith he, "take good at God's hands, and not be content to take evil also?" And so of friends in a proportion. This is certain, that a man that studieth revenge keeps his own wounds green, which otherwise would heal and do well. Public revenges are for the most part fortunate, as that for the death of Cæsar[2]; for the death of Pertinax[3]; for the death of Henry the Third[4] of France; and many more. But in private revenges it is not so. Nay rather, vindictive persons live the life of witches; who, as they are mischievous, so end they infortunate.

OF MARRIAGE AND SINGLE LIFE

He that hath wife and children hath given hostages to fortune; for they are impediments to great enterprises, either of virtue or mischief. Certainly, the best works, and of greatest merit for the public, have proceeded from the unmarried or childless men, which both in affection and means have married and endowed the public. Yet it were great reason that those that have children should have greatest care of future times; unto which they know they must transmit their dearest pledges. Some there are, who though they lead a single life, yet their thoughts do end with themselves, and account future times impertinences. Nay, there are some other that account wife and children but as bills of charges. Nay more, there are some foolish rich covetous men that take a pride in having no children, because they may be thought so much the richer. For

[1] Cosmo (or Cosimo) de' Medici (1519–1574).
[2] Julius Cæsar, assassinated 44 B.C.
[3] A Roman emperor, murdered by the Prætorian Guards, 193 A.D.
[4] Assassinated in 1589.

The Aphoristic Essay

perhaps they have heard some talk, "Such an one is a great rich man," and another except to it, "Yea, but he hath a great charge of children"; as if it were an abatement to his riches. But the most ordinary cause of a single life is liberty; especially in certain self-pleasing and humorous[1] minds, which are so sensible of every restraint, as they will ᵼᵒ near to think their girdles and garters to be bonds and shackles. Unmarried men are best friends, best masters, best servants, but not always best subjects; for they are light to run away, and almost all fugitives are of that condition. A single life doth well with churchmen[2]; for charity will hardly water the ground where it must first fill a pool. It is indifferent for judges and magistrates; for if they be facile and corrupt, you shall have a servant five times worse than a wife. For soldiers, I find the generals commonly in their hortatives put men in mind of their wives and children; and I think the despising of marriage amongst the Turks maketh the vulgar soldier more base. Certainly wife and children are a kind of discipline of humanity; and single men, though they be many times more charitable, because their means are less exhaust,[3] yet, on the other side, they are more cruel and hardhearted (good to make severe inquisitors), because their tenderness is not so oft called upon. Grave natures, led by custom, and therefore constant, are commonly loving husbands; as was said of Ulysses, *Vetulam suam prætulit immortalitati*.[4] Chaste women are often proud and froward, as presuming upon the merit of their chastity. It is one of the best bonds both of chastity and obedience in the wife, if she think her husband wise; which she will never do if she find him jealous. Wives are young men's mistresses; companions for middle age; and old men's nurses. So as a man may have a quarrel[5] to marry when he will. But yet he was reputed one of the wise men,

---

[1] whimsical.　　　　　　[2] clergymen.　　　　　　[3] exhausted.
[4] "He preferred his aged wife to immortality." (The goddess Calypso had urged Ulysses to share her immortality instead of returning to Ithaca.)
[5] reason, excuse.

[8]

Sir Francis Bacon

that made answer to the question when a man should marry? "A young man not yet, an elder man not at all."[1] It is often seen that bad husbands have very good wives; whether it be that it raiseth the price of their husband's kindness when it comes, or that the wives take a pride in their patience. But this never fails, if the bad husbands were of their own choosing, against their friends' consent; for then they will be sure to make good their own folly.

OF BOLDNESS

It is a trivial grammar-school text, but yet worthy a wise man's consideration. Question was asked of Demosthenes,[2] "What was the chief part of an orator?" He answered "Action." What next? "Action." What next again? "Action." He said it that knew it best, and had by nature himself no advantage in that he commended. A strange thing, that that part of an orator which is but superficial, and rather the virtue of a player, should be placed so high above those other noble parts of invention, elocution, and the rest; nay, almost alone, as if it were all in all. But the reason is plain. There is in human nature generally more of the fool than of the wise; and therefore those faculties by which the foolish part of men's minds is taken are most potent. Wonderful like is the case of boldness in civil business: What first? "Boldness." What second and third? "Boldness." And yet boldness is a child of ignorance and baseness, far inferior to other parts. But nevertheless it doth fascinate and bind hand and foot those that are either shallow in judgment or weak in courage, which are the greatest part; yea, and prevaileth with wise men at weak times. Therefore we see it hath done wonders in popular[3] states, but with senates and princes less; and more ever upon the first entrance of bold persons into action than soon after; for boldness is an ill keeper

---

[1] A saying attributed to Thales (640–546 B.C.), one of the Seven Wise Men of Greece.

[2] The greatest Greek orator (384?–322 B.C.).   [3] democratic.

[9]

The Aphoristic Essay

of promise. Surely, as there are mountebanks[1] for the natural body, so are there mountebanks for the politic body; men that undertake great cures, and perhaps have been lucky in two or three experiments, but want the grounds[2] of science, and therefore cannot hold out. Nay, you shall see a bold fellow many times do Mahomet's miracle. Mahomet made the people believe that he would call an hill to him, and from the top of it offer up his prayers for the observers of his law. The people assembled; Mahomet called the hill to come to him, again and again; and when the hill stood still, he was never a whit abashed, but said, "If the hill will not come to Mahomet, Mahomet will go to the hill." So these men, when they have promised great matters and failed most shamefully, yet (if they have the perfection of boldness) they will but slight it over, and make a turn, and no more ado. Certainly, to men of great judgment, bold persons are a sport to behold; nay, and to the vulgar also, boldness hath somewhat of the ridiculous. For if absurdity be the subject of laughter, doubt you not but great boldness is seldom without some absurdity. Especially it is a sport to see, when a bold fellow is out of countenance, for that puts his face into a most shrunken and wooden posture, as needs it must; for in bashfulness the spirits do a little go and come, but with bold men, upon like occasion, they stand at a stay, like a stale[3] at chess, where it is no mate, but yet the game cannot stir. But this last were fitter for a satire than for a serious observation. This is well to be weighed, that boldness is ever blind; for it seeth not dangers and inconveniences. Therefore it is ill in counsel, good in execution; so that the right use of bold persons is, that they never command in chief, but be seconds, and under the direction of others. For in counsel it is good to see dangers; and in execution not to see them, except they be very great.

[1] Quack doctors (who mount benches to sell their wares).
[2] foundations.
[3] Stalemate, a situation in chess, where the king, not in check, must move, but cannot move except into check. The game is drawn.

Sir Francis Bacon

OF YOUTH AND AGE

A man that is young in years may be old in hours, if he have
lost no time. But that happeneth rarely. Generally, youth is
like the first cogitations, not so wise as the second. For there is
a youth in thoughts as well as in ages. And yet the invention
of young men is more lively than that of old; and imaginations stream into their minds better, and, as it were, more
divinely. Natures that have much heat, and great and violent
desires and perturbations, are not ripe for action till they have
passed the meridian of their years: as it was with Julius Cæsar
and Septimius Severus. Of the latter of whom it is said, *Juventu-
tem egit erroribus, imo furoribus, plenam.*[1] And yet he was the
ablest emperor, almost, of all the list. But reposed natures may
do well in youth. As it is seen in Augustus Cæsar, Cosmus,[2]
duke of Florence, Gaston de Foix,[3] and others. On the other
side, heat and vivacity in age is an excellent composition for
business. Young men are fitter to invent than to judge; fitter
for execution than for counsel; and fitter for new projects than
for settled business. For the experience of age, in things that
fall within the compass of it, directeth them; but in new things,
abuseth them. The errors of young men are the ruin of business;
but the errors of aged men amount but to this, that more might
have been done, or sooner. Young men, in the conduct and
manage[4] of actions, embrace more than they can hold; stir
more than they can quiet; fly to the end, without consideration
of the means and degrees; pursue some few principles which
they have chanced upon absurdly; care[5] not to innovate, which
draws unknown inconveniences; use extreme remedies at first;
and, that which doubleth all errors, will not acknowledge or
retract them, like an unready horse, that will neither stop nor
turn. Men of age object too much, consult too long, adventure

---

[1] "He spent his youth in errors, nay rather, it was full of madnesses."
[2] See the essay "Of Revenge," p. 7.
[3] A celebrated French general (1489–1512).   [4] management.   [5] hesitate.

The Aphoristic Essay

too little, repent too soon, and seldom drive business home to the full period, but content themselves with a mediocrity of success. Certainly, it is good to compound employments of both; for that will be good for the present, because the virtues of either age may correct the defects of both; and good for succession, that young men may be learners, while men in age are actors; and, lastly, good for extern[1] accidents, because authority followeth old men, and favor and popularity youth. But for the moral part, perhaps youth will have the preëminence, as age hath for the politic. A certain rabbin, upon the text "Your young men shall see visions, and your old men shall dream dreams,"[2] inferreth that young men are admitted nearer to God than old, because vision is a clearer revelation than a dream. And certainly, the more a man drinketh of the world, the more it intoxicateth; and age doth profit rather in the powers of understanding, than in the virtues of the will and affections. There be some have an over-early ripeness in their years, which fadeth betimes. These are, first, such as have brittle wits, the edge whereof is soon turned; such as was Hermogenes the rhetorician, whose books are exceeding subtle, who afterwards waxed stupid. A second sort is of those that have some natural dispositions which have better grace in youth than in age; such as is a fluent and luxuriant speech, which becomes youth well, but not age: so Tully[3] saith of Hortensius, *Idem manebat, neque idem decebat.*[4] The third is of such as take too high a strain at the first, and are magnanimous more than tract of years can uphold. As was Scipio Africanus, of whom Livy saith in effect, *Ultima primis cedebant.*[5]

---

[1] external. [2] Joel ii, 28.
[3] Marcus Tullius Cicero (106–43 B.C.), Roman orator.
[4] "He remained the same, but the same was no longer becoming."
[5] "His latter days fell short of the first."

Sir Francis Bacon

OF BEAUTY

Virtue is like a rich stone, best plain set; and surely virtue is best in a body that is comely, though not of delicate features; and that hath rather dignity of presence than beauty of aspect. Neither is it almost[1] seen, that very beautiful persons are otherwise of great virtue; as if nature were rather busy not to err, than in labor to produce excellency. And therefore they prove accomplished, but not of great spirit; and study rather behavior than virtue. But this holds not always: for Augustus Cæsar, Titus Vespasianus, Philip le Bel of France, Edward the Fourth of England, Alcibiades of Athens, Ismael the Sophy of Persia, were all high and great spirits; and yet the most beautiful men of their times. In beauty, that of favor[2] is more than that of color; and that of decent and gracious motion more than that of favor. That is the best part of beauty, which a picture cannot express; no, nor the first sight of the life. There is no excellent beauty that hath not some strangeness in the proportion. A man cannot tell whether Apelles[3] or Albert Dürer[4] were the more trifler; whereof the one would make a personage by geometrical proportions; the other, by taking the best parts out of divers[5] faces, to make one excellent. Such personages, I think, would please nobody but the painter that made them. Not but I think a painter may make a better face than ever was; but he must do it by a kind of felicity (as a musician that maketh an excellent air in music), and not by rule. A man shall see faces, that if you examine them part by part, you shall find never a good; and yet altogether do well. If it be true that the principal part of beauty is in decent motion, certainly it is no marvel though persons in years seem many times more amiable; *pulchrorum autumnus pulcher*[6]; for no youth can be comely

[1] for the most part.　　　[2] looks.
[3] Apelles, a Greek painter of the fourth century B.C.
[4] Dürer (1471–1528) was a German painter and engraver.
[5] several.　　[6] "The autumn of the beautiful is beautiful."

but by pardon, and considering the youth as to make up the comeliness. Beauty is as summer fruits, which are easy to corrupt, and cannot last; and for the most part it makes a dissolute youth, and an age a little out of countenance; but yet certainly again, if it light well, it maketh virtue shine, and vices blush.

OF STUDIES

Studies serve for delight, for ornament, and for ability. Their chief use for delight is in privateness and retiring; for ornament, is in discourse; and for ability, is in the judgment and disposition of business. For expert men can execute, and perhaps judge of particulars, one by one; but the general counsels, and the plots and marshaling of affairs, come best from those that are learned. To spend too much time in studies is sloth; to use them too much for ornament is affectation; to make judgment wholly by their rules is the humor of a scholar. They perfect nature, and are perfected by experience; for natural abilities are like natural plants, that need pruning by study; and studies themselves do give forth directions too much at large, except they be bounded in by experience. Crafty men contemn studies, simple men admire them, and wise men use them, for they teach not their own use: but that is a wisdom without them and above them, won by observation. Read not to contradict and confute; nor to believe and take for granted; nor to find talk and discourse; but to weigh and consider. Some books are to be tasted, others to be swallowed, and some few to be chewed and digested; that is, some books are to be read only in parts; others to be read, but not curiously[1]; and some few to be read wholly, and with diligence and attention. Some books also may be read by deputy, and extracts made of them by others; but that would be only in the less important arguments, and the meaner sort of books; else distilled books are like common distilled waters, flashy[2] things. Reading maketh a full man; con-

[1] attentively. [2] insipid, tasteless.

Sir Francis Bacon

ference a ready man; and writing an exact man. And therefore, if a man write little, he had need have a great memory; if he confer little, he had need have a present wit; and if he read little, he had need have much cunning, to seem to know that he doth not. Histories make men wise; poets witty; the mathematics subtle; natural philosophy deep; moral grave; logic and rhetoric able to contend. *Abeunt studia in mores.*[1] Nay, there is no stond[2] or impediment in the wit, but may be wrought out by fit studies: like as diseases of the body may have appropriate exercises. Bowling is good for the stone and reins[3]; shooting, for the lungs and breast; gentle walking, for the stomach; riding, for the head; and the like. So if a man's wit be wandering, let him study the mathematics; for in demonstrations, if his wit be called away never so little, he must begin again. If his wit be not apt to distinguish or find differences, let him study the schoolmen; for they are *cymini sectores.*[4] If he be not apt to beat over matters, and to call one thing to prove and illustrate another, let him study the lawyers' cases. So every defect of the mind may have a special receipt.

[1] "Studies develop into manners."
[2] hindrance.
[3] the loins; the kidneys.
[4] "splitters of cumin" (hairsplitters).

Seventeenth-Century Characters

There are three distinct stages in the development of the "character" essay.

1. The Greek writer Theophrastus (fourth century B. C.) had sketched twenty-eight human qualities, representing these abstractions by typical actions. In 1592 a French scholar translated these "characters" from Greek into the more familiar Latin language, and they became the model for all English writers of "characters" during the seventeenth century. The people described were not named and were not individualized, but remained as examples of various qualities and types of human nature. In the hands of the court wits the "character" became a thing of paradox and wit; in Earle's writings it was keenly observant of the small details of life; with Butler it was bitterly satirical.

2. A French writer, La Bruyère, extended the idea by giving to his characters names (of Greek or Latin origin, but still suggesting something of individuality). He also added concrete details until he gave the impression of writing about characters who were typical, but nevertheless real, individuals. "Les Caractères" (1688) was widely known in England, and was translated into English in 1699. In addition, pamphleteers of the day seized on the idea of naming and characterizing the supposed authors of their own pamphlets. Swift, for instance, professed that his satires against an astrologer were the work of a rival astrologer, one Isaac Bickerstaff, Esq. This name became immediately popular and was widely used; Steele represented Bickerstaff as the editor of the *Tatler* papers, and Bickerstaff was represented in contemporary pictures as an old gentleman sitting in his study among his instruments and books.

[17]

Seventeenth-Century Characters

3. The third step, in the eighteenth-century periodicals, was that of giving these characters a world to live in by the creation of clubs of such personages. At first the characters in these clubs were highly generalized; in the Spectator Club, for example, Captain Sentry was the soldier, Sir Andrew Freeport the merchant, and Sir Roger de Coverley (named for an old country dance) the country gentleman. But this was not for long; Sir Roger de Coverley grew out of the rigid frame in which he was placed, and became one of the most beloved individuals in literature. The same movement toward individuality of character portrayal continued in the novel, in the drama, and in some of the poetry, as well as in the essay. Eighteenth-century literature is largely devoted to the portrayal of types; but these types were afterwards so vividly conceived that many of them, such as Uncle Toby and Parson Adams and Dr. Primrose,[1] are among the supreme artistic creations of the English language.

Examples of the later portrayal of characters will be found in the periodical essays of the eighteenth century. The selections given here from Earle and Butler illustrate the earlier stage of character-writing, before the figures were given individual names.

[1] Three characters in eighteenth-century novels. Uncle Toby occurs in "Tristram Shandy," by Sterne; Parson Adams in "Joseph Andrews," by Fielding; Dr. Primrose in "The Vicar of Wakefield," by Goldsmith.

JOHN EARLE

[1601–1665]

A CHILD[1]

Is a man in a small letter, yet the best copy of Adam before he tasted of Eve or the apple; and he is happy whose small practice in the world can only write this character. He is nature's fresh picture newly drawn in oil, which time and much handling dims and defaces. His soul is yet a white paper unscribbled with observations of the world, wherewith at length it becomes a blurred notebook. He is purely happy, because he knows no evil, nor hath made means by sin to be acquainted with misery. He arrives not at the mischief of being wise, nor endures evils to come by foreseeing them. He kisses and loves all, and when the smart of the rod is past, smiles on his beater. Nature and his parents alike dandle him, and tice him on with a bait of sugar to a draft of wormwood. He plays yet, like a young prentice the first day, and is not come to his task of melancholy. All the language he speaks yet is tears, and they serve him well enough to express his necessity.[2] His hardest labor is his tongue, as if he were loath to use so deceitful an organ; and he is best company with it when he can but prattle. We laugh at his foolish sports, but his game is our earnest: and his drums, rattles, and hobbyhorses, but the emblems and mocking of man's business. His father hath writ him as his own little story, wherein he reads those days of his life that he cannot remember, and sighs to see what innocence he has outlived. The elder he grows, he is a stair lower from God; and, like his first

---

[1] From "Microcosmographie" (1628).
[2] This sentence is not in the first edition.

father, much worse in his breeches.[1] He is the Christian's example, and the old man's relapse; the one imitates his pureness, and the other falls into his simplicity. Could he put off his body with his little coat, he had got eternity without a burden, and exchanged but one heaven for another.

[1] Like Adam, who, in the words of the old Geneva Bible, did not "make himself breeches" until after he had sinned.

SAMUEL BUTLER

[1612–1680]

A ROMANCE WRITER[1]

Pulls down old histories to build them up finer again, after a new model of his own designing. He takes away all the lights of truth in history to make it the fitter tutoress of life; for Truth herself has little or nothing to do in the affairs of the world, although all matters of the greatest weight and moment are pretended and done in her name, like a weak princess that has only the title, and falsehood all the power. He observes one very fit decorum in dating his histories in the days of old and putting all his own inventions upon ancient times; for when the world was younger, it might perhaps love and fight and do generous things at the rate he describes them; but since it is grown old, all these heroic feats are laid by and utterly given over, nor ever like to come in fashion again; and therefore all his images of those virtues signify no more than the statues upon dead men's tombs, that will never make them live again. He is like one of Homer's gods, that sets men together by the ears and fetches them off again how he pleases; brings armies into the field like Janello's[2] leaden soldiers; leads up both sides himself, and gives the victory to which he pleases, according as he finds it fit the design of his story; makes love and lovers too, brings them acquainted, and appoints meetings when and where he pleases, and at the same time betrays them in the

[1] From "Characters," first published from Butler's manuscript in 1759.
[2] According to Robert Thyer, the first editor of Butler's miscellaneous writings (1759), Janello is referred to by Butler in another passage as a famous puppet master.

height of all their felicity to miserable captivity, or some other horrid calamity; for which he makes them rail at the gods and curse their own innocent stars when he only has done them all the injury; makes men villains, compels them to act all barbarous inhumanities by his own directions, and after inflicts the cruelest punishments upon them for it. He makes all his knights fight in fortifications, and storm one another's armor before they can come to encounter body for body, and always matches them so equally one with another that it is a whole page before they can guess which is likely to have the better; and he that has it is so mangled that it had been better for them both to have parted fair at first; but when they encounter with those that are no knights, though ever so well armed and mounted, ten to one goes for nothing. As for the ladies, they are every one the most beautiful in the whole world, and that's the reason why no one of them, nor all together with all their charms, have power to tempt away any knight from another. He differs from a just historian as a joiner does from a carpenter : the one does things plainly and substantially for use, and the other carves and polishes merely for show and ornament.

The Periodical Essay

The essential features of the periodical essays of the eighteenth century arose from the conditions of their publication and from the special abilities and interests of four remarkable writers: Steele, Addison, Johnson, and Goldsmith.

The periodicals were intended for middle-class readers primarily — the newly arrived merchant class, themselves descended from the Puritans of the previous century. This accounts for the Saturday discourses on moral and religious themes; for the attacks on dueling and heavy drinking, on fans and face patches; for the interest in education and religious worship, in marriage and public morals; and for the cautious tone with regard to literature, and the rather hesitant use of classical allusions, as if the writer were conscious of being on ground unfamiliar to the readers.

They were intended for a much wider reading public than the seventeenth-century volumes of essays had been, and for women as well as for men. This accounts for the usual avoidance of political subjects through fear of giving offense, for the gradual dropping out of all topics which had little general appeal or which could not be treated in a pleasing way, and for the great emphasis on social interests and especially on the concerns of women. Swift turned away from Steele in disgust at last, writing in his journal, "Let him fair sex it to the end of the world." But there is every reason to suppose that the skill of Steele and Addison in enlisting the interest of women readers accounted for much of the success of the *Tatler* and the *Spectator*.

They were issued once, twice, or three times a week (the *Spectator* daily except Sunday) on a single sheet; and this determined the approximate length of an essay. *The Tatler*

[23]

The Periodical Essay

began by printing several short sections devoted to news of various kinds, supposedly written in different parts of London; but it eventually adopted the method of having a single essay in each number, and this practice became usual in the later periodicals. "The Citizen of the World," like a few other series of essays, was published serially as a contribution to a periodical, not on a separate sheet as an independent project.

The frequent appearance of the essays and, with it, the urgent need of interesting many readers made variety necessary. Not only were contributions from other hands accepted, especially in the *Spectator* and the *Guardian*, and not only were all the older essay subjects developed more fully (such as the "characters" and the reflections on abstract subjects), but a considerable number of new types of essays were developed. There were early attempts at short stories, letters and stories of real life, the newly popular Oriental tales and allegories, literary criticisms, poems, social satire, and serious efforts at moral reform. In many ways the periodicals seem surprisingly modern; they carried some advertisements, they not infrequently left stories to be continued in the next issue, and (especially in the *Tatler*) they worked hard to arouse public indignation by a series of articles dealing with the same wrong.

Of the four principal writers, Steele had most originality and most initiative; he was the business man of the *Tatler* and the *Spectator*, and he began more enterprises than all the others together. He was also a man of very genuine humanitarian interests, apparently writing from his own heart when he espoused a public cause. His interest in politics was so strong that it hampered his work as a literary essayist. Addison was a finer literary artist, was more systematic and more steady in his work, and had more learning, a more perfect style, and a keener sense of humor. He was so perfectly a man of his own age that his charm has faded a little; some of the moral essays which were most highly prized seem cold and lifeless today. But it was Addison who finished the portraits of the Spectator Club which

The Periodical Essay

Steele had begun rather baldly, and Sir Roger de Coverley is virtually his original creation. Of the four, Johnson achieved perhaps least success in current periodicals; but the *Rambler*, when reissued in book form, had a profound influence for at least two generations afterwards. It afforded probably the most popular statement of moral philosophy during the century. Johnson could be humorous when he chose, especially in his riper years; his conversation in private life displayed a wealth of humor which far surpasses the polite and somewhat thin vein of Addison, but in his essays he usually appears as the "periodical mentor." To many readers Goldsmith is the most charming of the four. He had something of the humanitarian interests of Steele and of Johnson, something of the shrewd critical sagacity of Johnson, and more than Addison's humor and gift of style.

Each of these writers had a share in other periodical ventures than those which are represented here, and the vogue of the periodical essay throughout the century is difficult to conceive. Professor Crane has stated that two hundred and twenty such ventures had been undertaken in London or other cities of the British Isles by 1809.

Two other authors whose essays are here represented call for special mention. "The Short Club" is a very good-natured skit by Alexander Pope, himself one of the shortest of men and not always as good-natured as he appears in this composition. The essay by Lord Chesterfield is the somewhat aloof and superior moralizing of a very rich and very fashionable nobleman writing for the *World*, a magazine whose contributors were men of wealth and social distinction. *The World* achieved great popularity, partly on account of the aristocratic names of its contributors; but it is the only periodical represented here which is consciously aimed at readers above the merchant class.

[25]

THE TATLER

[1709–1711]

A CURE FOR FITS IN MARRIED LADIES

No. 23. Thursday, June 2, 1709. [By STEELE]

Quicquid agunt homines . . . nostri est farrago libelli.[1] — JUVENAL

WHITE'S CHOCOLATE-HOUSE, May 31

The generality of mankind are so very fond of this world, and of staying in it, that a man cannot have eminent skill in any one art but they will, in spite of his teeth, make him a physician also, that being the science the worldlings have most need of. I pretended, when I first set up, to astrology only; but I am told I have deep skill also in medicine. I am applied to now by a gentleman for my advice in behalf of his wife, who, upon the least matrimonial difficulty, is excessively troubled with fits, and can bear no manner of passion without falling into immediate convulsions. I must confess it is a case I have known before, and remember the party was recovered by certain words pronounced in the midst of the fit by the learned doctor who performed the cure. These ails have usually their beginning from the affections of the mind; therefore you must have patience to let me give you an instance, whereby you may discern the cause of the distemper, and then proceed in the cure as follows:

A fine town-lady was married to a gentleman of ancient descent in one of the counties of Great Britain, who had good

---

[1] "Whatever men do is fodder for our booklet" (Juvenal, "Satires," I, 85, 86). This motto was repeated at the head of each of the first forty numbers in the folio issue.

[26]

humor to a weakness, and was the sort of person of whom it
is usually said, he is no man's enemy but his own: one who
had too much tenderness of soul to have any authority with his
wife; and she had too little sense to give him any authority,
for that reason. His kind wife observed this temper in him and
made proper use of it. But knowing it was below a gentlewoman to wrangle, she resolved upon an expedient to save
decorum, and wear her dear to her point at the same time. She
therefore took upon her to govern him by falling into fits whenever she was repulsed in a request or contradicted in a discourse.
It was a fish day when, in the midst of her husband's good
humor at table, she bethought herself to try her project. She
made signs that she had swallowed a bone. The man grew pale
as ashes, and ran to her assistance, calling for drink. "No, my
dear," said she, recovering, "it is down; do not be frightened."
This accident betrayed his softness enough. The next day she
complained a lady's chariot, whose husband had not half his
estate, had a crane-neck and hung with twice the air that hers
did. He answered, "Madam, you know my income; you know
I lost two coach horses this spring." — Down she fell — "Hartshorn! Betty, Susan, Alice, throw water in her face." With
much care and pains she was brought to herself, and the vehicle
in which she visited was amended in the nicest manner, to prevent relapses; but they frequently happened during that husband's whole life, which he had the good fortune to end in a few
years after. The disconsolate soon pitched upon a very agreeable successor, whom she very prudently designed to govern by
the same method. This man knew her little arts, and resolved to
break through all tenderness and be absolute master as soon as
occasion offered. One day it happened that a discourse arose
about furniture. He was very glad of the occasion, and fell into
an invective against china, protesting he would never let five
pounds more of his money be laid out that way as long as he
breathed. She immediately fainted — he starts up as amazed,
and calls for help — the maids run to the closet. He chafes her

[27]

The Periodical Essay

face, bends her forward, and beats the palms of her hands; her convulsions increase, and down she tumbles on the floor, where she lies quite dead, in spite of what the whole family, from the nursery to the kitchen, could do for her relief.

While every servant was thus helping or lamenting their mistress, he, fixing his cheek to hers, seemed to be following in a trance of sorrow; but secretly whispers her, "My dear, this will never do; what is within my power and fortune, you may always command; but none of your artifices; you are quite in other hands than those you passed these pretty passions upon." This made her almost in the condition she pretended; her convulsions now came thicker, nor was she to be held down. The kind man doubles his care, helps the servants to throw water in her face by full quarts; and when the sinking part of the fit came again: "Well, my dear," said he, "I applaud your action, but I must take my leave of you until you are more sincere with me. Farewell forever; you shall always know where to hear of me, and want for nothing." With that, he ordered the maids to keep plying her with hartshorn, while he went for a physician; he was scarce at the stairhead when she followed, and, pulling him into a closet, thanked him for her cure, which was so absolute that she gave me this relation herself, to be communicated for the benefit of all the voluntary invalids of her sex.

FROZEN WORDS

No. 254. Thursday, November 23, 1710. [By ADDISON and STEELE]

Splendide mendax.[1] — HORACE

MY OWN APARTMENT, November 22

There are no books which I more delight in than in travels, especially those that describe remote countries, and give the writer an opportunity of showing his parts without incurring

[1] "Gloriously false" (Horace, "Odes," III, xi, 35).

[28]

The Tatler

any danger of being examined or contradicted. Among all the authors of this kind, our renowned countryman Sir John Mandeville[1] has distinguished himself by the copiousness of his invention and the greatness of his genius. The second to Sir John I take to have been Ferdinand Mendez Pinto,[2] a person of infinite adventure and unbounded imagination. One reads the voyages of these two great wits with as much astonishment as the travels of Ulysses in Homer, or of the Red-Cross Knight in Spenser. All is enchanted ground and fairyland.

I have got into my hands, by great chance, several manuscripts of these two eminent authors, which are filled with greater wonders than any of those they have communicated to the public; and indeed, were they not so well attested, they would appear altogether improbable. I am apt to think the ingenious authors did not publish them with the rest of their works, lest they should pass for fictions and fables: a caution not unnecessary, when the reputation of their veracity was not yet established in the world. But as this reason has now no farther weight, I shall make the public a present of these curious pieces, at such times as I shall find myself unprovided with other subjects.

The present paper I intend to fill with an extract from Sir John's Journal, in which that learned and worthy knight gives an account of the freezing and thawing of several short speeches which he made in the territories of Nova Zembla.[3] I need not inform my reader, that the author of "Hudibras"[4] alludes to this strange quality in that cold climate, when, speaking of abstracted notions clothed in a visible shape, he adds that apt simile,

Like words congealed in northern air.

[1] The supposed travels of Sir John Mandeville are regarded as a fictitious narrative by a French writer, Jehan de Bourgogne, who died in 1372.
[2] The account of the adventures of this Portuguese traveler was published in 1614.   [3] A group of Arctic islands north of Russia.
[4] A satiric poem by Samuel Butler; the quotation is from Part I, Canto i, 148.

The Periodical Essay

Not to keep my reader any longer in suspense, the relation put into modern language is as follows:

We were separated by a storm in the latitude of seventy-three, insomuch, that only the ship which I was in, with a Dutch and French vessel, got safe into a creek of Nova Zembla. We landed, in order to refit our vessels, and store ourselves with provisions. The crew of each vessel made themselves a cabin of turf and wood, at some distance from each other, to fence themselves against the inclemencies of the weather, which was severe beyond imagination. We soon observed, that in talking to one another we lost several of our words, and could not hear one another at above two yards' distance, and that too when we sat very near the fire. After much perplexity, I found that our words froze in the air before they could reach the ears of the persons to whom they were spoken. I was soon confirmed in this conjecture, when, upon the increase of the cold, the whole company grew dumb, or rather deaf; for every man was sensible, as we afterwards found, that he spoke as well as ever, but the sounds no sooner took air than they were condensed and lost. It was now a miserable spectacle to see us nodding and gaping at one another, every man talking, and no man heard. One might observe a seaman that could hail a ship at a league's distance, beckoning with his hand, straining his lungs, and tearing his throat; but all in vain.

Nec vox nec verba sequuntur.[1]

We continued here three weeks in this dismal plight. At length, upon a turn of wind, the air about us began to thaw. Our cabin was immediately filled with a dry clattering sound, which I afterwards found to be the crackling of consonants that broke above our heads, and were often mixed with a gentle hissing, which I imputed to the letter *s*, that occurs so frequently in the English tongue. I soon after felt a breeze of whispers rushing by my ear; for those, being of a soft and gentle substance, immediately liquefied in the warm wind that blew across our cabin. These were soon followed by syllables and short words, and at length by entire sentences, that melted sooner or later, as they were more or less congealed; so that we now heard everything that had been *spoken* during the whole three weeks that

[1] "Nor voice, nor words ensue" (Ovid, "Metamorphoses," XI, 326).

[30]

we had been *silent*, if I may use that expression. It was now very early in the morning, and yet, to my surprise, I heard somebody say, "Sir John, it is midnight, and time for the ship's crew to go to bed." This I knew to be the pilot's voice; and, upon recollecting myself, I concluded that he had spoken these words to me some days before, though I could not hear them until the present thaw. My reader will easily imagine how the whole crew was amazed to hear every man talking, and see no man opening his mouth. In the midst of this great surprise we were all in, we heard a volley of oaths and curses, lasting for a long while, and uttered in a very hoarse voice which I knew belonged to the boatswain, who was a very choleric fellow, and had taken his opportunity of cursing and swearing at me when he thought I could not hear him; for I had several times given him the strappado on that account, as I did not fail to repeat it for these his pious soliloquies, when I got him on shipboard.

I must not omit the names of several beauties in Wapping,[1] which were heard every now and then, in the midst of a long sigh that accompanied them; as, "Dear Kate!" "Pretty Mrs. Peggy!" "When shall I see my Sue again!" This betrayed several amours which had been concealed until that time, and furnished us with a great deal of mirth in our return to England.

When this confusion of voices was pretty well over, though I was afraid to offer at speaking, as fearing I should not be heard, I proposed a visit to the Dutch cabin, which lay about a mile farther up in the country. My crew were extremely rejoiced to find they had again recovered their hearing; though every man uttered his voice with the same apprehensions that I had done,

Et timide verba intermissa retentat.[2]

At about half a mile's distance from our cabin we heard the groanings of a bear, which at first startled us; but upon inquiry we were informed by some of our company that he was dead, and now lay in salt, having been killed upon that very spot about a fortnight before,

---

[1] A riverside district in the eastern part of London, south of London Docks. Nine years before this essay was written Captain Kidd was hanged at Execution Dock in Wapping.

[2] "And timidly attempts again interrupted words" (Ovid, "Metamorphoses," I, 746).

in the time of the frost. Not far from the same place we were like-wise entertained with some posthumous snarls and barkings of a fox.

We at length arrived at the little Dutch settlement; and, upon entering the room, found it filled with sighs that smelled of brandy, and several other unsavory sounds, that were altogether inarticulate. My valet, who was an Irishman, fell into so great a rage at what he heard that he drew his sword; but not knowing where to lay the blame, he put it up again. We were stunned with these confused noises, but did not hear a single word until about half an hour after; which I ascribed to the harsh and obdurate sounds of that language, which wanted more time than ours to melt and become audible.

After having here met with a very hearty welcome, we went to the cabin of the French, who, to make amends for their three weeks' silence, were talking and disputing with greater rapidity and con-fusion than I ever heard in an assembly, even of that nation. Their language, as I found, upon the first giving of the weather, fell asunder and dissolved. I was here convinced of an error, into which I had before fallen; for I fancied, that for the freezing of the sound, it was necessary for it to be wrapped up and, as it were, preserved in breath; but I found my mistake when I heard the sound of a kit[1] playing a minuet over our heads. I asked the occasion of it; upon which one of the company told me that it would play there above a week longer; "for," says he, "finding ourselves bereft of speech, we prevailed upon one of the company, who had his musical instrument about him, to play to us from morning to night; all which time was employed in dancing in order to dissipate our chagrin, *et tuer le temps*."[2]

Here Sir John gives very good philosophical reasons why the kit could not be heard during the frost; but, as they are some-thing prolix, I pass them over in silence, and shall only observe, that the honorable author seems, by his quotations, to have been well versed in the ancient poets, which perhaps raised his fancy above the ordinary pitch of historians and very much contributed to the embellishment of his writings.

[1] A small violin with three strings, commonly used by a dancing master.
[2] "and to kill time."

THE SPECTATOR

[1711–1712]

SIR ROGER AT CHURCH

No. 112. Monday, July 9, 1711. [By ADDISON]

Ἀθανάτους μὲν πρῶτα θεούς, νόμῳ ὡς διάκειται, Τίμα.[1] — PYTHAGORAS

I am always very well pleased with a country Sunday, and think, if keeping holy the seventh day were only a human institution, it would be the best method that could have been thought of for the polishing and civilizing of mankind. It is certain the country people would soon degenerate into a kind of savages and barbarians were there not such frequent returns of a stated time, in which the whole village meet together with their best faces, and in their cleanliest habits, to converse with one another upon indifferent subjects, hear their duties explained to them, and join together in adoration of the Supreme Being. Sunday clears away the rust of the whole week, not only as it refreshes in their minds the notions of religion, but as it puts both the sexes upon appearing in their most agreeable forms and exerting all such qualities as are apt to give them a figure in the eye of the village. A country fellow distinguishes himself as much in the churchyard as a citizen does upon the 'Change, the whole parish politics being generally discussed in that place either after sermon or before the bell rings.

My friend Sir Roger, being a good churchman, has beautified the inside of his church with several texts of his own choosing; he has likewise given a handsome pulpit cloth, and railed in the communion table at his own expense. He has often told

---

[1] " First reverence the immortal gods, as custom decrees."

[33]

me that, at his coming to his estate, he found his parishioners very irregular; and that, in order to make them kneel and join in the responses, he gave every one of them a hassock and a common-prayer book, and at the same time employed an itinerant singing master, who goes about the country for that purpose, to instruct them rightly in the tunes of the psalms; upon which they now very much value themselves, and, indeed, outdo most of the country churches that I have ever heard.

As Sir Roger is landlord to the whole congregation, he keeps them in very good order, and will suffer nobody to sleep in it besides himself; for if by chance he has been surprised into a short nap at sermon, upon recovering out of it he stands up and looks about him, and if he sees anybody else nodding, either wakes them himself or sends his servant to them. Several other of the old knight's particularities break out upon these occasions; sometimes he will be lengthening out a verse in the singing-psalms half a minute after the rest of the congregation have done with it; sometimes, when he is pleased with the matter of his devotion, he pronounces "Amen" three or four times to the same prayer; and sometimes stands up when everybody else is upon their knees, to count the congregation or see if any of his tenants are missing.

I was yesterday very much surprised to hear my old friend, in the midst of the service, calling out to one John Matthews to mind what he was about, and not disturb the congregation. This John Matthews, it seems, is remarkable for being an idle fellow, and at that time was kicking his heels for his diversion. This authority of the knight, though exerted in that odd manner which accompanies him in all circumstances of life, has a very good effect upon the parish, who are not polite enough to see anything ridiculous in his behavior; besides that the general good sense and worthiness of his character makes his friends observe these little singularities as foils that rather set off than blemish his good qualities.

As soon as the sermon is finished, nobody presumes to stir till Sir Roger is gone out of the church. The knight walks down from his seat in the chancel between a double row of his tenants, that stand bowing to him on each side, and every now and then inquires how such an one's wife, or mother, or son, or father do, whom he does not see at church, which is understood as a secret reprimand to the person that is absent.

The chaplain has often told me that, upon a catechizing day, when Sir Roger had been pleased with a boy that answers well, he has ordered a Bible to be given him next day for his encouragement, and sometimes accompanies it with a flitch of bacon to his mother. Sir Roger has likewise added five pounds a year to the clerk's place; and, that he may encourage the young fellows to make themselves perfect in the church service, has promised, upon the death of the present incumbent, who is very old, to bestow it according to merit.[1]

The fair understanding between Sir Roger and his chaplain, and their mutual concurrence in doing good, is the more remarkable because the very next village is famous for the differences and contentions that rise between the parson and the squire, who live in a perpetual state of war. The parson is always preaching at the squire, and the squire, to be revenged on the parson, never comes to church. The squire has made all his tenants atheists and tithe-stealers[2]; while the parson instructs them every Sunday in the dignity of his order, and insinuates to them in almost every sermon that he is a better man than his patron. In short, matters are come to such an extremity that the squire has not said his prayers either in public or private this half year; and that the parson threatens him, if he does not mend his manners, to pray for him in the face of the whole congregation.

[1] Such appointments were usually awarded as a matter of personal patronage, not by merit.

[2] Withholders of the tithes, or taxes for clergy and church.

The Periodical Essay

Feuds of this nature, though too frequent in the country, are very fatal to the ordinary people, who are so used to be dazzled with riches that they pay as much deference to the understanding of a man of an estate as of a man of learning; and are very hardly brought to regard any truth, how important soever it may be, that is preached to them, when they know there are several men of five hundred a year [1] who do not believe it.

A HUNTING SCENE WITH SIR ROGER

No. 116. Friday, July 13, 1711. [By BUDGELL]

Vocat ingenti clamore Cithaeron Taygetique canes. [2] — VIRGIL

Those who have searched into human nature observe that nothing so much shows the nobleness of the soul as that its felicity consists in action. Every man has such an active principle in him that he will find out something to employ himself upon, in whatever place or state of life he is posted. I have heard of a gentleman who was under close confinement in the Bastile [3] seven years; during which time he amused himself in scattering a few small pins about his chamber, gathering them up again, and placing them in different figures on the arm of a great chair. He often told his friends afterwards that unless he had found out this piece of exercise he verily believed he should have lost his senses.

After what has been said, I need not inform my readers that Sir Roger, with whose character I hope they are at present pretty well acquainted, has in his youth gone through the whole course of those rural diversions which the country abounds in,

---

[1] Men with incomes of five hundred pounds a year (usually implying landed estates).

[2] "The echoing hills and chiding hounds invite" (Virgil, "Georgics," III, 43-44).

[3] A former castle, or fortress, in Paris, used as a prison until demolished by the populace in 1789; usually spelled "Bastille."

[36]

and which seem to be extremely well suited to that laborious industry a man may observe here in a far greater degree than in towns and cities. I have before hinted at some of my friend's exploits: He has in his youthful days taken forty coveys of partridges in a season, and tired many a salmon with a line consisting but of a single hair. The constant thanks and good wishes of the neighborhood always attended him on account of his remarkable enmity toward foxes; having destroyed more of those vermin in one year that it was thought the whole country could have produced. Indeed, the knight does not scruple to own, among his most intimate friends, that in order to establish his reputation this way, he has secretly sent for great numbers of them out of other counties, which he used to turn loose about the country by night, that he might the better signalize himself in their destruction the next day. His hunting horses were the finest and best managed in all these parts; his tenants are still full of the praises of a gray stone-horse[1] that unhappily staked himself several years since, and was buried with great solemnity in the orchard.

Sir Roger, being at present too old for fox-hunting, to keep himself in action has disposed of his beagles and got a pack of stop-hounds.[2] What these want in speed he endeavors to make amends for by the deepness of their mouths and the variety of their notes, which are suited in such manner to each other that the whole cry makes up a complete concert. He is so nice in this particular that a gentleman having made him a present of a very fine hound the other day, the knight returned it by the servant with a great many expressions of civility, but desired him to tell his master that the dog he had sent was indeed a most excellent bass, but that at present he only wanted a counter-tenor. Could I believe my friend had ever read Shakespeare, I should certainly conclude he had taken the hint from Theseus, in the "Midsummer Night's Dream"[3]:

[1] A stallion.   [2] Hounds trained to stop at the hunter's signal.
[3] IV, i, 123–129.

The Periodical Essay

My hounds are bred out of the Spartan kind,
So flew'd,[1] so sanded[2]; and their heads are hung
With ears that sweep away the morning dew;
Crook-knee'd, and dew-lapp'd like Thessalian bulls;
Slow in pursuit, but match'd in mouth like bells,
Each under each. A cry more tuneable
Was never holla'd to, nor cheer'd with horn.

Sir Roger is so keen at this sport that he has been out almost every day since I came down; and upon the chaplain's offering to lend me his easy pad, I was prevailed on yesterday morning to make one of the company. I was extremely pleased, as we rid along, to observe the general benevolence of all the neighborhood toward my friend. The farmers' sons thought themselves happy if they could open a gate for the good old knight as he passed by; which he generally requited with a nod or a smile, and a kind inquiry after their fathers or uncles.

After we had rid about a mile from home, we came upon a large heath, and the sportsmen began to beat. They had done so for some time, when, as I was at a little distance from the rest of the company, I saw a hare pop out from a small furze-brake almost under my horse's feet. I marked the way she took, which I endeavored to make the company sensible of by extending my arm; but to no purpose, till Sir Roger, who knows that none of my extraordinary motions are insignificant, rode up to me, and asked me if puss was gone that way. Upon my answering "Yes," he immediately called in the dogs and put them upon the scent. As they were going off, I heard one of the country fellows muttering to his companion that 'twas a wonder they had not lost all their sport, for want of the silent gentleman's crying "Stole away!"

This, with my aversion to leaping hedges, made me withdraw to a rising ground, from whence I could have the picture of the whole chase without the fatigue of keeping in with the hounds. The hare immediately threw them above a mile behind her;

[1] with large, hanging chaps.   [2] sand-colored, sandy.

but I was pleased to find that instead of running straight forward, or, in hunter's language, "flying the country," as I was afraid she might have done, she wheeled about and described a sort of circle round the hill where I had taken my station, in such manner as gave me a very distinct view of the sport. I could see her first pass by, and the dogs some time afterwards unraveling the whole track she had made, and following her through all her doubles. I was at the same time delighted in observing that deference which the rest of the pack paid to each particular hound, according to the character he had acquired amongst them. If they were at fault, and an old hound of reputation opened but once, he was immediately followed by the whole cry; while a raw dog, or one who was a noted liar, might have yelped his heart out without being taken notice of.

The hare now, after having squatted two or three times, and been put up again as often, came still nearer to the place where she was at first started. The dogs pursued her, and these were followed by the jolly knight, who rode upon a white gelding, encompassed by his tenants and servants, and cheering his hounds with all the gayety of five-and-twenty. One of the sportsmen rode up to me, and told me that he was sure the chase was almost at an end, because the old dogs, which had hitherto lain behind, now headed the pack. The fellow was in the right. Our hare took a large field just under us, followed by the full cry in view. I must confess the brightness of the weather, the cheerfulness of everything around me, the chiding of the hounds, which was returned upon us in a double echo from two neighboring hills, with the hollowing of the sportsmen, and the sounding of the horn, lifted my spirits into a most lively pleasure, which I freely indulged because I was sure it was innocent. If I was under any concern, it was on the account of the poor hare, that was now quite spent, and almost within the reach of her enemies; when the huntsman, getting forward, threw down his pole before the dogs. They were now within eight yards of that game which they had been pursuing for almost as many hours; yet, on the signal before mentioned, they all made a sudden stand, and though they continued opening as much as before, durst not once attempt to pass beyond the pole. At the same time Sir Roger rode forward, and, alighting, took up the hare in his arms, which he soon after delivered to one of his servants, with an order, if she could be kept alive, to let her go in his great orchard, where it seems he has several of these prisoners of war, who live together in a very comfortable captivity. I was highly pleased to see the discipline of the pack, and the good nature of the knight, who could not find in his heart to murder a creature that had given him so much diversion.

As we were returning home I remembered that Monsieur Pascal, in his most excellent discourse on the "Misery of Man," tells us that all our endeavors after greatness proceed from nothing but a desire of being surrounded by a multitude of persons and affairs that may hinder us from looking into ourselves, which is a view we cannot bear. He afterwards goes on to show that our love of sports comes from the same reason, and is particularly severe upon hunting. "What," says he, "unless it be to drown thought, can make men throw away so much time and pains upon a silly animal, which they might buy cheaper in the market?" The foregoing reflection is certainly just when a man suffers his whole mind to be drawn into his sports, and altogether loses himself in the woods; but does not affect those who propose a far more laudable end from this exercise,— I mean the preservation of health and keeping all the organs of the soul in a condition to execute her orders. Had that incomparable person whom I last quoted been a little more indulgent to himself in this point, the world might probably have enjoyed him much longer; whereas through too great an application to his studies in his youth, he contracted that ill habit of body which, after a tedious sickness, carried him off in the fortieth year of his age; and the whole history we have of his life till that time is but one continued account of the behavior of a noble soul struggling under innumerable pains and distempers.

For my own part, I intend to hunt twice a week during my stay with Sir Roger, and shall prescribe the moderate use of this exercise to all my country friends as the best kind of physic for mending a bad constitution and preserving a good one.

I cannot do this better than in the following lines out of Mr. Dryden:[1]

> The first physicians by debauch were made;
> Excess began, and sloth sustains the trade.
> By chase our long-lived fathers earned their food;
> Toil strung the nerves, and purified the blood;
> But we their sons, a pamper'd race of men,
> Are dwindled down to threescore years and ten.
> Better to hunt in fields for health unbought
> Than fee the doctor for a nauseous draught.
> The wise for cure on exercise depend:
> God never made his work for man to mend.

MOLL WHITE

No. 117. Saturday, July 14, 1711. [By ADDISON]

Ipsi sibi somnia fingunt.[2] — VIRGIL

There are some opinions in which a man should stand neuter, without engaging his assent to one side or the other. Such a hovering faith as this, which refuses to settle upon any determination, is absolutely necessary in a mind that is careful to avoid errors and prepossessions. When the arguments press equally on both sides, in matters that are indifferent to us, the safest method is to give up ourselves to neither.

It is with this temper of mind that I consider the subject of

[1] From an epistle to his kinsman John Driden, Esq.
[2] "With voluntary dreams they cheat their minds" (Virgil, "Eclogues," VIII, 108).

The Periodical Essay

witchcraft.[1] When I hear the relations that are made from all parts of the world, not only from Norway and Lapland, from the East and West Indies, but from every particular nation in Europe, I cannot forbear thinking that there is such an intercourse and commerce[2] with evil spirits as that which we express by the name of witchcraft. But when I consider that the ignorant and credulous parts of the world abound most in these relations, and that the persons among us who are supposed to engage in such an infernal commerce are people of a weak understanding and crazed imagination, and at the same time reflect upon the many impostures and delusions of this nature that have been detected in all ages, I endeavor to suspend my belief till I hear more certain accounts than any which have yet come to my knowledge. In short, when I consider the question whether there are such persons in the world as those we call witches, my mind is divided between the two opposite opinions; or rather (to speak my thoughts freely), I believe in general that there is, and has been, such a thing as witchcraft, but at the same time can give no credit to any particular instance of it.

I am engaged in this speculation by some occurrences that I met with yesterday, which I shall give my reader an account of at large. As I was walking with my friend Sir Roger by the side of one of his woods, an old woman applied herself to me for my charity. Her dress and figure put me in mind of the following description in Otway[3]:

> In a close lane as I pursued my journey,
> I spied a wrinkled hag, with age grown double,
> Picking dry sticks, and mumbling to herself.
> Her eyes with scalding rheum were gall'd and red;
> Cold palsy shook her head; her hands seem'd wither'd;
> And on her crooked shoulders had she wrapp'd
> The tatter'd remnants of an old striped hanging,

---

[1] Witchcraft was still commonly believed in at this time. Prosecutions for witchcraft were not abolished until 1736.

[2] fellowship, communication. [3] "The Orphan," II, iv.

The Spectator

Which served to keep her carcase from the cold:
So there was nothing of a piece about her.
Her lower weeds[1] were all o'er coarsely patch'd
With diff'rent color'd rags, black, red, white, yellow,
And seem'd to speak variety of wretchedness.

As I was musing on this description and comparing it with the object before me, the knight told me that this very old woman had the reputation of a witch all over the country, that her lips were observed to be always in motion, and that there was not a switch about her house which her neighbors did not believe had carried her several hundreds of miles. If she chanced to stumble, they always found sticks or straws that lay in the figure of a cross before her. If she made any mistake at church, and cried "Amen" in a wrong place, they never failed to conclude that she was saying her prayers backward. There was not a maid in the parish that would take a pin of her, though she would offer a bag of money with it. She goes by the name of Moll White, and has made the country ring with several imaginary exploits which are palmed upon her. If the dairymaid does not make her butter come so soon as she should have it, Moll White is at the bottom of the churn. If a horse sweats in the stable, Moll White has been upon his back. If a hare makes an unexpected escape from the hounds, the huntsman curses Moll White. "Nay," (says Sir Roger), "I have known the master of the pack, upon such an occasion, send one of his servants to see if Moll White had been out that morning."

This account raised my curiosity so far that I begged my friend Sir Roger to go with me into her hovel, which stood in a solitary corner under the side of the wood. Upon our first entering, Sir Roger winked to me and pointed at something that stood behind the door, which, upon looking that way, I found to be an old broomstaff. At the same time he whispered me in the ear to take notice of a tabby cat that sat in the chimney corner, which, as the old knight told me, lay under as bad a

[1] garments.

[43]

The Periodical Essay

report as Moll White herself; for besides that Moll is said often to accompany her in the same shape, the cat is reported to have spoken twice or thrice in her life, and to have played several pranks above the capacity of an ordinary cat.

I was secretly concerned to see human nature in so much wretchedness and disgrace, but at the same time could not forbear smiling to hear Sir Roger, who is a little puzzled about the old woman, advising her, as a justice of peace, to avoid all communication with the devil, and never to hurt any of her neighbor's cattle. We concluded our visit with a bounty, which was very acceptable.

In our return home Sir Roger told me that old Moll had been often brought before him for making children spit pins, and giving maids the nightmare; and that the country people would be tossing her into a pond and trying experiments with her every day, if it was[1] not for him and his chaplain.

I have since found, upon inquiry, that Sir Roger was several times staggered with the reports that had been brought him concerning this old woman, and would frequently have bound her over to the county sessions had not his chaplain with much ado persuaded him to the contrary.

I have been the more particular in this account because I hear there is scarce a village in England that has not a Moll White in it. When an old woman begins to dote, and grow chargeable to a parish, she is generally turned into a witch, and fills the whole country with extravagant fancies, imaginary distempers, and terrifying dreams. In the meantime the poor wretch that is the innocent occasion of so many evils begins to be frighted at herself, and sometimes confesses secret commerce and familiarities that her imagination forms in a delirious old age. This frequently cuts off charity from the greatest objects of compassion, and inspires people with a malevolence toward those poor decrepit parts of our species in whom human nature is defaced by infirmity and dotage.

[1] were.

The Spectator

A STAGECOACH JOURNEY

No. 132. Wednesday, August 1, 1711. [By STEELE]

Qui, aut tempus quid postulet non videt, aut plura loquitur aut se ostentat, aut eorum quibuscum est rationem non habet, is ineptus esse dicitur.[1] — TULLY

Having notified to my good friend Sir Roger that I should set out for London the next day, his horses were ready at the appointed hour in the evening; and attended by one of his grooms, I arrived at the county town at twilight, in order to be ready for the stagecoach the day following. As soon as we arrived at the inn, the servant who waited upon me inquired of the chamberlain, in my hearing, what company he had for the coach. The fellow answered, "Mrs.[2] Betty Arable, the great fortune, and the widow, her mother; a recruiting officer (who took a place because they were to go); young Squire Quickset, her cousin (that her mother wished her to be married to); Ephraim the Quaker,[3] her guardian; and a gentleman that had studied himself dumb from Sir Roger de Coverley's." I observed, by what he said of myself, that according to his office, he dealt much in intelligence[4]; and doubted not but there was some foundation for his reports of the rest of the company, as well as for the whimsical account he gave of me.

The next morning at daybreak we were all called; and I, who know my own natural shyness, and endeavor to be as little liable to be disputed with as possible, dressed immediately, that I might make no one wait. The first preparation for our setting out was that the captain's half-pike was placed near the coachman, and a drum behind the coach. In the meantime the drummer,

[1] "That man may be called impertinent who considers not the circumstances of time, or engrosses the conversation, or makes himself the subject of his discourse, or pays no regard to the company he is in" (Cicero).

[2] In the eighteenth century the title "Mrs." was given to any woman, married or single, who was not called by a superior title.

[3] The Quaker is called Ephraim because he objected to fighting (Psalm lxxviii, 9).   [4] news.

The Periodical Essay

the captain's equipage,[1] was very loud that none of the captain's things should be placed so as to be spoiled; upon which his cloak bag was fixed in the seat of the coach; and the captain himself, according to a frequent though invidious behavior of military men, ordered his man to look sharp that none but one of the ladies should have the place he had taken fronting to the coach box.

We were in some little time fixed in our seats, and sat with that dislike which people not too good-natured usually conceive of each other at first sight. The coach jumbled us insensibly into some sort of familiarity, and we had not moved above two miles when the widow asked the captain what success he had in his recruiting. The officer, with a frankness he believed very graceful, told her that indeed he had but very little luck, and had suffered much by desertion, therefore should be glad to end his warfare in the service of her or her fair daughter. "In a word," continued he, "I am a soldier, and to be plain is my character; you see me, madam, young, sound, and impudent; take me yourself, widow, or give me to her; I will be wholly at your disposal. I am a soldier of fortune, ha!" This was followed by a vain laugh of his own and a deep silence of all the rest of the company. I had nothing left for it but to fall fast asleep, which I did with all speed. "Come," said he, "resolve upon it, we will make a wedding at the next town; we will wake this pleasant companion who is fallen asleep, to be the bride-man, and" (giving the Quaker a clap on the knee), he concluded, "this sly saint, who, I'll warrant, understands what's what as well as you or I, widow, shall give the bride as father."

The Quaker, who happened to be a man of smartness, answered: "Friend, I take it in good part, that thou hast given me the authority of a father over this comely and virtuous child; and I must assure thee that, if I have the giving her, I shall not bestow her on thee. Thy mirth, friend, savoreth of folly; thou art a person of a light mind; thy drum is a type of thee — it soundeth because it is empty. Verily, it is not from thy fullness

[1] retinue, followers; here, only one man.

but thy emptiness that thou hast spoken this day. Friend,
friend, we have hired this coach in partnership with thee, to
carry us to the great city; we cannot go any other way. This
worthy mother must hear thee if thou wilt needs utter thy
follies; we cannot help it, friend, I say; if thou wilt, we must
hear thee; but if thou wert a man of understanding, thou
wouldst not take advantage of thy courageous countenance to
abash us children of peace. Thou art, thou sayest, a soldier;
give quarter to us, who cannot resist thee. Why didst thou
fleer at our friend who feigned himself asleep? He said nothing, but how dost thou know what he containeth? If thou
speakest improper things in the hearing of this virtuous young
virgin, consider it is an outrage against a distressed person that
cannot get from thee; to speak indiscreetly what we are obliged
to hear, by being hasped up with thee in this public vehicle, is
in some degree assaulting on the high road."

Here Ephraim paused, and the captain, with a happy and
uncommon impudence (which can be convicted and support
itself at the same time), cries: "Faith, friend, I thank thee; I
should have been a little impertinent if thou hadst not repri-
manded me. Come, thou art, I see, a smoky old fellow, and I'll
be very orderly the ensuing part of the journey. I was going to
give myself airs, but, ladies, I beg pardon."

The captain was so little out of humor, and our company was
so far from being soured by this little ruffle, that Ephraim and
he took a particular delight in being agreeable to each other for
the future, and assumed their different provinces in the conduct
of the company. Our reckonings, apartments, and accommodation fell under Ephraim; and the captain looked to all dis-
putes on the road, as the good behavior of our coachmen, and
the right we had of taking place as going to London of all
vehicles coming from thence.[1] The occurrences we met with

[1] On bad roads only the center was passable. When vehicles met, one
had to pull aside to let the other pass; the vehicle going to London had the
right of way ("taking place").

The Periodical Essay

were ordinary, and very little happened which could entertain by the relation of them; but when I considered the company we were in, I took it for no small good fortune that the whole journey was not spent in impertinences, which to one part of us might be an entertainment, to the other a suffering.

What, therefore, Ephraim said when we were almost arrived at London, had to me an air not only of good understanding but good breeding. Upon the young lady's expressing her satisfaction in the journey and declaring how delightful it had been to her, Ephraim delivered himself as follows: "There is no ordinary part of human life which expresseth so much a good mind, and a right inward man, as his behavior upon meeting with strangers, especially such as may seem the most unsuitable companions to him. Such a man, when he falleth in the way with persons of simplicity and innocence, however knowing he may be in the ways of men, will not vaunt himself thereof; but will the rather hide his superiority to them, that he may not be painful unto them. My good friend," continued he, turning to the officer, "thee and I are to part by and by, and peradventure we may never meet again. But be advised by a plain man; modes and apparel are but trifles to the real man, therefore do not think such a man as thyself terrible for thy garb, nor such a one as me contemptible for mine. When two such as thee and I meet, with affections as we ought to have toward each other, thou shouldst rejoice to see my peaceable demeanor, and I should be glad to see thy strength and ability to protect me in it."

The Spectator

THE TRUNK-MAKER

No. 235. Thursday, November 29, 1711. [By ADDISON]

Populares vincentem strepitus.[1] — HORACE

There is nothing which lies more within the province of a
Spectator than public shows and diversions; and as among these
there are none which can pretend to vie with those elegant entertainments that are exhibited in our theaters, I think it particularly incumbent on me to take notice of everything that is
remarkable in such numerous and refined assemblies.

It is observed that, of late years, there has been a certain
person in the upper gallery of the playhouse who, when he is
pleased with anything that is acted upon the stage, expresses his
approbation by a loud knock upon the benches or the wainscot,
which may be heard over the whole theater. This person is commonly known by the name of the Trunk-maker in the Upper
Gallery. Whether it be that the blow he gives on these occasions
resembles that which is often heard in the shops of such artisans,
or that he was supposed to have been a real trunk-maker who,
after the finishing of his day's work, used to unbend his mind
at these public diversions with his hammer in his hand, I cannot
certainly tell. There are some, I know, who have been foolish
enough to imagine it is a spirit which haunts the upper gallery,
and from time to time makes those strange noises; and the
rather, because he is observed to be louder than ordinary every
time the ghost of Hamlet appears. Others have reported that it
is a dumb man, who has chosen this way of uttering himself
when he is transported with anything he sees or hears. Others
will have it to be the playhouse thunderer, that exerts himself
after this manner in the upper gallery when he has nothing to
do upon the roof.

But having made it my business to get the best information I
could in a matter of this moment, I find that the Trunk-maker,

[1] "Winning the noisy approval of the people" (Horace, "Ars Poetica," 81).

The Periodical Essay

as he is commonly called, is a large black[1] man whom nobody knows. He generally leans forward on a huge oaken plant[2] with great attention to everything that passes upon the stage. He is never seen to smile; but upon hearing anything that pleases him, he takes up his staff with both hands and lays it upon the next piece of timber that stands in his way with exceeding vehemence; after which he composes himself in his former posture, till such time as something new sets him again at work.

It has been observed his blow is so well timed that the most judicious critic could never except against it.[3] As soon as any shining thought is expressed in the poet, or any uncommon grace appears in the actor, he smites the bench or wainscot. If the audience does not concur with him, he smites a second time; and if the audience is not yet awaked, looks round him with great wrath and repeats the blow a third time, which never fails to produce the clap. He sometimes lets the audience begin the clap of themselves, and at the conclusion of their applause ratifies it with a single thwack.

He is of so great use to the playhouse that it is said a former director of it, upon his not being able to pay his attendance by reason of sickness, kept one in pay to officiate for him till such time as he recovered; but the person so employed, though he laid about him with incredible violence, did it in such wrong places that the audience soon found out it was not their old friend the Trunk-maker.

It has been remarked that he has not yet exerted himself with vigor this season. He sometimes plies at the opera; and upon Nicolini's first appearance was said to have demolished three benches in the fury of his applause. He has broken half a dozen oaken plants upon Doggett,[4] and seldom goes away from a tragedy of Shakespeare without leaving the wainscot extremely shattered.

The players do not only connive at this his obstreperous ap-

[1] dark-complexioned, brunette.   [2] cudgel, staff.
[3] make objection against it.   [4] A popular comic actor who died in 1721.

[50]

probation, but very cheerfully repair at their own cost whatever damages he makes. They had once a thought of erecting a kind of wooden anvil for his use, that should be made of a very sounding plank, in order to render his strokes more deep and mellow; but as this might not have been distinguished from the music of a kettledrum, the project was laid aside.

In the meanwhile I cannot but take notice of the great use it is to an audience that a person should thus preside over their heads,[1] like the director of a concert, in order to awaken their attention and beat time to their applauses. Or to raise my simile, I have sometimes fancied the Trunk-maker in the Upper Gallery to be like Virgil's Ruler of the Winds, seated upon the top of a mountain, who, when he struck his scepter upon the side of it, roused an hurricane, and set the whole cavern in an uproar.[2]

It is certain the Trunk-maker has saved many a good play and brought many a graceful actor into reputation who would not otherwise have been taken notice of. It is very visible, as the audience is not a little abashed if they find themselves betrayed into a clap when their friend in the upper gallery does not come into it; so the actors do not value themselves upon the clap, but regard it as a mere *brutum fulmen*, or empty noise, when it has not the sound of the oaken plant in it. I know it has been given out by those who are enemies to the Trunk-maker that he has sometimes been bribed to be in the interest of a bad poet or a vicious player; but this is a surmise which has no foundation: his strokes are always just, and his admonitions seasonable; he does not deal about his blows at random, but always hits the right nail upon the head. The inexpressible force wherewith he lays them on sufficiently shows the evidence and strength of his conviction. His zeal for a good author is indeed outrageous, and breaks down every force and

---

[1] The entire essay is a satire on the use of hired applause to win approval of a play by the audience.

[2] Æneid, I, 81.

The Periodical Essay

partition, every board and plank, that stands within the expression of his applause.

As I do not care for terminating my thoughts in barren speculations, or in reports of pure matter of fact, without drawing something from them for the advantage of my countrymen, I shall take the liberty to make an humble proposal, that whenever the Trunk-maker shall depart this life, or whenever he shall have lost the spring of his arm by sickness, old age, infirmity, or the like, some able-bodied critic should be advanced to this post, and have a competent salary settled on him for life, to be furnished with bamboos for operas, crab-tree cudgels for comedies, and oaken plants for tragedy, at the public expense. And to the end that this place should always be disposed of according to merit, I would have none preferred to it who has not given convincing proofs both of a sound judgment and a strong arm, and who could not upon occasion either knock down an ox or write a comment upon Horace's "Art of Poetry." In short, I would have him a due composition of Hercules and Apollo, and so rightly qualified for this important office that the Trunk-maker may not be missed by our posterity.

THE GUARDIAN

[1713]

THE SHORT CLUB

No. 91. Thursday, June 25, 1713. [By POPE]

Inest sua gratia parvis.[1]

It is the great rule of behavior "to follow nature." The author of the following letter is so much convinced of this truth that he turns what would render a man of little soul exceptious, humorsome, and particular in all his actions, to a subject of raillery and mirth. He is, you must know, but half as tall as an ordinary man, but is contented to be still at his friend's elbow, and has set up a club, by which he hopes to bring those of his own size into a little reputation.

TO NESTOR IRONSIDE, ESQ.

SIR,

I remember a saying of yours concerning persons in low circumstances of stature, that their littleness would hardly be taken notice of, if they did not manifest a consciousness of it themselves in all their behavior. Indeed, the observation that no man is ridiculous for being what he is, but only in the affectation of being somebody more, is equally true in regard to the mind and the body.

I question not but it will be pleasing to you to hear that a set of us have formed a society, who are sworn to "dare to be short," and boldly bear out the dignity of littleness under the noses of those enormous engrossers of manhood, those hyperbolical monsters of the species, the tall fellows that overlook us.

[1] "Little things have their value."

The Periodical Essay

The day of our institution was the tenth of December,[1] being the shortest of the year, on which we are to hold an annual feast over a dish of shrimps.

The place we have chosen for this meeting is in the Little Piazza, not without an eye to the neighborhood of Mr. Powell's opera, for the performers of which we have, as becomes us, a brotherly affection.[2]

At our first resort hither an old woman brought her son to the clubroom, desiring he might be educated in this school, because she saw here were finer boys than ordinary. However, this accident no way discouraged our designs. We began with sending invitations to those of a stature not exceeding five foot, to repair to our assembly; but the greater part returned excuses or pretended they were not qualified.

One said he was indeed but five foot at present, but represented he should soon exceed that proportion, his periwig-maker and shoemaker having lately promised him three inches more betwixt them.

Another alleged he was so unfortunate as to have one leg shorter than the other, and whoever had determined his stature to five foot had taken him at a disadvantage; for when he was mounted on the other leg, he was at least five foot two inches and a half.

There were some who questioned the exactness of our measures; and others, instead of complying, returned us informations of people yet shorter than themselves. In a word, almost every one recommended some neighbor or acquaintance, whom he was willing we should look upon to be less than he. We were not a little ashamed that those who are past the years of growth, and whose beards pronounce them men, should be guilty of as many unfair tricks in this point as the most aspiring children when they are measured.

We therefore proceeded to fit up the clubroom and provide conveniences for our accommodation. In the first place, we caused a total removal of all chairs, stools, and tables, which had served the gross of mankind for many years. The disadvantages we had undergone while we made use of these were unspeakable. The president's whole body was sunk in the elbow chair, and when his arms were spread over it he appeared (to the great lessening of his dignity) like

---

[1] December 10, in the Old Style, or Julian, calendar, corresponded to December 21 in the Gregorian, or New Style, calendar.

[2] Martin Powell's puppet shows were exhibited in the galleries of Covent Garden, the operas of which they were jokingly supposed to rival.

a child in a gocart. It was also so wide in the seat as to give a wag occasion of saying that notwithstanding the president sat in it, there was a *sede vacante.*[1]

The table was so high that one who came by chance to the door, seeing our chins just above the pewter dishes, took us for a circle of men that sat ready to be shaved, and sent in half a dozen barbers. Another time one of the club spoke contumeliously of the president, imagining he had been absent, when he was only eclipsed by a flask of Florence which stood on the table in a parallel line before his face. We therefore new-furnished the room in all respects proportionably to us, and had the door made lower so as to admit no man above five foot high without brushing his foretop, which whoever does is utterly unqualified to sit among us.

Some of the statutes of the club are as follows:

"I. If it be proved upon any member, though never so duly qualified, that he strives as much as possible to get above his size by stretching, cocking, or the like; or that he hath stood on tiptoe in a crowd, with design to be taken for as tall a man as the rest: or hath privily conveyed any large book, cricket,[2] or other device under him, to exalt him on his seat; every such offender shall be sentenced to walk in pumps [3] for a whole month.

"II. If any member shall take advantage from the fullness or length of his wig, or any part of his dress, or the immoderate extent of his hat, or otherwise to seem larger and higher than he is, it is ordered he shall wear red heels to his shoes and a red feather in his hat, which may apparently mark and set bounds to the extremities of his small dimension, that all people may readily find out between his hat and his shoes.

"III. If any member shall purchase a horse for his own riding above fourteen hands and a half in height, that horse shall forthwith be sold, a Scotch galloway [4] bought in its stead for him, and the overplus of the money shall treat the club.

"IV. If any member, in direct contradiction to the fundamental laws of the society, shall wear the heels of his shoes exceeding one inch and a half, it shall be interpreted as an open renunciation of lit-

---

[1] "a vacant seat."   [2] a low stool.
[3] Low-heeled shoes for dancing; men's shoes had high heels.
[4] A horse of a small strong breed from Galloway, in Scotland.

The Periodical Essay

tleness, and the criminal shall be instantly expelled. NOTE. The form to be used in expelling a member shall be in these words, "Go from among us, and be tall if you can!"

It is the unanimous opinion of our whole society that, since the race of mankind is granted to have decreased in stature from the beginning to this present, it is the intent of nature itself that men should be little; and we believe that all human kind shall at last grow down to perfection, that is to say, be reduced to our own measure.

I am, very literally,
Your humble servant,
BOB SHORT.

THE RAMBLER

[1750–1752]

THE EMPLOYMENTS OF A HOUSEWIFE IN THE COUNTRY

No. 51. Tuesday, September 11, 1750. [By JOHNSON]

Stultis labor est ineptiarum.[1] — MARTIAL

TO THE RAMBLER

SIR,

As you have allowed a place in your paper to Euphelia's letters from the country, and appear to think no form of human life unworthy of your attention, I have resolved, after many struggles with idleness and diffidence, to give you some account of my entertainment in this sober season of universal retreat, and to describe to you the employments of those who look with contempt on the pleasures and diversions of polite life, and employ all their powers of censure and invective upon the uselessness, vanity, and folly of dress, visits, and conversation.[2]

When a tiresome and vexatious journey of four days had brought me to the house where invitation, regularly sent for seven years together, had at last induced me to spend the summer, I was surprised, after the civilities of my first reception, to find, instead of the leisure and tranquillity which a rural life always promises, and, if well conducted, might always afford, a confused wildness of care and a tumultuous hurry of diligence, by which every face was clouded and every motion agitated.

[1] "How foolish is the toil of trifling cares." Martial, II, 86, 10.
[2] The pompous beginning is a characteristic fault of Johnson's essays, just as the shrewd humor, the realistic details, and the wisdom of the essay itself are characteristic virtues.

The Periodical Essay

The old lady, who was my father's relation, was, indeed, very full of the happiness which she received from my visit, and, according to the forms of obsolete breeding, insisted that I should recompense the long delay of my company with a promise not to leave her till winter. But, amidst all her kindness and caresses, she very frequently turned her head aside and whispered, with anxious earnestness, some order to her daughters, which never failed to send them out with unpolite precipitation. Sometimes her impatience would not suffer her to stay behind; she begged my pardon, she must leave me for a moment; she went, and returned and sat down again, but was again disturbed by some new care, dismissed her daughters with the same trepidation, and followed them with the same countenance of business and solicitude.

However I was alarmed at this show of eagerness and disturbance, and however my curiosity was excited by such busy preparations as naturally promised some great event, I was yet too much a stranger to gratify myself with inquiries; but, finding none of the family in mourning, I pleased myself with imagining that I should rather see a wedding than a funeral.

At last we sat down to supper, when I was informed that one of the young ladies, after whom I thought myself obliged to inquire, was under a necessity of attending some affair that could not be neglected; soon afterwards my relation began to talk of the regularity of her family and the inconvenience of London hours; and at last let me know that they had purposed that night to go to bed sooner than was usual, because they were to rise early in the morning to make cheesecakes. This hint sent me to my chamber, to which I was accompanied by all the ladies, who begged me to excuse some large sieves of leaves and flowers that covered two thirds of the floor, for they intended to distil them when they were dry, and they had no other room that so conveniently received the rising sun.

The scent of the plants hindered me from rest, and therefore I rose early in the morning with a resolution to explore my new habitation. I stole unperceived by my busy cousins into the garden, where I found nothing either more great or elegant than in the same number of acres cultivated for the market. Of the gardener I soon learned that his lady was the greatest manager in that part of the country, and that I was come hither at the time in which I might learn to make more pickles and conserves than could be seen at any other house a hundred miles round.

It was not long before her ladyship gave me sufficient opportunities of knowing her character, for she was too much pleased with her own accomplishments to conceal them, and took occasion, from some sweetmeats which she set next day upon the table, to discourse for two long hours upon robs[1] and jellies; laid down the best methods of conserving, reserving, and preserving all sorts of fruit; told us with great contempt of the London lady in the neighborhood, by whom these terms were very often confounded; and hinted how much she should be ashamed to set before company, at her own house, sweetmeats of so dark a color as she had often seen at Mistress Sprightly's.

It is, indeed, the great business of her life to watch the skillet on the fire, to see it simmer with the due degree of heat, and to snatch it off at the moment of projection; and the employments to which she has bred her daughters are to turn rose leaves in the shade, to pick out the seeds of currants with a quill, to gather fruit without bruising it, and to extract beanflower water for the skin. Such are the tasks with which every day, since I came hither, has begun and ended, to which the early hours of life are sacrificed, and to which that time is passing away which never shall return.

But to reason or expostulate are hopeless attempts. The lady has settled her opinions, and maintains the dignity of her own performances with all the firmness of stupidity accustomed to be flattered. Her daughters, having never seen any house

[1] preserved fruit juices.

The Periodical Essay

but their own, believe their mother's excellence on her own word. Her husband is a mere sportsman, who is pleased to see his table well furnished, and thinks the day sufficiently successful in which he brings home a leash of hares to be potted by his wife.

After a few days I pretended to want books, but my lady soon told me that none of her books would suit my taste; for her part she never loved to see young women give their minds to such follies, by which they would only learn to use hard words; she bred up her daughters to understand a house, and whoever should marry them, if they knew anything of good cookery, would never repent it.

There are, however, some things in the culinary science too sublime for youthful intellects, mysteries into which they must not be initiated till the years of serious maturity, and which are referred to the day of marriage as the supreme qualification for connubial life. She makes an orange pudding which is the envy of all the neighborhood, and which she has hitherto found means of mixing and baking with such secrecy that the ingredient to which it owes its flavor has never been discovered. She, indeed, conducts this great affair with all the caution that human policy can suggest. It is never known beforehand when this pudding will be produced: she takes the ingredients privately into her own closet, employs her maids and daughters in different parts of the house, orders the oven to be heated for a pie, and places the pudding in it with her own hands; the mouth of the oven is then stopped, and all inquiries are vain.

The composition of the pudding she has, however, promised Clarinda, that if she pleases her in marriage she shall be told without reserve. But the art of making English capers[1] she has not yet persuaded herself to discover,[2] but seems resolved that secret shall perish with her, as some alchemists have obstinately suppressed the art of transmuting metals.

I once ventured to lay my fingers on her book of receipts, which she left upon the table, having intelligence that a vessel

[1] pickled buds of the caper plant.   [2] reveal.

of gooseberry wine had burst the hoops. But though the importance of the event sufficiently engrossed her care to prevent any recollection of the danger to which her secrets were exposed, I was not able to make use of the golden moments; for this treasure of hereditary knowledge was so well concealed by the manner of spelling used by her grandmother, her mother, and herself, that I was totally unable to understand it, and lost the opportunity of consulting the oracle, for want of knowing the language in which its answers were returned.

It is, indeed, necessary, if I have any regard to her ladyship's esteem, that I should apply myself to some of these economical accomplishments; for I overheard her, two days ago, warning her daughters, by my mournful example, against negligence of pastry and ignorance in carving; "for you saw," said she, "that, with all her pretensions to knowledge, she turned the partridge the wrong way when she attempted to cut it, and, I believe, scarcely knows the difference between paste raised and paste in a dish."

The reason, Mr. Rambler, why I have laid Lady Bustle's character before you is a desire to be informed whether in your opinion it is worthy of imitation, and whether I shall throw away the books which I have hitherto thought it my duty to read for "The Lady's Closet Opened," "The Complete Servant Maid," and "The Court Cook," and resign all curiosity after right and wrong for the art of scalding damascenes without bursting them, and preserving the whiteness of pickled mushrooms.

Lady Bustle has, indeed, by this incessant application to fruits and flowers, contracted her cares into a narrow space, and set herself free from many perplexities with which other minds are disturbed. She has no curiosity after the events of a war or the fate of heroes in distress; she can hear without the least emotion the ravage of a fire or devastations of a storm; her neighbors grow rich or poor, come into the world or go out of it, without regard, while she is pressing the jelly bag or airing

The Periodical Essay

the storeroom; but I cannot perceive that she is more free from disquiet than those whose understandings take a wider range. Her marigolds, when they are almost cured, are often scattered by the wind, the rain sometimes falls upon fruit when it ought to be gathered dry. While her artificial wines are fermenting, her whole life is restlessness and anxiety. Her sweetmeats are not always bright, and the maid sometimes forgets the just proportion of salt and pepper when venison is to be baked. Her conserves mold, her wines sour, and pickles mother[1]; and, like all the rest of mankind, she is every day mortified with the defeat of her schemes and the disappointments of her hopes.

With regard to vice and virtue she seems a kind of neutral being. She has no crime but luxury, nor any virtue but chastity; she has no desire to be praised but for her cookery; nor wishes any ill to the rest of mankind, but that whenever they aspire to a feast their custards may be wheyish and their pie crusts tough.

I am now very impatient to know whether I am to look on these ladies as the great pattern of our sex, and to consider conserves and pickles as the business of my life; whether the censures which I now suffer be just, and whether the brewers of wines and the distillers of washes have a right to look with insolence on the weakness of

CORNELIA

[1] thicken, become viscid.

[62]

THE WORLD

[1753–1756]

ON THE SUPPOSED DEGENERACY OF
HUMAN NATURE

No. 197. Thursday, October 7, 1756. [By CHESTERFIELD]

If we give credit to the vulgar opinion, or even to the asser-
tions of some reputable authors both ancient and modern, poor
human nature was not originally formed for keeping: age has
degenerated; and from the fall of the first man, my unfortunate
ancestor, our species has been tumbling on, century by century,
from bad to worse, for about six thousand years.

Considering this progressive state of deterioration, it is a very,
great mercy that things are no worse with us at present; 'since,
geometrically speaking, the human ought by this time to have
sunk infinitely below the brute and the vegetable species, which
are neither of them supposed to have dwindled or degenerated
considerably, except in very few instances: for it must be
owned that our modern oaks are inferior to those of Dodona,[1]
our breed of horses to that of the centaurs,[2] and our breed of
fowls to that of the phœnixes.[3]

But is this really the case? Certainly not. It is only one of
those many errors which are artfully scattered by the designs
of a few, and blindly adopted by the ignorance and folly of the
many. The moving exclamations of *these sad times! this de-*

[1] The grove surrounding the temple of Zeus at Dodona could speak; the
oaks uttered oracles.

[2] The centaurs were half man, half horse.

[3] The phœnix was fabled to live five hundred years, be consumed in fire,
and rise youthful from its own ashes.

[63]

The Periodical Essay

generate age! the affecting lamentations over *declining virtue* and *triumphant vice,* and the tender and final farewell bidden every day to unrewarded and discouraged public spirit, arts and sciences, are the commonplace topics of the pride, the envy, and the malignity of the human heart, that can more easily forgive, and even commend, antiquated and remote than contemporary and contiguous merit. Men of these mean sentiments have always been the satirists of their own and the panegyrists of former times. They give this tone, which fools, like birds in the dark,[1] catch by ear and whistle all day long.

As it has constantly been my endeavor to root out if I could, or, if I could not, to expose the vices of the human heart, it shall be the object of this day's paper to examine this strange inverted entail[2] of virtue and merit upward, according to priority of birth and seniority of age. I shall prove it to be forged, and consequently null and void to all intents and purposes whatever.

If I loved to jingle, I would say that human nature has always been invariably the same, though always varying; that is, the same in substance, but varying in forms and modes, from many concurrent causes, of which perhaps we know but few. Climate, education, accidents, severally contribute to change those modes; but in all climates and in all ages we discover through them the same passions, affections, and appetites, and the same degree of virtues and vices.

This being unquestionably the true state of the case, which it would be endless to bring instances to prove from the histories of all times and of all nations, I shall, by way of warning to the incautious and of reproof to the designing, proceed to explain the reasons, which I have but just hinted at above, why the human nature of the time being has always been reckoned the worst and most degenerate.

[1] Canaries are taught in this way.

[2] An act by which an estate is settled inalienably on a person and his descendants; often limited to settlement on the male heirs.

The World

Authors, especially poets, though great men are, alas! but men, and, like other men, subject to the weaknesses of human nature, though perhaps in a less degree. But it is, however, certain that their breasts are not absolutely strangers to the passions of jealousy, pride, and envy. Hence it is that they are very apt to measure merit by the century; to love dead authors better than living ones, and to love them the better the longer they have been dead. The Augustan Age is therefore their favorite era, being at least seventeen hundred years distant from the present. That emperor was not only a judge of wit, but, for an emperor, a tolerable performer too; and Mæcenas, his first minister, was both a patron and a poet. He not only encouraged and protected but fed and fattened men of wit at his own table, as appears from Horace — no small encouragement for panegyric. Those were times indeed for genius to display itself in! It was honored, tasted, and rewarded. But now — *O tempora! O mores!*[1] One must, however, do justice to the authors who thus declaim against their own times, by acknowledging that they are seldom the aggressors; their own times have commonly begun with them. It is their resentment, not their judgment (if they have any), that speaks this language. Anger and despair make them endeavor to lower that merit which, till brought very low indeed, they are conscious they cannot equal.

There is another and more numerous set of much greater men who still more loudly complain of the ignorance, the corruption, and the degeneracy of the present age. These are the consummate volunteer, but unregarded and unrewarded, politicians, who at a modest computation amount to at least three millions of souls in this political country, and who are all of them both able and willing to steer the great vessel of the state and to take upon themselves the whole load of business and burden of employments for the service of their dear country. The administration for the time being is always the worst,

[1] "O the times! O the manners!"

[65]

The Periodical Essay

the most incapable, the most corrupt that ever was, and negligent of everything but their own interest. *Where are now your Cecils and your Walsinghams?*[1] Those who ask that question could answer it if they would speak out, *Themselves*; for they are all that and more too.

I stepped the other day, in order only to inquire how my poor country did, into a coffeehouse, that is without dispute the seat of the soundest politics in this great metropolis, and sat myself down within earshot of the principal council table. Fortunately for me, the president, a person of age, dignity, and becoming gravity, had just begun to speak. He stated with infinite perspicuity and knowledge the present state of affairs in other countries, and the lamentable situation of our own. He traced with his finger upon the table, by the help of some coffee which he had spilled in the warmth of his exordium, the whole course of the Ohio[2] and the boundaries of the Russian, Prussian, Austrian, and Saxon dominions; foresaw a long and bloody war upon the Continent, calculated the supplies necessary for carrying it on, and pointed out the best methods of raising them, which for that very reason he intimated would not be pursued. He wound up his discourse with a most pathetic peroration, which he concluded with saying, *Things were not carried on in this way in Queen Elizabeth's day; the public was considered, and able men were consulted and employed. Those were days!* "Ay, sir, and nights too, I presume," said a young fellow who stood near him; "some longer, and some shorter, according to the variation of the seasons; pretty much like ours." Mr. President was a little surprised at the suddenness and pertness of this interruption; but, recomposing himself, answered with that cool contempt that becomes a great man, "I did not mean astronomical days, but political ones." The young fellow replied, "Oh, then, sir, I am your servant," and went off in a laugh.

Thus informed and edified, I went off too, but could not help

[1] Two families prominent in public affairs under Elizabeth.
[2] There the French and Indian War was in progress.

[66]

reflecting in my way upon the singular ill luck of this my dear country, which, as long as ever I remember it, and as far back as I have read, has always been governed by the only two or three people, out of two or three millions, totally incapable of governing and unfit to be trusted. But these reflections were soon interrupted by numbers of people whom I observed crowding into a public house. Among them I discovered my worthy friend and tailor, that industrious mechanic, Mr. Regnier. I applied to him to know the meaning of that concourse; to which, with his usual humanity, he answered, "We are the master tailors, who are to meet tonight to consider what is to be done about our journeymen, who insult and impose upon us to the great detriment of trade." I asked him whether under his protection I might slip in and hear their deliberations. He said Yes, and welcome; for that they should do nothing to be ashamed of. I profited of this permission, and, following him into the room, found a considerable number of these ingenious artists assembled, and waiting only for the arrival of my friend, who it seems was too considerable for business to begin without him. He accordingly took the lead, opened the meeting with a very handsome speech, in which he gave many instances of the insolence, the unreasonableness, and the exorbitant demands of the journeymen tailors, and concluded with observing that if the government minded anything nowadays but themselves, such abuses would have not been suffered; and had they been but attempted in Queen Elizabeth's days, she would have *worked* them with a witness.

Another orator then rose up to speak ; but as I was sure that he could say nothing better than what had just fallen from my worthy friend, I stole off unobserved, and was pursuing my way home, when in the very next street I discovered a much greater number of people (though, by their dress, of seemingly inferior note) rushing into another public house. As numbers always excite my curiosity almost as much as they mutually do each other's passions, I crowded in with them, in order to discover the

The Periodical Essay

object of this meeting, not without some suspicion that this frequent[1] senate might be composed of the journeymen tailors, and convened in opposition to that which I had just left. My suspicion was soon confirmed by the eloquence of a journeyman, a finisher, I presume, who expatiated with equal warmth and dignity upon the injustice and oppression of the master tailors, to the utter ruin of thousands of poor journeymen and their families; and concluded with asserting, "It was a shame that the government and the Parliament did not take notice of such abuses; and that had the master tailors done these things in Queen Elizabeth's time, she would have *mastered* them with a vengeance, so she would."

I confess I could not help smiling at this singular conformity of sentiments, and almost of expressions, of the master politicians, the master tailors, and the journeymen tailors. I am convinced that the two latter really and honestly believed what they said, it not being in the least improbable that their understandings should be the dupes of their interests. But I will not so peremptorily answer for the interior conviction of the political orator; though at the same time I must do him the justice to say he seemed full dull enough to be very much in earnest.

The several scenes of this day suggested to me, when I got home, various reflections, which perhaps I may communicate to my readers in some future paper.

[1] thronged, crowded.

THE CITIZEN OF THE WORLD[1]

[1760–1761]

IN RIDICULE OF FUNERAL ELEGIES FOR THE GREAT [Letter 106]

It was formerly the custom here, when men of distinction died, for their surviving acquaintances to throw each a slight present into the grave. Several things of little value were made use of for that purpose — perfumes, relics, spices, bitter herbs, camomile, wormwood, and verses. This custom, however, is almost discontinued, and nothing but verses alone are now lavished on such occasions — an oblation which they suppose may be interred with the dead, without any injury to the living.

Upon the death of the great, therefore, the poets and undertakers are sure of employment. While one provides the long cloak, black staff, and mourning coach, the other produces the pastoral or elegy, the monody or apotheosis. The nobility need be under no apprehensions, but die as fast as they think proper — the poet and undertaker are ready to supply them; these can find metaphorical tears and family escutcheons at an hour's warning; and when the one has soberly laid the body in the grave, the other is ready to fix it figuratively among the stars.

There are several ways of being poetically sorrowful on such occasions. The bard is now some pensive youth of science, who sits deploring among the tombs; again, he is Thyrsis complain-

---

[1] "The Citizen of the World" was not a separate journal devoted to essays, but a series of letters published in the *Public Ledger*; and it was not written by a group of contributors or by one man with occasional assistance, but entirely by one man, Oliver Goldsmith. The author professes to be a Chinese visitor in England.

The Periodical Essay

ing in a circle of harmless sheep. Now Britannia sits upon her
own shore, and gives a loose[1] to maternal tenderness; at another
time Parnassus, even the mountain Parnassus, gives way to sorrow, and is bathed in tears of distress.

But the most usual manner is this: Damon meets Menalcas,
who has got a most gloomy countenance. The shepherd asks
his friend whence that look of distress? To which the other
replies that Pollio is no more. "If that be the case, then," cries
Damon, "let us retire to yonder bower at some distance off,
where the cypress and the jasmine add fragrance to the breeze;
and let us weep alternately for Pollio, the friend of shepherds,
and the patron of every muse." "Ah!" returns his fellow shepherd, "what think you rather of that grotto by the fountain
side? The murmuring stream will help to assist our complaints,
and a nightingale on a neighboring tree will join her voice to
the concert!" When the place is thus settled, they begin: the
brook stands still to hear their lamentations; the cows forget
to graze; and the very tigers start from the forest with sympathetic concern. By the tombs of our ancestors, my dear Fum,
I am quite unaffected in all this distress; the whole is liquid
laudanum to my spirits; and a tiger of common sensibility has
twenty times more tenderness than I.

But though I could never weep with the complaining shepherd, yet I am sometimes induced to pity the poet, whose trade
is thus to make demigods and heroes for a dinner. There is not
in nature a more dismal figure than a man who sits down to pre-
meditated flattery: every stanza he writes tacitly reproaches
the meanness of his occupation, till at last his stupidity becomes more stupid and his dullness more diminutive.

I am amazed, therefore, that none have yet found out the
secret of flattering the worthless, and yet of preserving a safe
conscience. I have often wished for some method by which a
man might do himself and his deceased patron justice without
being under the hateful reproach of self-conviction. After long

[1] gives free expression.

[70]

The Citizen of the World

lucubration I have hit upon such an expedient, and sent you the specimen of a poem upon the decease of a great man, in which the flattery is perfectly fine, and yet the poet perfectly innocent.

ON THE DEATH OF THE RIGHT HONORABLE ——

Ye muses, pour the pitying tear
  For Pollio snatch'd away:
Oh, had he liv'd another year!
  — *He had not died today.*

Oh, were ye born to bless mankind
  In virtuous times of yore,
Heroes themselves had fallen behind!
  — *Whene'er he went before.*

How sad the groves and plains appear,
  And sympathetic sheep;[1]
E'en pitying hills would drop a tear:
  — *If hills could learn to weep.*

His bounty in exalted strain
  Each bard might well display,
Since none implored relief in vain!
  — *That went relieved away.*

And hark! I hear the tuneful throng
  His obsequies forbid;
He still shall live, shall live as long
  — *As ever dead man did.*

[1] The poem is based partly on anticlimax, partly on ridicule of pastoral poetry (which Goldsmith despised).

The Periodical Essay

BELIEF IN IDLE RUMORS [Letter 107]

It is the most usual method in every report first to examine its probability, and then act as the conjecture may require. The English, however, exert a different spirit in such circumstances; they first act, and when too late begin to examine. From a knowledge of this disposition, there are several here who make it their business to frame new reports at every convenient interval, all tending to denounce ruin, both on their contemporaries and their posterity. This denunciation is eagerly caught up by the public: away they fling to propagate the distress; sell out at one place, buy in at another, grumble at their governors, shout in mobs, and when they have for some time behaved like fools, sit down coolly to argue and talk wisdom, to puzzle each other with syllogism, and prepare for the next report that prevails, which is always attended with the same success.

Thus are they ever rising above one report, only to sink into another. They resemble a dog in a well, pawing to get free. When he has raised his upper parts above water, and every spectator imagines him disengaged, his lower parts drag him down again and sink him to the nose; he makes new efforts to emerge, and every effort, increasing his weakness, only tends to sink him the deeper.

There are some here who, I am told, make a tolerable subsistence by the credulity of their countrymen. As they find the public fond of blood, wounds, and death, they contrive political ruins suited to every month in the year. This month the people are to be eaten up by the French in flat-bottomed boats; the next by the soldiers, designed to beat the French back; now the people are going to jump down the gulf of luxury, and now nothing but a herring subscription can fish them up again. Time passes on; the report proves false; new circumstances produce new changes; but the people never change — they are persevering in folly.

[72]

The Citizen of the World

In other countries these boding politicians would be left to fret over their own schemes alone, and grow splenetic without hopes of infecting others, but England seems to be the very region where spleen delights to dwell: a man not only can give an unbounded scope to the disorder in himself, but may, if he pleases, propagate it over the whole kingdom, with a certainty of success. He has only to cry out that the government, the government is all wrong; that their schemes are leading to ruin; that Britons are no more: every good member of the commonwealth thinks it his duty, in such a case, to deplore the universal decadence with sympathetic sorrow, and, by fancying the constitution in a decay, absolutely to impair its vigor.

This people would laugh at my simplicity should I advise them to be less sanguine in harboring gloomy predictions, and examine coolly before they attempted to complain. I have just heard a story which, though transacted in a private family, serves very well to describe the behavior of the whole nation in cases of threatened calamity. As there are public so there are private incendiaries here. One of the last, either for the amusement of his friends or to divert a fit of the spleen, lately sent a threatening letter to a worthy family in my neighborhood, to this effect:

SIR:

Knowing you to be very rich, and finding myself to be very poor, I think it proper to inform you that I have learned the secret of poisoning man, woman, and child without danger of detection. Don't be uneasy, sir; you may take your choice of being poisoned in a fortnight, or poisoned in a month, or poisoned in six weeks; you shall have full time to settle all your affairs. Though I am poor, I love to do things like a gentleman. But, sir, you must die; I have determined it within my own breast that you must die. Blood, sir, blood is my trade; so I could wish you would this day six weeks take leave of your friends, wife, and family, for I cannot possibly allow you longer time. To convince you more certainly of the power of my art, by which you may know I speak truth, take this letter; when you have read it, tear off the seal, fold it up, and give it to

[73]

The Periodical Essay

your favorite Dutch mastiff that sits by the fire; he will swallow it, sir, like a buttered toast; in three hours four minutes after he has taken it he will attempt to bite off his own tongue, and half an hour after burst asunder in twenty pieces. Blood! blood! blood! So no more at present from, sir, your most obedient, most devoted, humble servant to command, till death.

You may easily imagine the consternation into which this letter threw the whole good-natured family. The poor man to whom it was addressed was the more surprised, as not knowing how he could merit such inveterate malice. All the friends of the family were convened; it was universally agreed that it was a most terrible affair, and that the government should be solicited to offer a reward and a pardon: a fellow of this kind would go on poisoning family after family, and it was impossible to say where the destruction would end. In pursuance of these determinations the government was applied to; strict search was made after the incendiary, but all in vain. At last, therefore, they recollected that the experiment was not yet tried upon the dog; the Dutch mastiff was brought up and placed in the midst of the friends and relations, the seal was torn off, the packet folded up with care, and soon they found, to the great surprise of all — that the dog would not eat the letter. Adieu.

The Familiar Essay

The essays of Bacon and of Addison, although often included in the general classification of familiar essays, are obviously quite different in spirit, in purpose, and in style from those of Lamb or of Hazlitt. Bacon's are primarily a continuation of the older "wisdom" writings — aphoristic advice on the conduct of life. Addison's are like the periodicals in which they appeared, and are often so impersonal that the authorship is not easy to determine at first sight. But with Lamb we come upon the author talking familiarly with his reader. He may call himself Elia, and his sister Mary may masquerade as his cousin Bridget; but the disguise is all too thin. It is not by chance that Lamb's personal letters and manuscripts are in such great request among collectors: he is to all readers a personality and to many a lifelong friend.

However, even in this intimate sense the familiar essay did not entirely begin with Lamb. It is to be found in its essential qualities in a few seventeenth-century writers, such as Sir William Temple and Samuel Pepys. The "Diary" of Pepys, although meant for no reader but himself and although written as a series of formless daily entries, illustrates perfectly the spirit of the familiar essay. No author has ever laid aside his pen with a more touching regret than did Pepys, when he discontinued his writing through fear of blindness:

And thus ends all that I doubt I shall ever be able to do with my own eyes in the keeping of my Journal, I being not able to do it any longer, having done now so long as to undo my eyes almost every time that I take a pen in my hand; and, therefore, whatever comes of it, I must forbear; and, therefore, resolve, from this time forward,

The Familiar Essay

to have it kept by my people in longhand, and must therefore be contented to set down no more than is fit for them and all the world to know. . . .

And so I betake myself to that course, which is almost as much as to see myself go into my grave: for which, and all the discomforts that will accompany my being blind, the good God prepare me!

Although it was in the periodicals that the eighteenth century made its special contribution to the essay, it advanced the spirit of the familiar essay by the personal letters of such writers as Lady Mary Wortley Montagu, Lord Chesterfield, and Horace Walpole. It also contributed to the direct forerunners of the descriptive nature essay in the writings of Gilbert White. In spite of the formlessness of these letters addressed to two of his correspondents, White still remains one of the most charming of all the nature essayists. He observes keenly, but his observation is not dissected by the minute scientific studies of a later age; he loves nature, but he does not look for his own moods in "the meanest flower that blows." To him a house cricket is a house cricket, a very interesting object in itself, not a mere *gryllus domesticus* and not a mere object for romantic contemplation.

In the nineteenth century the familiar essay reached its fullest development in the writings of such men as Lamb, Hazlitt, and Stevenson. This advance was aided by many influences, such as the individualism of the age, the prevalence of magazines which called for longer and more personal essays, the revival of interest in Montaigne, and the examples of Lamb and of Hazlitt. Lamb, although too individualistic in style and manner to be very successfully imitated, became the most beloved and most widely read of all English essayists. Hazlitt became for a century afterwards what Montaigne had been before him — the chief exemplar of the familiar essay, the model and inspiration for his followers.

The character essay had already reached its fullest possible development, and it was now being absorbed into the short story

The Familiar Essay

and the novel; but in the hands of some writers, especially Carlyle, the sharp portrayal of detached characters still continued as a fine art.

The descriptive essay has reached a very high level in the last century, lending itself admirably to the increased interest in nature, in travels, and in out-of-the-way places and people. It serves equally well to describe strange jungles in South America and unfamiliar aspects of New York.

But even in the familiar essay the moral tone is not altogether lacking. It has been said of Stevenson that he was a Scotchman, and therefore a preacher. It might be said of all English literature, from "Beowulf" to our own time, that there is an incessant questioning of life, of character, and of human conduct. Hazlitt's "Travelling Abroad" is so complete an exposure of the English tourist of his day that it applies almost equally to the American tourist of our time. Stevenson's "Æs Triplex" states what is perhaps the favorite thesis of all the essayists — that life is to be lived, not hoarded up or shirked.

SIR WILLIAM TEMPLE

[1628-1699]

OF POETRY AND MUSIC [1]

Among the Romans the last and great Scipio passed the soft
hours of his life in the conversation of Terence, and was thought
to have a part in the composition of his comedies. Cæsar was
an excellent poet as well as orator, and composed a poem in his
voyage from Rome to Spain, relieving the tedious difficulties
of his march with the entertainments of his muse. Augustus
was not only a patron, but a friend and companion of Virgil
and Horace, and was himself both an admirer of poetry and a
pretender too, as far as his genius would reach or his busy scene
allow. 'Tis true, since his age we have few such examples of
great princes favoring or affecting poetry, and as few perhaps
of great poets deserving it. Whether it be that the fierceness of
the Gothic humors, or noise of their perpetual wars, frighted it
away, or that the unequal mixture of the modern languages
would not bear it, certain it is, that the great heights and excellency both of poetry and music fell with the Roman learning
and empire, and have never since recovered the admiration and
applauses that before attended them.[2] Yet such as they are
amongst us, they must be confessed to be the softest and sweet-
est, the most general and most innocent amusements of common
time and life. They still find room in the courts of princes and
the cottages of shepherds. They serve to revive and animate
the dead calm of poor or idle lives and to allay or divert the

[1] The passage given here is the conclusion of the essay "Of Poetry."
[2] The relative excellence of the ancients and moderns was hotly contested
in Temple's time.

[78]

Sir William Temple

violent passions and perturbations of the greatest and the busiest men. And both these effects are of equal use to human life, for the mind of man is like the sea, which is neither agreeable to the beholder nor the voyager in a calm or in a storm, but is so to both when a little agitated by gentle gales; and so the mind, when moved by soft and easy passions or affections. I know very well that many, who pretend to be wise by the forms of being grave, are apt to despise both poetry and music as toys and trifles too light for the use or entertainment of serious men. But whoever find themselves wholly insensible to these charms would, I think, do well to keep their own counsel, for fear of reproaching their own temper and bringing the goodness of their natures, if not of their understandings, into question. It may be thought at least an ill sign, if not an ill constitution, since some of the Fathers[1] went so far as to esteem the love of music a sign of predestination, as a thing divine, and reserved for the felicities of heaven itself. While this world lasts, I doubt not but the pleasure and request of these two entertainments will do so too; and happy those that content themselves with these or any other so easy and so innocent, and do not trouble the world or other men, because they cannot be quiet themselves, though nobody hurts them!

When all is done, human life is, at the greatest and the best, but like a froward child, that must be played with and humored a little to keep it quiet till it falls asleep, and then the care is over.

[1] Early Christian writers.

CHARLES LAMB

[1775–1834]

MRS. BATTLE'S OPINIONS ON WHIST

"A clear fire, a clean hearth, and the rigor of the game."
This was the celebrated *wish* of old Sarah Battle (now with
God), who, next to her devotions, loved a good game at whist.
She was none of your lukewarm gamesters, your half-and-half
players, who have no objection to take a hand, if you want one
to make up a rubber; who affirm that they have no pleasure in
winning; that they like to win one game and lose another; that
they can while away an hour very agreeably at a card-table, but
are indifferent whether they play or no; and will desire an adversary, who has slipped a wrong card, to take it up and play
another. These insufferable triflers are the curse of a table. One
of these flies will spoil a whole pot. Of such it may be said that
they do not play at cards, but only play at playing at them.

Sarah Battle was none of that breed. She detested them,
as I do, from her heart and soul, and would not, save upon
a striking emergency, willingly seat herself at the same table
with them. She loved a thorough-paced partner, a determined
enemy. She took, and gave, no concessions. She hated favors.
She never made a revoke, nor ever passed it over in her adversary without exacting the utmost forfeiture. She fought a
good fight: cut and thrust. She held not her good sword (her
cards) "like a dancer." She sate bolt upright; and neither
showed you her cards, nor desired to see yours. All people
have their blind side — their superstitions; and I have heard
her declare, under the rose,[1] that Hearts was her favorite suit.

[1] *Sub rosa*, confidentially.

[80]

Charles Lamb

I never in my life — and I knew Sarah Battle many of the best years of it — saw her take out her snuffbox when it was her turn to play; or snuff a candle in the middle of a game; or ring for a servant, till it was fairly over. She never introduced, or connived at, miscellaneous conversation during its process. As she emphatically observed, cards were cards; and if I ever saw unmingled distaste in her fine last-century countenance, it was at the airs of a young gentleman of a literary turn, who had been with difficulty persuaded to take a hand, and who, in his excess of candor, declared that he thought there was no harm in unbending the mind now and then, after serious studies, in recreations of that kind! She could not bear to have her noble occupation, to which she wound up her faculties, considered in that light. It was her business, her duty, the thing she came into the world to do — and she did it. She unbent her mind afterwards — over a book.

Pope was her favorite author; his "Rape of the Lock" her favorite work. She once did me the favor to play over with me (with the cards) his celebrated game of Omber in that poem; and to explain to me how far it agreed with, and in what points it would be found to differ from, tradrille. Her illustrations were apposite and poignant; and I had the pleasure of sending the substance of them to Mr. Bowles,[1] but I suppose they came too late to be inserted among his ingenious notes upon that author.

Quadrille, she has often told me, was her first love; but whist had engaged her maturer esteem. The former, she said, was showy and specious, and likely to allure young persons. The uncertainty and quick shifting of partners — a thing which the constancy of whist abhors; the dazzling supremacy and regal investiture of Spadille — absurd, as she justly observed, in the pure aristocracy of whist, where his crown and garter give him no proper power above his brother nobility of the Aces; the giddy vanity, so taking to the inexperienced, of playing alone;

[1] William Lisle Bowles brought out an edition of Pope in 1806.

above all, the overpowering attractions of a *Sans Prendre Vole*,[1] to the triumph of which there is certainly nothing parallel or approaching, in the contingencies of whist — all these, she would say, make quadrille a game of captivation to the young and enthusiastic. But whist was the *solider* game: that was her word. It was a long meal; not like quadrille, a feast of snatches. One or two rubbers might coextend in duration with an evening. They gave time to form rooted friendships, to cultivate steady enmities. She despised the chance-started, capricious, and ever-fluctuating alliances of the other. The skirmishes of quadrille, she would say, reminded her of the petty ephemeral embroilments of the little Italian states, depicted by Machiavel[2]: perpetually changing postures and connections; bitter foes today, sugared darlings tomorrow; kissing and scratching in a breath; but the wars of whist were comparable to the long, steady, deep-rooted, rational antipathies of the great French and English nations.

A grave simplicity was what she chiefly admired in her favorite game. There was nothing silly in it, like the nob in cribbage — nothing superfluous. No *flushes* — that most irrational of all pleas that a reasonable being can set up: that anyone should claim four by virtue of holding cards of the same mark and color, without reference to the playing of the game, or the individual worth or pretensions of the cards themselves! She held this to be a solecism; as pitiful an ambition at cards as alliteration is in authorship. She despised superficiality, and looked deeper than the colors of things. Suits were soldiers, she would say, and must have a uniformity of array to distinguish them; but what should we say to a foolish squire who should claim a merit from dressing up his tenantry in red jackets that never were to be marshaled — never to take the field? She even wished that whist were more simple than it is; and in my mind, would have stripped it of some appendages which

[1] Taking a slam without a partner; winning all tricks alone.
[2] Machiavelli, a Florentine statesman and political writer (1469-1527).

Charles Lamb

in the state of human frailty may be venially, and even commendably, allowed of. She saw no reason for the deciding of the trump by the turn of the card. Why not one suit always trumps? Why two colors, when the mark of the suits would have sufficiently distinguished them without it?

"But the eye, my dear madam, is agreeably refreshed with the variety. Man is not a creature of pure reason — he must have his senses delightfully appealed to. We see it in Roman Catholic countries, where the music and the paintings draw in many to worship, whom your quaker spirit of unsensualizing would have kept out. You, yourself, have a pretty collection of paintings — but confess to me, whether, walking in your gallery at Sandham, among those clear Vandykes,[1] or among the Paul Potters[2] in the anteroom, you ever felt your bosom glow with an elegant delight at all comparable to *that* you have it in your power to experience most evenings over a well-arranged assortment of the court cards? — the pretty antic habits, like heralds in a procession — the gay triumph-assuring scarlets — the contrasting deadly killing sables — the 'hoary majesty of spades' — Pam[3] in all his glory! —

"All these might be dispensed with; and, with their naked names upon the drab pasteboard, the game might go on very well, pictureless, but the *beauty* of cards would be extinguished forever. Stripped of all that is imaginative in them, they must degenerate into mere gambling. Imagine a dull deal board or drumhead to spread them on, instead of that nice verdant carpet (next to nature's), fittest arena for those courtly combatants to play their gallant justs and tourneys in! Exchange those delicately turned ivory markers (work of Chinese artist, unconscious of their symbol, or as profanely slighting their true application as the arrantest Ephesian[4] journeyman that

---

[1] Van Dyck (1599-1641) was a Flemish portrait painter.
[2] Potter (1625-1654) was a Dutch painter of cattle and landscapes.
[3] The knave of clubs, the highest trump in the game of loo.
[4] Ephesus was famous for its temple of Diana.

turned out those little shrines for the goddess) — exchange them for little bits of leather (our ancestors' money), or chalk and a slate!"

The old lady, with a smile, confessed the soundness of my logic; and to her approbation of my arguments on her favorite topic that evening I have always fancied myself indebted for the legacy of a curious cribbage board, made of the finest Sienna marble, which her maternal uncle (old Walter Plumer,[1] whom I have elsewhere celebrated) brought with him from Florence — this, and a trifle of five hundred pounds, came to me at her death.

The former bequest (which I do not least value) I have kept with religious care; though she herself, to confess a truth, was never greatly taken with cribbage. It was an essentially vulgar game, I have heard her say, disputing with her uncle, who was very partial to it. She could never heartily bring her mouth to pronounce "*Go,*" or "*That's a go.*" She called it an ungrammatical game. The pegging teased her. I once knew her to forfeit a rubber (a five-dollar[2] stake) because she would not take advantage of the turn-up knave, which would have given it her, but which she must have claimed by the disgraceful tenure of declaring "*two for his heels.*" There is something extremely genteel in this sort of self-denial. Sarah Battle was a gentlewoman born.

Piquet she held the best game at the cards for two persons, though she would ridicule the pedantry of the terms, such as pique, repique, the capot; they savored (she thought) of affectation. But games for two, or even three, she never greatly cared for. She loved the quadrate, or square. She would argue thus: Cards are warfare — the ends are gain, with glory. But cards are war in disguise of a sport: when single adversaries encounter, the ends proposed are too palpable. By themselves it is too close a fight; with spectators it is not much bettered.

[1] Mentioned also in "The South-Sea House," the first of Lamb's "Essays of Elia."   [2] dollar, English slang for the old five-shilling piece, or crown.

Charles Lamb

No looker-on can be interested, except for a bet, and then it is a mere affair of money; he cares not for your luck *sympathetically*, or for your play. Three are still worse: a mere naked war of every man against every man, as in cribbage, without league or alliance; or a rotation of petty and contradictory interests, a succession of heartless leagues, and not much more hearty infractions of them, as in tradrille. But in square games (*she meant whist*) all that is possible to be attained in card-playing is accomplished. There are the incentives of profit with honor, common to every species, though the *latter* can be but very imperfectly enjoyed in those other games, where the spectator is only feebly a participator. But the parties in whist are spectators and principals too. They are a theater to themselves, and a looker-on is not wanted. He is rather worse than nothing, and an impertinence. Whist abhors neutrality, or interests beyond its sphere. You glory in some surprising stroke of skill or fortune, not because a cold — or even an interested — bystander witnesses it, but because your *partner* sympathizes in the contingency. You win for two. You triumph for two. Two are exalted. Two again are mortified; which divides their disgrace, as the conjunction doubles (by taking off the invidiousness) your glories. Two losing to two are better reconciled than one to one in that close butchery. The hostile feeling is weakened by multiplying the channels. War becomes a civil game. By such reasonings as these the old lady was accustomed to defend her favorite pastime.

No inducement could ever prevail upon her to play at any game, where chance entered into the composition, *for nothing*. Chance, she would argue — and here, again, admire the subtlety of her conclusion!— chance is nothing, but where something else depends upon it. It is obvious that cannot be *glory*. What rational cause of exultation could it give to a man to turn up size ace a hundred times together by himself? or before spectators, where no stake was depending? Make a lottery of a hundred thousand tickets with but one fortunate number, and

The Familiar Essay

what possible principle of our nature, except stupid wonderment, could it gratify to gain that number as many times successively, without a prize? Therefore she disliked the mixture of chance in backgammon where it was not played for money. She called it foolish, and those people idiots who were taken with a lucky hit under such circumstances. Games of pure skill were as little to her fancy. Played for a stake, they were a mere system of over-reaching. Played for glory, they were a mere setting of one man's wit — his memory, or combination-faculty rather — against another's; like a mock engagement at a review, bloodless and profitless. She could not conceive a *game* wanting the sprightly infusion of chance, the handsome excuses of good fortune. Two people playing at chess in a corner of a room, whilst whist was stirring in the center, would inspire her with insufferable horror and ennui. Those well-cut similitudes of Castles and Knights, the *imagery* of the board, she would argue (and I think in this case justly), were entirely misplaced and senseless. Those hard head-contests can in no instance ally with the fancy. They reject form and color. A pencil and dry slate (she used to say) were the proper arena for such combatants.

To those puny objectors against cards, as nurturing the bad passions, she would retort that man is a gaming animal. He must be always trying to get the better in something or other; that this passion can scarcely be more safely expended than upon a game at cards; that cards are a temporary illusion — in truth, a mere drama, for we do but *play* at being mightily concerned, where a few idle shillings are at stake, yet during the illusion we *are* as mightily concerned as those whose stake is crowns and kingdoms. They are a sort of dream-fighting; much ado, great battling, and little bloodshed; mighty means for disproportioned ends; quite as diverting, and a great deal more innoxious, than many of those more serious *games* of life, which men play without esteeming them to be such.

With great deference to the old lady's judgment in these matters, I think I have experienced some moments in my life when playing at cards *for nothing* has even been agreeable. When I am in sickness or not in the best spirits I sometimes call for the cards, and play a game at piquet *for love* with my cousin Bridget — Bridget Elia.[1]

I grant there is something sneaking in it; but with a toothache or a sprained ankle — when you are subdued and humble — you are glad to put up with an inferior spring of action.

There is such a thing in nature, I am convinced, as *sick whist.*

I grant it is not the highest style of man; I deprecate the manes[2] of Sarah Battle — she lives not, alas! to whom I should apologize.

At such times those *terms* which my old friend objected to come in as something admissible. I love to get a tierce or a quatorze, though they mean nothing. I am subdued to an inferior interest. Those shadows of winning amuse me.

That last game I had with my sweet cousin (I capotted[3] her) — (dare I tell thee, how foolish I am?) — I wished it might have lasted forever, though we gained nothing and lost nothing, though it was a mere shade of play: I would be content to go on in that idle folly forever. The pipkin[4] should be ever boiling that was to prepare the gentle lenitive to my foot, which Bridget was doomed to apply after the game was over; and, as I do not much relish appliances, there it should ever bubble. Bridget and I should be ever playing.

[1] Mary Lamb, his sister.
[2] To seek by prayer to avert the spirit (said of the dead).
[3] Won all the tricks from.
[4] A small earthen pot.

The Familiar Essay

DREAM–CHILDREN: A REVERIE

Children love to listen to stories about their elders when *they* were children; to stretch their imagination to the conception of a traditionary great-uncle, or grandame, whom they never saw. It was in this spirit that my little ones crept about me the other evening to hear about their great-grandmother Field,[1] who lived in a great house in Norfolk (a hundred times bigger than that in which they and papa lived) which had been the scene — so at least it was generally believed in that part of the country — of the tragic incidents which they had lately become familiar with from the ballad of the "Children in the Wood." Certain it is that the whole story of the children and their cruel uncle was to be seen fairly carved out in wood upon the chimney piece of the great hall, the whole story down to the Robin Redbreasts, till a foolish rich person pulled it down to set up a marble one of modern invention in its stead, with no story upon it. Here Alice put out one of her dear mother's looks, too tender to be called upbraiding. Then I went on to say how religious and how good their great-grandmother Field was; how beloved and respected by everybody, though she was not indeed the mistress of this great house, but had only the charge of it (and yet in some respects she might be said to be the mistress of it too) committed to her by the owner, who preferred living in a newer and more fashionable mansion which he had purchased somewhere in the adjoining county; but still she lived in it in a manner as if it had been her own, and kept up the dignity of the great house in a sort while she lived, which afterwards came to decay, and was nearly pulled down, and all its old ornaments stripped and carried away to the owner's other house, where they were set up, and looked as awkward as if someone were to carry away the old tombs they had seen lately at the Abbey and stick them up in Lady C's tawdry gilt drawing-room. Here John smiled, as much as to say, "That would

[1] Lamb's grandmother, Mary Field.

[88]

be foolish indeed." And then I told how, when she came to die, her funeral was attended by a concourse of all the poor, and some of the gentry too, of the neighborhood for many miles around, to show their respect for her memory, because she had been such a good and religious woman; so good indeed that she knew all the Psaltery by heart — ay, and a great part of the Testament besides. Here little Alice spread her hands. Then I told what a tall, upright, graceful person their great-grandmother Field once was; and how in her youth she was esteemed the best dancer — here Alice's little right foot played an involuntary movement, till, upon my looking grave, it desisted — the best dancer, I was saying, in the county, till a cruel disease, called a cancer, came, and bowed her down with pain; but it could never bend her good spirits or make them stoop, but they were still upright, because she was so good and religious. Then I told how she was used to sleep by herself in a lone chamber of the great lone house; and how she believed that an apparition of two infants[1] was to be seen at midnight gliding up and down the great staircase near where she slept, but she said "those innocents would do her no harm"; and how frightened I used to be, though in those days I had my maid to sleep with me, because I was never half so good or religious as she — and yet I never saw the infants. Here John expanded all his eyebrows and tried to look courageous. Then I told how good she was to all her grandchildren, having us to the great house in the holidays, where I in particular used to spend many hours by myself in gazing upon the old busts of the Twelve Cæsars, that had been emperors of Rome, till the old marble heads would seem to live again, or I to be turned into marble with them; how I never could be tired with roaming about that huge mansion, with its vast empty rooms with their worn-out hangings, fluttering tapestry, and carved oaken panels with the gilding almost rubbed out — sometimes in the spacious old-fashioned gardens, which I had almost to myself, unless when now and then a soli-

---

[1] The two Children in the Wood, referred to above.

tary gardening man would cross me; and how the nectarines
and peaches hung upon the walls, without my ever offering to
pluck them, because they were forbidden fruit, unless now and
then, and because I had more pleasure in strolling about among
the old melancholy looking yew trees or the firs and picking up
the red berries and the fir apples, which were good for nothing
but to look at, or in lying about upon the fresh grass with all the
fine garden smells around me, or basking in the orangery till I
could almost fancy myself ripening too along with the oranges
and the limes in that grateful warmth, or in watching the dace
that darted to and fro in the fishpond at the bottom of the
garden, with here and there a great sulky pike hanging midway
down the water in silent state, as if it mocked at their impertinent friskings, — I had more pleasure in these busy-idle diversions than in all the sweet flavors of peaches, nectarines, oranges,
and suchlike common baits of children. Here John slyly de-
posited back upon the plate a bunch of grapes which, not unobserved by Alice, he had meditated dividing with her, and
both seemed willing to relinquish them for the present as irrelevant. Then, in somewhat a more heightened tone, I told how,
though their great-grandmother Field loved all her grandchildren, yet in an especial manner she might be said to love their
uncle John L ——,[1] because he was so handsome and spirited a
youth, and a king to the rest of us; and instead of moping about
in solitary corners, like some of us, he would mount the most
mettlesome horse he could get, when but an imp no bigger than
themselves, and make it carry him half over the county in a
morning, and join the hunters when there were any out, and
yet he loved the old great house and gardens too, but had too
much spirit to be always pent up within their boundaries; and
how their uncle grew up to man's estate as brave as he was
handsome, to the admiration of everybody, but of their great-
grandmother Field most especially; and how he used to carry

[1] Lamb's brother, John, who had died a month or two before this essay
was written.

me upon his back when I was a lame-footed boy — for he was a
good bit older than me — many a mile when I could not walk
for pain; and how in after life he became lame-footed[1] too,
and I did not always (I fear) make allowances enough for him
when he was impatient and in pain, nor remember sufficiently
how considerate he had been to me when I was lame-footed;
and how when he died, though he had not been dead an hour,
it seemed as if he had died a great while ago, such a distance
there is betwixt life and death; and how I bore his death as I
thought pretty well at first, but afterwards it haunted and
haunted me, and though I did not cry or take it to heart as
some do and as I think he would have done if I had died, yet I
missed him all day long, and knew not till then how much I had
loved him. I missed his kindness, and I missed his crossness,
and wished him to be alive again, to be quarreling with him
(for we quarreled sometimes), rather than not have him again,
and was as uneasy without him as he, their poor uncle, must
have been when the doctor took off his limb. Here the children
fell a-crying, and asked if their little mourning which they had
on was not for Uncle John, and they looked up, and prayed me
not to go on about their uncle, but to tell them some stories
about their pretty dead mother. Then I told how for seven
long years, in hope sometimes, sometimes in despair, yet persisting ever, I courted the fair Alice W——n[2]; and, as much as
children could understand, I explained to them what coyness,
and difficulty, and denial meant in maidens — when suddenly,
turning to Alice, the soul of the first Alice looked out at her
eyes with such a reality of represenment that I became in doubt
which of them stood there before me, or whose that bright hair
was; and while I stood gazing, both the children gradually grew
fainter to my view, receding, and still receding, till nothing at

[1] It is not known whether Charles Lamb was ever lame. John suffered
some such injury, and made it an excuse for shirking.

[2] Alice Winterton, a feigned name for a girl whom Lamb had loved in
youth; apparently Ann Simmons, who afterwards married Mr. Bartram.

last but two mournful features were seen in the uttermost distance, which, without speech, strangely impressed upon me the effects of speech: "We are not of Alice, nor of thee, nor are we children at all. The children of Alice call Bartrum father. We are nothing, less than nothing, and dreams. We are only what might have been, and must wait upon the tedious shores of Lethe[1] millions of ages before we have existence, and a name"; and immediately awaking, I found myself quietly seated in my bachelor armchair, where I had fallen asleep, with the faithful Bridget[2] unchanged by my side — but John L. (or James Elia) was gone forever.

THE CONVALESCENT

A pretty severe fit of indisposition which, under the name of a nervous fever, has made a prisoner of me for some weeks past, and is but slowly leaving me, has reduced me to an incapacity of reflecting upon any topic foreign to itself. Expect no healthy conclusions from me this month, Reader; I can offer you only sick men's dreams.

And truly the whole state of sickness is such; for what else is it but a magnificent dream for a man to lie a-bed, and draw daylight curtains about him; and, shutting out the sun, to induce a total oblivion of all the works which are going on under it? To become insensible to all the operations of life, except the beatings of one feeble pulse?

If there be a regal solitude, it is a sick-bed. How the patient lords it there; what caprices he acts without control! how king-like he sways his pillow — tumbling, and tossing, and shifting, and lowering, and thumping, and flatting, and molding it, to the ever-varying requisitions of his throbbing temples.

He changes *sides* oftener than a politician. Now he lies full length, then half length, obliquely, transversely, head and feet quite across the bed; and none accuses him of tergiversation.

[1] The river of forgetfulness.   [2] Mary Lamb, as always in the essays.

Charles Lamb

Within the four curtains he is absolute. They are his *mare clausum*.[1]

How sickness enlarges the dimensions of a man's self to himself! he is his own exclusive object. Supreme selfishness is inculcated upon him as his only duty. 'Tis the Two Tables of the Law[2] to him. He has nothing to think of but how to get well. What passes out of doors or within them, so he hear not the jarring of them, affects him not.

A little while ago he was greatly concerned in the event of a lawsuit, which was to be the making or the marring of his dearest friend. He was to be seen trudging about upon this man's errand to fifty quarters of the town at once, jogging this witness, refreshing that solicitor. The cause was to come on yesterday. He is absolutely as indifferent to the decision as if it were a question to be tried at Pekin. Peradventure from some whispering going on about the house, not intended for his hearing, he picks up enough to make him understand that things went cross-grained in the court yesterday and his friend is ruined. But the word "friend" and the word "ruin" disturb him no more than so much jargon. He is not to think of anything but how to get better.

What a world of foreign cares are merged in that absorbing consideration!

He has put on the strong armor of sickness, he is wrapped up in the callous hide of suffering; he keeps his sympathy, like some curious vintage, under trusty lock and key, for his own use only.

He lies pitying himself, honing and moaning to himself; he yearneth over himself; his bowels are even melted within him, to think what he suffers; he is not ashamed to weep over himself.

He is forever plotting how to do some good to himself; studying little stratagems and artificial alleviations.

[1] "closed sea" (one subject to a particular nation, as distinct from the open sea).
[2] The stone slabs on which Moses brought the Law from Mount Sinai.

The Familiar Essay

He makes the most of himself — dividing himself, by an allowable fiction, into as many distinct individuals as he hath sore and sorrowing members. Sometimes he meditates — as of a dull thing apart from him — upon his poor aching head, and that dull pain which, dozing or waking, lay in it all the past night like a log, or palpable substance of pain, not to be removed without opening the very skull, as it seemed, to take it thence. Or he pities his long, clammy, attenuated fingers. He compassionates himself all over; and his bed is a very discipline of humanity and tender heart.

He is his own sympathizer, and instinctively feels that none can so well perform that office for him. He cares for few spectators to his tragedy. Only that punctual face of the old nurse pleases him that announces his broths and his cordials. He likes it because it is so unmoved, and because he can pour forth his feverish ejaculations before it as unreservedly as to his bedpost.

To the world's business he is dead. He understands not what the callings and occupations of mortals are; only he has a glimmering conceit of some such thing, when the doctor makes his daily call; and even in the lines of that busy face he reads no multiplicity of patients, but solely conceives of himself as *the sick man*. To what other uneasy couch the good man is hastening, when he slips out of his chamber, folding up his thin douceur[1] so carefully for fear of rustling, is no speculation which he can at present entertain. He thinks only of the regular return of the same phenomenon at the same hour tomorrow.

Household rumors touch him not. Some faint murmur, indicative of life going on within the house, soothes him, while he knows not distinctly what it is. He is not to know anything, not to think of anything. Servants gliding up and down the distant staircase, treading as upon velvet, gently keep his ear awake, so long as he troubles not himself further than with some feeble guess at their errands. Exacter knowledge would be a burden to him: he can just endure the pressure of con-

[1] a gratuity; here, a fee.

Charles Lamb

jecture. He opens his eye faintly at the dull stroke of the muffled knocker, and closes it again without asking "Who was it?" He is flattered by a general notion that inquiries are making after him, but he cares not to know the name of the inquirer. In the general stillness and awful hush of the house he lies in state and feels his sovereignty.

To be sick is to enjoy monarchal prerogatives. Compare the silent tread and quiet ministry, almost by the eye only, with which he is served, with the careless demeanor, the unceremonious goings in and out (slapping of doors or leaving them open) of the very same attendants, when he is getting a little better, and you will confess that from the bed of sickness (throne, let me rather call it) to the elbow chair of convalescence is a fall from dignity amounting to a deposition.

How convalescence shrinks a man back to his pristine stature! Where is now the space which he occupied so lately in his own, in the family's eye?

The scene of his regalities, his sick-room, which was his presence chamber, where he lay and acted his despotic fancies — how is it reduced to a common bedroom! The trimness of the very bed has something petty and unmeaning about it. It is *made* every day. How unlike to that wavy, many-furrowed, oceanic surface which it presented so short a time since, when to *make* it was a service not to be thought of at oftener than three- or four-day revolutions, when the patient was with pain and grief to be lifted for a little while out of it, to submit to the encroachments of unwelcome neatness, and decencies which his shaken frame deprecated; then to be lifted into it again for another three or four days' respite, to flounder it out of shape again, while every fresh furrow was an historical record of some shifting posture, some uneasy turning, some seeking for a little ease; and the shrunken skin scarce told a truer story than the crumpled coverlid.

Hushed are those mysterious sighs — those groans — so much more awful while we knew not from what caverns of vast hidden

[95]

The Familiar Essay

suffering they proceeded. The Lernean[1] pangs are quenched. The riddle of sickness is solved; and Philoctetes[2] is become an ordinary personage.

Perhaps some relic of the sick man's dream of greatness survives in the still lingering visitations of the medical attendant. But how is he, too, changed with everything else! Can this be he — this man of news — of chat — of anecdote — of everything but physic — can this be he who so lately came between the patient and his cruel enemy, as on some solemn embassy from nature, erecting herself into a high mediating party? Pshaw! 'tis some old woman.

Farewell with him all that made sickness pompous: the spell that hushed the household — the desert-like stillness, felt throughout its inmost chambers — the mute attendance — the inquiry by looks — the still softer delicacies of self-attention — the sole and single eye of distemper alonely fixed upon itself — world-thoughts excluded — the man a world unto himself — his own theater —

What a speck is he dwindled into!

In this flat swamp of convalescence, left by the ebb of sickness, yet far enough from the terra firma of established health, your note, dear Editor, reached me, requesting — an article. *In articulo mortis,*[3] thought I; but it is something hard — and the quibble, wretched as it was, relieved me. The summons, unseasonable as it appeared, seemed to link me on again to the petty businesses of life, which I had lost sight of; a gentle call to activity, however trivial; a wholesome weaning from that preposterous dream of self-absorption — the puffy state of sickness — in which I confess to have lain so long, insensible to the magazines and monarchies of the world alike, to its laws, and to its literature. The hypochondriac flatus is subsiding; the acres, which in imagination I had spread over — for the

[1] Hercules killed the Hydra in Lerna and poisoned his arrows with its blood.
[2] Philoctetes, to whom the arrows were given, wounded his own foot and suffered agony until he was cured.   [3] "at the point of death."

Charles Lamb

sick man swells in the sole contemplation of his single sufferings, till he becomes a Tityus[1] to himself — are wasting to a span; and for the giant of self-importance, which I was so lately, you have me once again in my natural pretensions — the lean and meager figure of your insignificant Essayist.

CAPTAIN JACKSON

Among the deaths in our obituary for this month, I observe with concern "At his cottage on the Bath Road, Captain Jackson." The name and attribution are common enough; but a feeling like reproach persuades me that this could have been no other in fact than my dear old friend, who some five-and-twenty years ago rented a tenement, which he was pleased to dignify with the appellation here used, about a mile from Westbourn Green. Alack, how good men, and the good turns they do us, slide out of memory, and are recalled but by the surprise of some such sad memento as that which now lies before us!

He whom I mean was a retired half-pay officer, with a wife and two grown-up daughters, whom he maintained with the port[2] and notions of gentlewomen upon that slender professional allowance. Comely girls they were, too.

And was I in danger of forgetting this man? — his cheerful suppers — the noble tone of hospitality, when first you set your foot in *the cottage* — the anxious ministerings about you, where little or nothing (God knows) was to be ministered. Althea's horn[3] in a poor platter — the power of self-enchantment, by which, in his magnificent wishes to entertain you, he multiplied his means to bounties.

You saw with your bodily eyes indeed what seemed a bare scrag — cold savings from the foregone meal — remnant hardly

---

[1] A giant in classical mythology.   [2] bearing; behavior.
[3] One of the horns of the goat Amalthæa, upon whose milk the infant Jupiter was fed; afterwards the cornucopia, or horn of plenty.

The Familiar Essay

sufficient to send a mendicant from the door contented. But in the copious will — the reveling imagination of your host — the "mind, the mind, Master Shallow,"[1] whole beeves were spread before you — hecatombs — no end appeared to the profusion.

It was the widow's cruse[2] — the loaves and fishes[3]; carving could not lessen, nor helping diminish it — the stamina were left — the elemental bone still flourished, divested of its accidents.

"Let us live while we can," methinks I hear the open-handed creature exclaim; "while we have, let us not want," "here is plenty left," "want for nothing" — with many more such hospitable sayings — the spurs of appetite, and old concomitants of smoking boards and feast-oppressed chargers. Then sliding a slender ratio of Single Gloucester[4] upon his wife's plate, or the daughter's, he would convey the remanent[5] rind into his own, with a merry quirk of "the nearer the bone," etc., and declaring that he universally preferred the outside. For we had our table distinctions, you are to know, and some of us in a manner sate above the salt.[6] None but his guest or guests dreamed of tasting flesh luxuries at night; the fragments were *vere hospitibus sacra.*[7] But of one thing or another there was always enough, and leavings; only he would sometimes finish the remainder crust, to show that he wished no savings.

Wine we had none; nor, except on very rare occasions, spirits; but the sensation of wine was there. Some thin kind of ale I remember — "British beverage," he would say! "Push about, my boys"; "Drink to your sweethearts, girls." At every meager draft a toast must ensue, or a song. All the forms of good liquor were there, with none of the effects wanting. Shut your eyes, and you would swear a capacious bowl of punch was foaming in the center, with beams of generous port or

[1] "Give me the spirit, Master Shallow" ("2 Henry IV," III, ii, 278).
[2] See 1 Kings xvii.　[3] The miracle recorded in all four of the Gospels.
[4] Gloucestershire cheese; the double cheese is made of richer milk than the single.　[5] remaining.　[6] near the head of the table.
[7] "in truth sacred to guests."

Charles Lamb

Madeira radiating to it from each of the table corners. You got flustered, without knowing whence; tipsy upon words; and reeled under the potency of his unperforming Bacchanalian encouragements.

We had our songs: "Why, Soldiers, Why," and the "British Grenadiers," in which last we were all obliged to bear chorus. Both the daughters sang. Their proficiency was a nightly theme — the masters he had given them, the "no-expense" which he spared to accomplish them in a science "so necessary to young women." But then — they could not sing "without the instrument."

Sacred, and, by me, never-to-be-violated Secrets of Poverty! Should I disclose your honest aims at grandeur, your makeshift efforts of magnificence? Sleep, sleep, with all thy broken keys, if one of the bunch be extant; thrummed by a thousand ancestral thumbs; dear, cracked spinet of dearer Louisa! Without mention of mine, be dumb, thou thin accompanier of her thinner warble! A veil be spread over the dear delighted face of the well-deluded father, who now haply listening to cherubic notes, scarce feels sincerer pleasure than when she awakened thy time-shaken chords responsive to the twitterings of that slender image of a voice.

We were not without our literary talk either. It did not extend far, but as far as it went it was good. It was bottomed well; had good grounds to go upon. In *the cottage* was a room which tradition authenticated to have been the same in which Glover, in his occasional retirements, had penned the greater part of his "Leonidas."[1] This circumstance was nightly quoted, though none of the present inmates, that I could discover, appeared ever to have met with the poem in question. But that was no matter. Glover had written there, and the anecdote was pressed into the account of the family importance. It diffused a learned air through the apartment, the little side casement of which (the poet's study window), opening upon

[1] Glover's "Leonidas" (1737) is a long epic poem, little read.

The Familiar Essay

a superb view as far as the pretty spire of Harrow,[1] over do-
mains and patrimonial acres, not a rood nor square yard
whereof our host could call his own, yet gave occasion to an
immoderate expansion of — vanity, shall I call it? — in his
bosom, as he showed them in a glowing summer evening. It
was all his; he took it all in, and communicated rich portions of
it to his guests. It was a part of his largess, his hospitality; it
was going over his grounds; he was lord for the time of showing them, and you the implicit lookers-up to his magnificence.

He was a juggler, who threw mists before your eyes — you had
no time to detect his fallacies. He would say, "Hand me the
silver sugar tongs"; and before you could discover it was a
single spoon, and that *plated*, he would disturb and captivate
your imagination by a misnomer of "the urn" for a teakettle,
or by calling a homely bench a sofa. Rich men direct you to
their furniture, poor ones divert you from it; he neither did
one nor the other, but by simply assuming that everything was
handsome about him, you were positively at a demur what you
did, or did not see, at *the cottage*. With nothing to live on, he
seemed to live on everything. He had a stock of wealth in his
mind; not that which is properly termed *Content*, for in truth
he was not to be *contained* at all, but overflowed all bounds by
the force of a magnificent self-delusion.

Enthusiasm is catching; and even his wife, a sober native
of North Britain, who generally saw things more as they were,
was not proof against the continual collision of his credulity.
Her daughters were rational and discreet young women; in
the main, perhaps, not insensible to their true circumstances. I
have seen them assume a thoughtful air at times. But such was
the preponderating opulence of his fancy, that I am persuaded
not for any half-hour together did they ever look their own pros-
pects fairly in the face. There was no resisting the vortex of his
temperament. His riotous imagination conjured up handsome

[1] The seat of the famous public school; now almost absorbed in the suburbs of London.

Charles Lamb

settlements before their eyes, which kept them up in the eye of the world too, and seem at last to have realized themselves; for they both have married since, I am told, more than respectably.

It is long since, and my memory waxes dim on some subjects, or I should wish to convey some notion of the manner in which the pleasant creature described the circumstances of his own wedding day. I faintly remember something of a chaise-and-four, in which he made his entry into Glasgow on that morning to fetch the bride home, or carry her thither, I forget which. It so completely made out the stanza of the old ballad

> When we came down through Glasgow town,
>   We were a comely sight to sèe;
> My love was clad in black velvet,
>   And I myself in cramasie.

I suppose it was the only occasion upon which his own actual splendor at all corresponded with the world's notions on that subject. In homely cart, or traveling caravan, by whatever humble vehicle they chanced to be transported in less prosperous days, the ride through Glasgow came back upon his fancy, not as a humiliating contrast, but as a fair occasion for reverting to that one day's state. It seemed an "equipage eterne" from which no power of fate or fortune, once mounted, had power thereafter to dislodge him.

There is some merit in putting a handsome face upon indigent circumstances. To bully and swagger away the sense of them before strangers may not be always discommendable. Tibbs[1] and Bobadil,[2] even when detected, have more of our admiration than contempt. But for a man to put the cheat upon himself; to play the Bobadil at home; and, steeped in poverty up to the lips, to fancy himself all the while chin-deep in riches, is a strain of constitutional philosophy and a mastery over fortune which was reserved for my old friend Captain Jackson.

[1] A threadbare beau in Goldsmith's "Citizen of the World."
[2] A braggart in "Every Man in his Humour," by Jonson.

KENNETH GRAHAME

[1859–   ]

THE SECRET DRAWER

It must surely have served as a boudoir for the ladies of old time, this little-used, rarely entered chamber where the neglected old bureau stood. There was something very feminine in the faint hues of its faded brocades, in the rose and blue of such bits of china as yet remained, and in the delicate, old-world fragrance of potpourri from the great bowl — blue and white, with funny holes in its cover — that stood on the bureau's flat top. Modern aunts disdained this out-of-the-way, backwater, upstairs room, preferring to do their accounts and grapple with their correspondence in some central position more in the whirl of things, whence one eye could be kept on the carriage drive, while the other was alert for malingering servants and marauding children. Those aunts of a former generation — I sometimes felt — would have suited our habits better. But even by us children, to whom few places were private or reserved, the room was visited but rarely. To be sure, there was nothing in particular in it that we coveted or required — only a few spindle-legged, gilt-backed chairs; an old harp on which, so the legend ran, Aunt Eliza herself used once to play in years remote, un-chronicled; a corner cupboard with a few pieces of china; and the old bureau. But one other thing the room possessed peculiar to itself: a certain sense of privacy, — a power of making the intruder feel that he *was* intruding, — perhaps even a faculty of hinting that someone might have been sitting on those chairs, writing at the bureau, or fingering the china just a second before one entered. No such violent word as "haunted" could possibly apply to this pleasant old-fashioned chamber, which indeed we all rather liked; but there was no doubt it was reserved and stand-offish, keeping itself to itself.

Uncle Thomas was the first to draw my attention to the possibilities of the old bureau. He was pottering about the house one afternoon, having ordered me to keep at his heels for company — he was a man who hated to be left one minute alone — when his eye fell on it. "H'm! Sheraton!" he remarked. (He had a smattering of most things, this uncle, especially the vocabularies.) Then he let down the flap and examined the empty pigeonholes and dusty paneling. "Fine bit of inlay," he went on; "good work, all of it. I know the sort. There's a secret drawer in there somewhere." Then, as I breathlessly drew near, he suddenly exclaimed, "By Jove, I do want to smoke!" And wheeling round, he abruptly fled for the garden, leaving me with the cup dashed from my lips. What a strange thing, I mused, was this smoking, that takes a man suddenly, — be he in the court, the camp, or the grove, — grips him like an afreet, and whirls him off to do its imperious behests! Would it be even so with myself, I wondered, in those unknown grown-up years to come?

But I had no time to waste in vain speculations. My whole being was still vibrating to those magic syllables "secret drawer"; and that particular chord had been touched that never fails to thrill responsive to such words as "cave," "trap-door," "sliding panel," "bullion," "ingots," or "Spanish dollars." For, besides its own special bliss who ever heard of a secret drawer with nothing in it? And oh, I did want money so badly! I mentally ran over the list of demands which were pressing me the most imperiously.

First, there was a pipe I wanted to give George Jannaway. George, who was Martha's young man, was a shepherd, and a great ally of mine; and the last fair he was at, when he bought his sweetheart fairings, as a right-minded shepherd should, he had purchased a lovely snake expressly for me — one of the wooden sort, with joints, waggling deliciously in the hand; with yellow spots on a green ground, sticky and strong-smelling, as a fresh-painted snake ought to be; and with a red-flannel tongue pasted cunningly into its jaws. I loved it much, and took it to bed with me every night till what time its spinal cord was loosed and it fell apart, and went the way of all mortal joys. I thought it very nice of George to think of me at the fair, and that's why I wanted to give him a pipe. When the young year was chill and lambing-time was on, George inhabited a little wooden house on wheels, far out on the wintry downs, and saw no faces but such as were sheepish and woolly and mute; and when he and Martha were married she was going to carry his dinner out to him every day, two miles, and after it, perhaps he would smoke my pipe. It seemed an idyllic sort of existence for both the parties concerned; but a pipe of quality, a pipe fitted to be part of such a life as this, could not be procured (so Martha informed me) for a smaller sum than eighteenpence. And meantime —!

Then there was the fourpence I owed Edward; not that he was bothering me for it, but I knew he was in need of it himself to pay back Selina, who wanted it to make up a sum of two shillings to buy Harold an ironclad for his approaching birthday — H.M.S. *Majestic*, now lying uselessly careened in the toy-shop window, just when her country had such sore need of her.

And then there was that boy in the village who had caught a young squirrel, and I had never possessed one; and he wanted a shilling for it, but I knew that for ninepence in cash — But what was the good of these sorry, threadbare reflections? I had wants enough to exhaust any possible find of bullion, even if it amounted to half a sovereign. My only hope now lay in the magic drawer; and here I was, standing and letting the precious minutes slip by! Whether "findings" of this sort could, morally speaking, be considered "keepings" was a point that did not occur to me.

The room was very still as I approached the bureau; possessed, it seemed to be, by a sort of hush of expectation. The faint odor of orris root that floated forth as I let down the flap seemed to identify itself with the yellows and browns of the old wood, till hue and scent were of one quality and interchangeable. Even so, ere this, the potpourri had mixed itself with the tints of the old brocade, and brocade and potpourri had long been one. With expectant fingers I explored the empty pigeonholes and sounded the depths of the softly sliding drawers. No books that I knew of gave any general recipe for a quest like this; but the glory, should I succeed unaided, would be all the greater.

To him who is destined to arrive, the fates never fail to afford on the way their small encouragements. In less than two minutes I had come across a rusty buttonhook. This was truly magnificent. In the nursery there existed, indeed, a general buttonhook, common to either sex; but none of us possessed a private and special buttonhook to lend or to refuse, as suited the high humor of the moment. I pocketed the treasure carefully, and proceeded. At the back of another drawer three old foreign stamps told me I was surely on the highroad to fortune.

Following on these bracing incentives came a dull, blank period of unrewarded search. In vain I removed all the drawers and felt over every inch of the smooth surfaces from front to back. Never a knob, spring, or projection met the thrilling finger tips; unyielding the old bureau stood, stoutly guarding its secret, if secret it really had. I began to grow weary and disheartened. This was not the first time that Uncle Thomas had proved shallow, uninformed — a guide into blind alleys where the echoes mocked you. Was it any good persisting longer? Was anything any good whatever? In my mind I began to review past disappointments, and life seemed one

The Familiar Essay

long record of failure and of nonarrival. Disillusioned and depressed, I left my work and went to the window. The light was ebbing from the room, and seemed outside to be collecting itself on the horizon for its concentrated effort of sunset. Far down in the garden, Uncle Thomas was holding Edward in the air reversed and smacking him. Edward, gurgling hysterically, was striking blind fists in the direction where he judged his uncle's stomach should rightly be; the contents of his pockets — a motley show — were strewing the lawn. Somehow, though I had been put through a similar performance myself an hour or two ago, it all seemed very far away and cut off from me.

Westward, the clouds were massing themselves in a low violet bank; below them, to north and south, as far round as eye could reach, a narrow streak of gold ran out and stretched away, straight along the horizon. Somewhere very far off a horn was blowing, clear and thin; it sounded like the golden streak grown audible, while the gold seemed the visible sound. It pricked my ebbing courage, this blended strain of music and color, and I turned for a last effort; and Fortune thereupon, as if half ashamed of the unworthy game she had been playing with me, relented, opening her clenched fist. Hardly had I put my hand once more to the obdurate wood, when with a sort of small sigh, almost a sob — as it were — of relief, the secret drawer sprang open.

I drew it out and carried it to the window to examine it in the failing light. Too hopeless had I gradually grown in my dispiriting search to expect very much, and yet at a glance I saw that my basket of glass lay in shivers at my feet. No ingots or dollars were here, to crown me the little Monte Cristo[1] of a week. Outside, the distant horn had ceased its gnat song, the gold was paling to primrose, and everything was lonely and still. Within, my confident little castles were tumbling down like so many card houses, leaving me

[1] The hero of a romance by Dumas; he escapes from prison and finds a hidden treasure.

Kenneth Grahame

stripped of estate, both real and personal, and dominated by the depressing reaction.

And yet, as I looked again at the small collection that lay within that drawer of disillusions, some warmth crept back to my heart as I recognized that a kindred spirit to my own had been at the making of it. Two tarnished gilt buttons — naval, apparently; a portrait of a monarch unknown to me, cut from some antique print and deftly colored by hand in just my own bold style of brushwork; some foreign copper coins, thicker and clumsier of make than those I hoarded myself; and a list of birds' eggs, with names of the places where they had been found. Also a ferret's muzzle, and a twist of tarry string still faintly aromatic! It was a real boy's hoard, then, that I had happened upon. He too had found out the secret drawer, this happy-starred young person; and here he had stowed away his treasures, one by one, and had cherished them secretly awhile, and then — what? Well, one would never know now the reason why these priceless possessions lay still here unreclaimed; but across the void stretch of years I seemed to touch hands a moment with my little comrade of seasons long since dead.

I restored the drawer, with its contents, to the trusty bureau, and heard the spring click with a certain satisfaction. Some other boy, perhaps, would some day release that spring again. I trusted he would be equally appreciative. As I opened the door to go, I could hear, from the nursery at the end of the passage, shouts and yells, telling that the hunt was up. Bears, apparently, or bandits were on the evening bill of fare, judging by the character of the noises. In another minute I would be in the thick of it, in all the warmth and light and laughter. And yet — what a long way off it all seemed, both in space and time, to me yet lingering on the threshold of that old-world chamber!

THOMAS CARLYLE

[1795–1881]

THOMAS DE QUINCEY

He was a pretty little creature, full of wire-drawn ingenuities; bankrupt enthusiasms, bankrupt pride; with the finest silver-toned low voice, and most elaborate gently winding courtesies and ingenuities in conversation: "What wouldn't one give to have him in a Box, and take him out to talk!" (That was *Her* criticism of him; and it was right good.) A bright, ready, and melodious talker; but in the end an inconclusive and long-winded. One of the smallest man-figures I ever saw; shaped like a pair of tongs; and hardly above five feet in all: when he sat, you would have taken him, by candle-light, for the beautifullest little child; blue-eyed, blonde-haired, sparkling face, — had there not been a something, too, which said, "*Eccovi, this Child has been in Hell!*"

TENNYSON

Alfred is the son of a Lincolnshire Gentleman Farmer,[1] I think; indeed, you see in his verses that he is a native of "moated granges," and green, fat pastures, not of mountains and their torrents and storms. He had his breeding at Cambridge, as if for the Law or Church; being master of a small

[1] Tennyson's father was rector of the parish church in a village in Lincolnshire.

Thomas Carlyle

annuity on his Father's decease, he preferred clubbing with his Mother and some Sisters, to live unpromoted and write Poems. In this way he lives still, now here, now there; the family always within reach of London, never in it; he himself making rare and brief visits, lodging in some old comrade's rooms. I think he must be under forty, not much under it. One of the finest-looking men in the world. A great shock of rough dusty-dark hair; bright-laughing hazel eyes; massive aquiline face, most massive yet most delicate; of sallow-brown complexion, almost Indian-looking; clothes cynically loose, free-and-easy; — smokes infinite tobacco. His voice is musical metallic, — fit for loud laughter and piercing wail, and all that may lie between; speech and speculation free and plenteous: I do not meet, in these late decades, such company over a pipe!

SAMUEL PEPYS

[1633–1703]

AN AFTERNOON IN THE FIELDS[1]

The women and W. Hewer and I walked upon the Downs, where a flock of sheep was; and the most pleasant and innocent sight that ever I saw in my life. We found a shepherd and his little boy reading, far from any houses or sight of people, the Bible to him; so I made the boy read to me, which he did, with the forced tone that children do usually read, that was mighty pretty, and then I did give him something, and went to the father, and talked with him; and I find he had been a servant in my cousin Pepys's house, and told me what was become of their old servants. He did content himself mightily in my liking his boy's reading, and did bless God for him, the most like one of the old patriarchs that ever I saw in my life, and it brought those thoughts of the old age of the world in my mind for two or three days after.

We took notice of his woolen knit stockings of two colors mixed, and of his shoes shod with iron, both at the toe and heels, and with great nails in the soles of his feet, which was mighty pretty: and, taking notice of them, "Why," says the poor man, "the downs, you see, are full of stones, and we are fain to shoe ourselves thus; and these," says he, "will make the stones fly till they ring before me." I did give the poor man something, for which he was mighty thankful, and I tried to cast stones with his horn crook. He values his dog mightily, that would turn a sheep any way which he would have him, when he goes to fold

[1] This is the concluding part of the long entry for July 14, 1667, in the "Diary."

[110]

Samuel Pepys

them: told me there was about eighteenscore sheep in his flock, and that he hath four shillings a week the year round for keeping of them: and Mrs. Turner, in the common fields here, did gather one of the prettiest nosegays that ever I saw in my life.

So to our coach, and through Mr. Minnes's wood, and looked upon Mr. Evelyn's house; and so over the common, and through Epsom town to our inn, in the way stopping a poor woman with her milk pail, and in one of my gilt tumblers did drink our bellyfuls of milk, better than any cream; and so to our inn, and there had a dish of cream, but it was sour, and so had no pleasure in it; and so paid our reckoning, and took coach, it being about seven at night, and passed and saw the people walking with their wives and children to take the air, and we set out for home, the sun by and by going down, and we in the cool of the evening all the way with much pleasure home, talking and pleasing ourselves with the pleasure of this day's work. Mrs. Turner mightily pleased with my resolution, which, I tell her, is never to keep a country house, but to keep a coach, and with my wife on the Saturday to go sometimes for a day to this place, and then quit to another place; and there is more variety and as little charge, and no trouble, as there is in a country house. Anon it grew dark, and we had the pleasure to see several glowworms, which was mighty pretty, but my foot begins more and more to pain me, which Mrs. Turner, by keeping her warm hand upon it, did much ease; but so that when we come home, which was just at eleven at night, I was not able to walk from the lane's end to my house without being helped. So to bed, and there had a cerecloth laid to my foot, but in great pain all night long.

GILBERT WHITE

[1720-1793]

THE HOUSE CRICKET[1]

Far from all resort of mirth
Save the cricket on the hearth. — MILTON, "Il Penseroso"

While many other insects must be sought after in fields and
woods, the *gryllus domesticus*, or *house cricket*, resides altogether
within our dwellings, intruding itself upon our notice whether we
will or no. This species delights in new-built houses, being, like
the spider, pleased with the moisture of the walls; and besides,
the softness of the mortar enables them to burrow and mine between the joints of the bricks or stones, and to open communications from one room to another. They are particularly fond of
kitchens and bakers' ovens, on account of their perpetual warmth.

Tender insects that live abroad either enjoy only the short
period of one summer, or else doze away the cold uncomfortable
months in profound slumbers; but these, residing as it were
in a torrid zone, are always alert and merry: a good *Christmas*
fire is to them like the heats of the dog days. Though they are
frequently heard by day, yet is their natural time of motion
only in the night. As soon as it grows dusk the chirping increases, and they come running forth, and are from the size
of a flea to that of their full stature. As one should suppose,
from the burning atmosphere which they inhabit, they are a
thirsty race, and show a great propensity for liquids, being

[1] In "The Natural History of Selborne" this appears as Letter XLVII,
in a series addressed "To the Honourable Daines Barrington," with Selborne as the place of composition. Although no date is given, the letter was
apparently written in the winter of 1778–1779.

Gilbert White

found frequently drowned in pans of water, milk, broth, or the like. Whatever is moist they affect, and therefore often gnaw holes in wet woolen stockings and aprons that are hung to the fire. They are the housewife's barometer, foretelling her when it will rain; and are prognostic sometimes, she thinks, of ill or good luck; of the death of a near relation, or the approach of an absent lover. By being the constant companions of her solitary hours they naturally become the objects of her superstition. These crickets are not only very thirsty, but very voracious; for they will eat the scummings of pots, and yeast, salt, and crumbs of bread; and any kitchen offal or sweepings. In the summer we have observed them to fly, when it became dusk, out of the windows, and over the neighboring roofs. This feat of activity accounts for the sudden manner in which they often leave their haunts, as it does for the method by which they come to houses where they were not known before. It is remarkable that many sorts of insects seem never to use their wings but when they have a mind to shift their quarters and settle new colonies. When in the air they move *volatu undoso*, in waves or curves, like woodpeckers, opening and shutting their wings at every stroke, and so are always rising or sinking.

When they increase to a great degree, as they did once in the house where I am now writing, they become noisome pests, flying into the candles and dashing into people's faces; but may be blasted and destroyed by gunpowder discharged into their crevices and crannies. In families, at such times, they are, like Pharaoh's plague of frogs, "in their bedchambers, and upon their beds, and in their ovens, and in their kneading troughs."[1] Their shrilling noise is occasioned by a brisk attrition of their wings. Cats catch hearth crickets, and, playing with them as they do with mice, devour them. Crickets may be destroyed, like wasps, by phials half filled with beer or any liquid, and set in their haunts; for, being always eager to drink, they will crowd in till the bottles are full.

[1] Adapted from Exodus viii, 3.

St. John de Crevecœur

[1735–1813]

A SNOWSTORM

Great rains at last replenish the springs, the brooks, the swamps, and impregnate the earth. Then a severe frost succeeds which prepares it to receive the voluminous coat of snow which is soon to follow; though it is often preceded by a short interval of smoke and mildness, called the Indian Summer. This is in general the invariable rule: winter is not said properly to begin until these few moderate days and the rising of the waters have announced it to man. This great mass of liquid once frozen spreads everywhere natural bridges; opens communications impassable before. The man of foresight neglects nothing; he has saved every object which might be damaged or lost; he is ready.

The wind, which is a great regulator of the weather, shifts to the northeast; the air becomes bleak and then intensely cold; the light of the sun becomes dimmed as if an eclipse had happened; a general night seems coming on. At last imperceptible atoms make their appearance; they are few and descend slowly, a sure prognostic of a great snow. Little or no wind is as yet felt. By degrees the number as well as the size of these white particles is increased; they descend in larger flakes; a distant wind is heard; the noise swells and seems to advance; the new element at last appears and overspreads everything. In a little time the heavy clouds seem to approach nearer the earth

St. John de Crèvecœur

and discharge a winged flood, driving along toward the southwest, howling at every door, roaring in every chimney, whistling
with asperous sound through the naked limbs of the trees;
these are the shrill notes which mark the weight of the storm.
Still the storm increases as the night approaches, and its great
obscurity greatly adds to the solemnity of the scene.

Sometimes the snow is preceded by melted hail, which, like
a shining varnish, covers and adorns the whole surface of the
earth of buildings and trees; a hurtful time for the cattle,
which it chills and oppresses. Mournful and solitary they retire
to what shelter they can get, and, forgetting to eat, they wait
with instinctive patience until the storm is over. How amazingly
changed is the aspect of nature! From the dusky hues of the
autumnal shades, everything becomes refulgently white; from
soft, miry roads, we pass all at once to solid icy bridges. What
could an inhabitant of Africa say or think in contemplating this
northern phenomenon? Would not it raise in his mind a
greater degree of astonishment than his thunderstorms and
his vertical suns?

A general alarm is spread through the farm. The master
calls all his hands; opens the gates; lets down the bars; calls
and counts all his stock as they come along. The oxen, the cows,
remembering ancient experience, repair to the place where
they were foddered the preceding winter; the colts wild, whilst
they could unrestrained bound on the grassy fields, suddenly
deprived of that liberty, become tame and docile to the hands
which stroke and feed them. The sheep, more encumbered
than the rest, slowly creep along, and by their incessant bleat-
ing show their instinctive apprehension; they are generally the
first which attract our attention and care. The horses are led
to their stables; the oxen to their stalls; the rest are confined
under their proper sheds and districts. All is safe, but no fodder
need be given them yet; the stings of hunger are necessary to
make them eat cheerfully the dried herbage and forget the
green one on which they so lately fed. Heaven be praised, no

The Familiar Essay

accident has happened; all is secured from the inclemency of the storm. The farmer's vigilant eye has seen every operation performed; has numbered every head; and as a good master provided for the good welfare of all.

At last he returns home loaded with hail and snow melting on his rough but warm clothes; his face is red with the repeated injury occasioned by the driving wind. His cheerful wife, not less pleased, welcomes him home with a mug of gingered cider; and whilst she helps him to dried and more comfortable clothes, she recounts to him the successful pains she has taken also in collecting all her ducks, geese, and all the rest of her numerous poultry, a province less extensive indeed but not less useful. But no sooner this simple tale is told than the cheerfulness of her mind is clouded by a sudden thought. Her children went to a distant school early in the morning whilst the sun shone, and ere any ideas were formed of this storm. They are not yet returned. What is become of them? Has the master had tenderness enough to tarry awhile and watch over his little flock until the arrival of some relief? Or has he rudely dismissed them in quest of his own safety?

These alarming thoughts are soon communicated to her husband, who, starting up in all the glow of paternal anxiety, orders one of his negroes to repair to the schoolhouse with Bonny, the old faithful mare, who, like his wife, by her fecundity has replenished his farm. 'Tis done: she is mounted bareback and hurried through the storm to the schoolhouse, at the door of which each child is impatiently waiting for this paternal assistance. At the sight of honest Tom, the negro, their joy is increased by the pleasure of going home on horseback. One is mounted before and two behind. Rachel, the poor widow's little daughter, with tears in her eyes, sees her playmates, just before her equals, as she thought, now provided with a horse and an attendant — a sad mortification. This is the first time she ever became sensible of the difference of her situation. Her distressed mother, not less anxious to fetch her child, prays to

St. John de Crèvecœur

heaven that some charitable neighbor may bring her along.
She too has a cow to take care of; a couple of pigs hitherto
tenderly fed at the door; three or four ewes, perhaps, demand-
ing her shelter round some part of her lonely log-house. Kind
heaven hears her prayers. Honest Tom lifts her [Rachel] up
and, for want of room, places her on Bonny's neck; there she
is upheld by the oldest boy. Thus fixed with difficulty, they
turn about and boldly face the driving storm; they all scream
and are afraid of falling; at last they clinch together and are
hushed. With cheerfulness and instinctive patience, Bonny
proceeds along, and, sensible of the valuable cargo, highly lifting her legs, she securely treads along, shaking now and then
her ears as the drifted snow penetrates into them.

A joyful meeting ensues. The thoughts of avoided danger
increase the pleasure of the family. The milk biscuit, the short-
cake, the newly baked apple pie are immediately produced,
and the sudden joy these presents occasion expels every idea of
cold and snow. In this country of hospitality and plenty it
would be a wonder indeed if little Rachel had not partaken of
the same bounty. She is fed, made to warm herself; she has
forgot the little reflections she had made at the schoolhouse
door; she is happy, and to complete the goodly act, she is sent
home on the same vehicle. The unfeigned thanks, the honest
blessings of the poor widow, who was just going to set out,
amply repays the trouble that has been taken—happy wages of
this charitable attention.

The messenger returns. Everything is safe both within and
without. At that instant the careful negro, Jack, who has been
busily employed in carrying wood to the shed that he may not
be at a loss to kindle fire in the morning, comes into his master's room carrying on his hip an enormous backlog, without
which a fire is supposed to be imperfectly made and to be de-
void of heat. All hands rise; the fire is made to blaze; the
hearth is cleaned; and all the cheerful family sit around. Rest
after so many laborious operations brings along with it an in-

voluntary silence, even among the children, who grow sleepy with their victuals in their hands, as they grow warm. "Lord, hear, how it blows!" says one. "My God, what a storm!" says another. "Mammy, where does all this snow come from?" asks a third. "Last year's storm, I think, was nothing to this," observes the wife. "I hope all is fast about the house. How happy it is for us that we had daylight to prepare us for it."

The father now and then opens the door to pass judgment and to contemplate the progress of the storm. "'Tis dark, 'tis dark," he says; "a fence four rods off cannot be distinguished. The locust trees hard by the door bend under the pressure of the loaded blast. Thank God, all is secured. I'll fodder my poor cattle well in the morning if it please Him I should live to see it." And this pious sentiment serves him as a reward for all his former industry, vigilance, and care. The negroes, friends to the fire, smoke and crack some coarse jokes; and, well fed and clad, they contentedly make their brooms and ladles without any further concerns on their minds. Thus the industrious family, all gathered together under one roof, eat their wholesome supper, drink their mugs of cider, and grow imperceptibly less talkative and more thoughtless as they grow more sleepy. Now and then, when the redoubled fury of the storm rattles in the chimney, they seem to awake. They look at the door again and again, but 'tis the work of omnipotence; it is unavoidable; their neighbors feel it as well as themselves. Finally they go to bed, not to that bed of slavery or sorrow as is the case in Europe with people of their class, but on the substantial collection of honest feathers picked and provided by the industrious wife. There, stretched between flannel sheets and covered with warm blankets made of their own sheep's wool, they enjoy the luxury of sound, undisturbed repose, earned by the fatigues of the preceding day. The Almighty has no crime to punish in this innocent family; why should He permit ominous dreams and terrific visions to disturb the imaginations of these good people?

As soon as day reappears the American farmer awakes and

calls all his hands. While some are busy in kindling the fires, the rest with anxiety repair to the barns and sheds. What a dismal aspect presents itself to their view! The roads, the paths are no longer visible. The drifted snow presents obstacles which must be removed with the shovel. The fences and the trees, bending under the weight of snow which encumbers them, bend in a thousand shapes; but by a lucky blast of wind they are discharged, and they immediately recover their natural situation. The cattle, who had hitherto remained immovable, their tails to the wind, appear strangely disfigured by the long accession and adherence of the snow to their bodies. On the sight of the master, suddenly animated, they heavily shake themselves clean, and crowd from all parts in expectation of that fodder which the industry of man has provided for them. Where their number is extensive, various and often distant are their allotments, which are generally in the vicinity of the stacks of hay. In that case, when the barnyard work is done, the farmer mounts his horse, followed by his men armed with pitchforks. He counts again the number of each sort, and sees that each receives a sufficient quantity. The strong are separated from the weak, oxen with oxen, yearlings with yearlings, and so on through every class. For cattle, like men, conscious of their superior force will abuse it when unrestrained by any law, and often live on their neighbor's property.

What a care, what an assiduity does this life require! Who on contemplating the great and important field of action performed every year by a large farmer can refrain from valuing and praising as they ought this useful, this dignified class of men? These are the people who, scattered on the edge of this great continent, have made it to flourish; and have, without the dangerous assistance of mines, gathered, by the sweat of their honest brows and by the help of their plows, such a harvest of commercial emoluments for their country, uncontaminated either by spoils or rapine. These are the men who in future will replenish this huge continent even to its utmost unknown

The Familiar Essay

limits, and render this new-found part of the world by far the happiest, the most potent, as well as the most populous of any. Happy people! May the poor, the wretched of Europe, animated by our example, invited by our laws, avoid the fetters of their country, and come in shoals to partake of our toils as well as of our happiness!

The next operation is to seek for convenient watering places. Holes must be cut through the ice; 'tis done. The veteran, experienced cattle lead the way, tread down the snow, and form a path; the rest soon follow. Two days' experience [teaches] them all the way to this place as well as the station they must occupy in their progress thither; the stoutest marching first and the weakest closing the rear. The succeeding operations with regard to the preservation of the cattle entirely depend on the judgment of the farmer. He knows, according to the weather, when it is best to give them either straw, cornstalks, or hay. In very hard weather they are more hungry and better able to consume the coarse fodder; corn stocks are reserved for sheep and young cattle; hay is given to all in thaws.

Soon after this great fall of snow the wind shifts to the northwest and blows with great impetuosity; it gathers and drives the loose element. Everything seems to be involved a second time in a general whirlwind of white atoms, not so dangerous indeed as those clouds of sand raised in the deserts of Arabia. This second scourge is rather worse than the first, because it renders parts of the roads seemingly impassable. 'Tis then that with empty sleighs the neighborhood gather, and by their united efforts open a communication along the road. If new snow falls, new endeavors must be made use of to guard against the worst of inconveniences. For, to live, it is necessary to go to market, to mill, to the woods. This is, besides, the season of merriment and mutual visiting. All the labors of the farm are now reduced to those of the barn, to the fetching of fuel, and to cleaning their own flax. The fatigues of the preceding summer require now some relaxation. What can be more conducive

St. John de Crèvecœur

to it than the great plenty of wholesome food we all have? Cider is to be found in every house. The convenience of traveling invites the whole country to society, pleasure, and visiting. Bees are made, by which a number of people with their sleighs resort to the inviter's house, and there in one day haul him as much wood as will serve him a whole year. Next day 'tis another man's turn; admirable contrivance which promotes good will, kindness, and mutual assistance. By means of these associations often the widows and orphans are relieved.

After two or three falls of snow the weather becomes serene though cold. New communications are opened over lakes and rivers and through forests hitherto impassable. The ox rests from his summer labor, and the horse, amply fed, now does all the work. His celerity is strengthened by the steel shoes with which his hoofs are armed; he is fit to draw on the snow as well as on the ice. Immense is the value of this season: logs for future buildings are easily drawn to the sawmills; ready piled stones are with equal ease brought to the intended spot; grain is conveyed to the different landings on our small rivers, from whence in the spring small vessels carry it to the seaport towns, and from which again larger ones convey it away to the different marts of the world. The constancy of this serenely cold weather is one of the greatest blessings which seldom fails us.

ALEXANDER WILSON

[1766–1813]

THE BLUEBIRD[1]

The pleasing manners and sociable disposition of this little
bird entitle him to particular notice. As one of the first mes-
sengers of spring, bringing the charming tidings to our very
doors, he bears his own recommendation always along with
him, and meets with a hearty welcome from everybody.

Though generally accounted a bird of passage, yet, so early
as the middle of February, if the weather be open, he usually
makes his appearance about his old haunts — the barn, orchard, and fence posts. Storms and deep snows sometimes succeeding, he disappears for a time; but about the middle of
March is again seen, accompanied by his mate, visiting the
box in the garden or the hole in the old apple tree, the cradle
of some generations of his ancestors. "When he first begins his
amours," says a curious and correct observer, "it is pleasing
to behold his courtship, his solicitude to please and to secure
the favor of his beloved female. He uses the tenderest expressions, sits close by her, caresses and sings to her his most en-
dearing warblings. When seated together, if he espies an insect
delicious to her taste, he takes it up, flies with it to her, spreads
his wings over her, and puts it in her mouth." If a rival makes
his appearance (for they are ardent in their loves), he quits
her in a moment, attacks and pursues the intruder as he shifts
from place to place, in tones that bespeak the jealousy of his
affection, conducts him, with many reproofs, beyond the extremities of his territory, and returns to warble out his transports
of triumph beside his beloved mate. The preliminaries being
thus settled, and the spot fixed on, they begin to clean out the

[1] From Wilson's great work, "American Ornithology."

Alexander Wilson

old nest and the rubbish of the former year, and to prepare for the reception of their future offspring. Soon after this another sociable little pilgrim (*motacilla domestica*, house wren) also arrives from the south, and, finding such a snug berth preoccupied, shows his spite by watching a convenient opportunity and, in the absence of the owner, popping in and pulling out sticks, but takes special care to make off as fast as possible.

The female lays five and sometimes six eggs, of a pale-blue color, and raises two and sometimes three broods in a season; the male taking the youngest under his particular care while the female is again setting. Their principal food is insects, particularly large beetles and other hard-shelled sorts that lurk among old, dead, and decaying trees. Spiders are also a favorite repast with them. In the fall they occasionally regale themselves on the berries of the sour gum, and, as winter approaches, on those of the red cedar, and on the fruit of a rough, hairy vine that runs up and cleaves fast to the trunks of trees. Ripe persimmons are another of their favorite dishes, and many other fruits and seeds which I have found in their stomachs at that season, which, being no botanist, I am unable to particularize. They are frequently pestered with a species of tapeworm, some of which I have taken from their intestines of an extraordinary size, and in some cases in great numbers. Most other birds are also plagued with these vermin, but the bluebird seems more subject to them than any I know, except the woodcock. An account of the different species of vermin, many of which, I doubt not, are nondescripts, that infest the plumage and intestines of our birds, would of itself form an interesting publication; but, as this belongs more properly to the entomologist, I shall only, in the course of this work, take notice of some of the most remarkable.

The usual spring and summer song of the bluebird is a soft, agreeable, and oft-repeated warble, uttered with open quivering wings, and is extremely pleasing. In his motions and general character he has great resemblance to the robin redbreast of

The Familiar Essay

Britain, and had he the brown olive of that bird, instead of his own blue, could scarcely be distinguished from him. Like him, he is known to almost every child, and shows as much confidence in man by associating with him in summer, as the other by his familiarity in winter. He is also of a mild and peaceful disposition, seldom fighting or quarreling with other birds. His society is courted by the inhabitants of the country, and few farmers neglect to provide for him, in some suitable place, a snug little summerhouse, ready fitted and rent free. For this he more than sufficiently repays them by the cheerfulness of his song and the multitudes of injurious insects which he daily destroys. Toward fall, that is, in the month of October, his song changes to a single plaintive note, as he passes over the yellow many-colored woods; and its melancholy air recalls to our minds the approaching decay of the face of nature. Even after the trees are stripped of their leaves, he still lingers over his native fields, as if loath to leave them. About the middle or end of November, few or none of them are seen; but with every return of mild and open weather we hear his plaintive note amidst the fields or in the air, seeming to deplore the devastations of winter. Indeed, he appears scarcely ever totally to forsake us, but to follow fair weather through all its journeyings till the return of spring.

Such are the mild and pleasing manners of the bluebird, and so universally is he esteemed that I have often regretted that no pastoral muse has yet arisen in this western woody world to do justice to his name, and endear him to us still more by the tenderness of verse, as has been done to his representative in Britain, the robin redbreast. A small acknowledgment of this kind I have to offer, which the reader, I hope, will excuse as a tribute to rural innocence.

When winter's cold tempests and snows are no more,
Green meadows and brown furrow'd fields reappearing,
The fishermen hauling their shad to the shore,
And cloud-cleaving geese to the lakes are a-steering,

Alexander Wilson

When first the lone butterfly flits on the wing,
  When red glow the maples, so fresh and so pleasing,
Oh, then comes the bluebird, the herald of spring!
  And hails with his warblings the charms of the season.

Then loud-piping frogs make the marshes to ring;
  Then warm glows the sunshine, and fine is the weather;
The blue woodland flowers just beginning to spring,
  And spicewood and sassafras budding together:
Oh, then to your gardens ye housewives repair,
  Your walks border up, sow and plant at your leisure;
The bluebird will chant from his box such an air,
  That all your hard toils will seem truly a pleasure!

He flits through the orchard, he visits each tree,
  The red flowering peach, and the apple's sweet blossoms;
He snaps up destroyers wherever they be,
  And seizes the caitiffs that lurk in their bosoms;
He drags the vile grub from the corn it devours,
  The worms from the webs, where they riot and welter;
His songs and his services freely are ours,
  And all that he asks is — in summer a shelter.

The plowman is pleased when he gleans in his train,
  Now searching the furrows — now mounting to cheer him;
The gard'ner delights in his sweet, simple strain,
  And leans on his spade to survey and to hear him;
The slow-ling'ring schoolboys forget they'll be chid,
  While gazing intent as he warbles before them
In mantle of sky-blue, and bosom so red,
  And each little loiterer seems to adore him.

When all the gay scenes of the summer are o'er,
  And autumn slow enters so silent and sallow,
And millions of warblers that charm'd us before
  Have fled in the train of the sun-seeking swallow,

[125]

The Familiar Essay

The bluebird, forsaken, yet true to his home,
  Still lingers, and looks for a milder tomorrow,
Till forced by the horrors of winter to roam,
  He sings his adieu in a lone note of sorrow.

While spring's lovely season, serene, dewy, warm,
  The green face of earth, and the pure blue of heaven,
Or love's native music have influence to charm,
  Or sympathy's glow to our feelings are given,
Still dear to each bosom the bluebird shall be,
  His voice, like the thrillings of hope, is a treasure,
For, through bleakest storms, if a calm he but see,
  He comes to remind us of sunshine and pleasure!

LEIGH HUNT

[1784–1859]

A "NOW"

Descriptive of a Hot Day

Now the rosy- (and lazy-) fingered Aurora,[1] issuing from her
saffron house, calls up the moist vapors to surround her, and
goes veiled with them as long as she can; till Phœbus,[2] coming
forth in his power, looks everything out of the sky, and holds
sharp, uninterrupted empire from his throne of beams. Now
the mower begins to make his sweeping cuts more slowly, and
resorts oftener to the beer. Now the carter sleeps a-top of his
load of hay, or plods with double slouch of shoulder, looking
out with eyes winking under his shading hat, and with a hitch
upward of one side of his mouth. Now the little girl at her
grandmother's cottage door watches the coaches that go by,
with her hand held up over her sunny forehead. Now laborers
look well resting in their white shirts at the doors of rural ale-
houses. Now an elm is fine there, with a seat under it; and
horses drink out of the trough, stretching their yearning necks
with loosened collars; and the traveler calls for his glass of ale,
having been without one for more than ten minutes; and his
horse stands wincing at the flies, giving sharp shivers of his
skin, and moving to and fro his ineffectual docked tail; and
now Miss Betty Wilson, the host's daughter, comes streaming
forth in a flowered gown and earrings, carrying with four of her
beautiful fingers the foaming glass, for which, after the traveler

[1] The goddess of dawn.
[2] The sun god. (The classical allusions prepare for the anticlimax of realistic detail.)

The Familiar Essay

has drunk it, she receives with an indifferent eye, looking another way, the lawful twopence. Now grasshoppers "fry," as Dryden says. Now cattle stand in water, and ducks are envied. Now boots, and shoes, and trees by the roadside are thick with dust; and dogs, rolling in it, after issuing out of the water, into which they have been thrown to fetch sticks, come scattering horror among the legs of the spectators. Now a fellow who finds he has three miles farther to go in a pair of tight shoes is in a pretty situation. Now rooms with the sun upon them become intolerable; and the apothecary's apprentice, with a bitterness beyond aloes,[1] thinks of the pond he used to bathe in at school. Now men with powdered heads (especially if thick) envy those that are unpowdered, and stop to wipe them uphill, with countenances that seem to expostulate with destiny. Now boys assemble round the village pump with a ladle to it, and delight to make a forbidden splash and get wet through the shoes. Now also they make suckers of leather, and bathe all day long in rivers and ponds, and make mighty fishings for "tittlebats." Now the bee, as he hums along, seems to be talking heavily of the heat. Now doors and brick walls are burning to the hand; and a walled lane, with dust and broken bottles in it, near a brickfield, is a thing not to be thought of. Now a green lane, on the contrary, thick-set with hedgerow elms, and having the noise of a brook "rumbling in pebblestones," is one of the pleasantest things in the world.

Now, in town, gossips talk more than ever to one another, in rooms, in doorways, and out of window, always beginning the conversation with saying that the heat is overpowering. Now blinds are let down, and doors thrown open, and flannel waistcoats left off, and cold meat preferred to hot, and wonder expressed why tea continues so refreshing, and people delight to sliver lettuces into bowls, and apprentices water doorways with tin canisters that lay several atoms of dust. Now the water cart, jumbling along the middle of the street, and jolting

[1] a bitter drug.

[128]

Leigh Hunt

the showers out of its box of water, really does something. Now
fruiterers' shops and dairies look pleasant, and ices are the only
things to those who can get them. Now ladies loiter in baths;
and people make presents of flowers; and wine is put into ice;
and the after-dinner lounger recreates his head with applica-
tions of perfumed water out of long-necked bottles. Now the
lounger, who cannot resist riding his new horse, feels his boots
burn him. Now buckskins are not the lawn of Cos.[1] Now
jockeys, walking in greatcoats to lose flesh, curse inwardly.
Now five fat people in a stagecoach hate the sixth fat one who
is coming in, and think he has no right to be so large. Now
clerks in office do nothing but drink soda water and spruce
beer and read the newspaper. Now the old-clothes man drops
his solitary cry more deeply into the areas[2] on the hot and
forsaken side of the street; and bakers look vicious; and cooks
are aggravated; and the steam of a tavern kitchen catches hold
of us like the breath of Tartarus.[3] Now delicate skins are be-
set with gnats; and boys make their sleeping companion start
up, with playing a burning-glass on his hand; and blacksmiths
are supercarbonated; and cobblers in their stalls almost feel
a wish to be transplanted; and butter is too easy to spread;
and the dragoons wonder whether the Romans liked their hel-
mets; and old ladies, with their lappets[4] unpinned, walk along
in a state of dilapidation; and the servant maids are afraid
they look vulgarly hot; and the author, who has a plate of
strawberries brought him, finds that he has come to the end
of his writing.

[1] Cos, an island of Asia Minor, was famous for its fine silks, which were
much worn in Rome.

[2] The sunken spaces between houses and the street, usually inclosed by
a railing.

[3] A deep abyss far below Hades; a place of punishment for sinners.

[4] streamers of a lady's headdress.

HENRY DAVID THOREAU

[1817–1862]

BRUTE NEIGHBORS

The mice which haunted my house were not the common ones, which are said to have been introduced into the country, but a wild native kind not found in the village. I sent one to a distinguished naturalist, and it interested him much. When I was building, one of these had its nest underneath the house, and before I had laid the second floor, and swept out the shavings, would come out regularly at lunch time and pick up the crumbs at my feet. It probably had never seen a man before; and it soon became quite familiar, and would run over my shoes and up my clothes. It could readily ascend the sides of the room by short impulses, like a squirrel, which it resembled in its motions. At length, as I leaned with my elbow on the bench one day, it ran up my clothes, and along my sleeve, and round and round the paper which held my dinner, while I kept the latter close, and dodged and played at bopeep with it; and when at last I held still a piece of cheese between my thumb and finger, it came and nibbled it, sitting in my hand, and afterwards cleaned its face and paws, like a fly, and walked away.

A phœbe soon built in my shed, and a robin for protection in a pine which grew against the house. In June the partridge (*Tetrao umbellus*), which is so shy a bird, led her brood past my windows, from the woods in the rear to the front of my house, clucking and calling to them like a hen, and in all her behavior proving herself the hen of the woods. The young suddenly disperse on your approach, at a signal from the mother, as if a whirlwind had swept them away, and they so exactly resemble the dried leaves and twigs that many a traveler has placed his foot in the midst of a brood, and heard the whir of the old bird as she flew off, and her anxious calls and mewing, or seen her trail her wings to attract his attention, without suspecting their neighborhood. The parent will sometimes roll and spin round before you in such a dishabille, that you cannot, for a few moments, detect what kind of creature it is. The young squat still and flat, often running their heads under a leaf, and mind only their mother's directions given from a distance, nor will your approach make them run again and betray themselves. You may even tread on them, or have your eyes on them for a minute, without discovering them. I have held them in my open hand at such a time, and still their only care, obedient to their mother and their instinct, was to squat there without fear or trembling. So perfect is this instinct, that once, when I had laid them on the leaves again, and one accidentally fell on its side, it was found with the rest in exactly the same position ten minutes afterwards. They are not callow like the young of most birds, but more perfectly developed and precocious even than chickens. The remarkably adult yet innocent expression of their open and serene eyes is very memorable. All intelligence seems reflected in them. They suggest not merely the purity of infancy, but a wisdom clarified by experience. Such an eye was not born when the bird was, but is coeval with the sky it reflects. The woods do not yield another such a gem. The traveler does not often look into such a limpid well. The ignorant or reckless sportsman often shoots the parent at such a time, and leaves these innocents to fall a prey to some prowling beast or bird, or gradually mingle with the decaying leaves which they so much resemble. It is said that when hatched by a hen they will directly disperse on some alarm, and so are lost, for they never hear the mother's call which gathers them again. These were my hens and chickens.

The Familiar Essay

It is remarkable how many creatures live wild and free though secret in the woods, and still sustain themselves in the neighborhood of towns, suspected by hunters only. How retired the otter manages to live here! He grows to be four feet long, as big as a small boy, perhaps without any human being getting a glimpse of him. I formerly saw the raccoon in the woods behind where my house is built, and probably still heard their whinnering at night. Commonly I rested an hour or two in the shade at noon, after planting, and ate my lunch, and read a little by a spring which was the source of a swamp and of a brook, oozing from under Brister's Hill, half a mile from my field. The approach to this was through a succession of descending grassy hollows, full of young pitch pines, into a larger wood about the swamp. There, in a very secluded and shaded spot, under a spreading white pine, there was yet a clean, firm sward to sit on. I had dug out the spring and made a well of clear gray water, where I could dip up a pailful without roiling it, and thither I went for this purpose almost every day in midsummer, when the pond was warmest. Thither too the woodcock led her brood, to probe the mud for worms, flying but a foot above them down the bank, while they ran in a troop beneath; but at last, spying me, she would leave her young and circle round and round me, nearer and nearer till within four or five feet, pretending broken wings and legs, to attract my attention, and get off her young, who would already have taken up their march, with faint, wiry peep, single file through the swamp, as she directed. Or I heard the peep of the young when I could not see the parent bird. There too the turtledoves sat over the spring, or fluttered from bough to bough of the soft white pines over my head; or the red squirrel, coursing down the nearest bough, was particularly familiar and inquisitive. You only need sit still long enough in some attractive spot in the woods that all its inhabitants may exhibit themselves to you by turns.

I was witness to events of a less peaceful character. One day when I went out to my woodpile, or rather my pile of stumps,

Henry David Thoreau

I observed two large ants, the one red, the other much larger, nearly half an inch long, and black, fiercely contending with one another. Having once got hold they never let go, but struggled and wrestled and rolled on the chips incessantly. Looking farther, I was surprised to find that the chips were covered with such combatants, that it was not a *duellum*,[1] but a *bellum*,[2] a war between two races of ants, the red always pitted against the black, and frequently two red ones to one black. The legions of these Myrmidons[3] covered all the hills and vales in my woodyard, and the ground was already strewn with the dead and dying, both red and black. It was the only battlefield which I have ever witnessed, the only battlefield I ever trod while the battle was raging; internecine war; the red republicans on the one hand, and the black imperialists on the other. On every side they were engaged in deadly combat, yet without any noise that I could hear, and human soldiers never fought so resolutely. I watched a couple that were fast locked in each other's embraces, in a little sunny valley amid the chips, now at noonday prepared to fight till the sun went down, or life went out. The smaller red champion had fastened himself like a vice to his adversary's front, and through all the tumblings on that field never for an instant ceased to gnaw at one of his feelers near the root, having already caused the other to go by the board; while the stronger black one dashed him from side to side, and, as I saw on looking nearer, had already divested him of several of his members. They fought with more pertinacity than bulldogs. Neither manifested the least disposition to retreat. It was evident that their battle cry was "Conquer or die." In the meanwhile there came along a single red ant on the hillside of this valley, evidently full of excitement, who either had dispatched his foe, or had not yet taken part in the battle; probably the latter, for he had lost none of his limbs; whose mother had charged him to return with his

[1] War between two parties (Thoreau uses the term here inexactly, to mean a duel).   [2] war.   [3] The fierce soldiers of Achilles.

The Familiar Essay

shield or upon it. Or perchance he was some Achilles, who had nourished his wrath apart and had now come to avenge or rescue his Patroclus. He saw this unequal combat from afar, for the blacks were nearly twice the size of the red; he drew near with rapid pace till he stood on his guard within half an inch of the combatants; then, watching his opportunity, he sprang upon the black warrior, and commenced his operations near the root of his right foreleg, leaving the foe to select among his own members; and so there were three united for life, as if a new kind of attraction had been invented which put all other locks and cements to shame. I should not have wondered by this time to find that they had their respective musical bands stationed on some eminent chip, and playing their national airs the while, to excite the slow and cheer the dying combatants. I was myself excited somewhat even as if they had been men. The more you think of it, the less the difference. And certainly there is not the fight recorded in Concord history, at least, if in the history of America, that will bear a moment's comparison with this, whether for the numbers engaged in it, or for the patriotism and heroism displayed. For numbers and for carnage it was an Austerlitz or Dresden. Concord Fight! Two killed on the patriots' side, and Luther Blanchard wounded! Why here every ant was a Buttrick, "Fire! for God's sake fire!" — and thousands shared the fate of Davis and Hosmer. There was not one hireling there. I have no doubt that it was a principle they fought for, as much as our ancestors, and not to avoid a threepenny tax on their tea; and the results of this battle will be as important and memorable to those whom it concerns as those of the battle of Bunker Hill, at least.

I took up the chip on which the three I have particularly described were struggling, carried it into my house, and placed it under a tumbler on my window sill, in order to see the issue. Holding a microscope to the first-mentioned red ant, I saw that, though he was assiduously gnawing at the near foreleg of his enemy, having severed his remaining feeler, his own breast

Henry David Thoreau

was all torn away, exposing what vitals he had there to the jaws of the black warrior, whose breastplate was apparently too thick for him to pierce; and the dark carbuncles of the sufferer's eyes shone with ferocity such as war only could excite. They struggled half an hour longer under the tumbler, and when I looked again the black soldier had severed the heads of his foes from their bodies, and the still living heads were hanging on either side of him like ghastly trophies at his saddle-bow, still apparently as firmly fastened as ever, and he was endeavoring with feeble struggles, being without feelers and with only the remnant of a leg, and I know not how many other wounds, to divest himself of them; which at length, after half an hour more, he accomplished. I raised the glass, and he went off over the window sill in that crippled state. Whether he finally survived that combat, and spent the remainder of his days in some Hôtel des Invalides, I do not know; but I thought that his industry would not be worth much thereafter. I never learned which party was victorious, nor the cause of the war; but I felt for the rest of that day as if I had my feelings excited and harrowed by witnessing the struggle, the ferocity and carnage, of a human battle before my door.

Kirby and Spence tell us that the battles of ants have long been celebrated and the date of them recorded, though they say that Huber is the only modern author who appears to have witnessed them. "Æneas Sylvius," say they, "after giving a very circumstantial account of one contested with great obstinacy by a great and small species on the trunk of a pear tree," adds that "'This action was fought in the pontificate of Eugenius the Fourth, in the presence of Nicholas Pistoriensis, an eminent lawyer, who related the whole history of the battle with the greatest fidelity.' A similar engagement between great and small ants is recorded by Olaus Magnus, in which the small ones, being victorious, are said to have buried the bodies of their own soldiers, but left those of their giant enemies a prey to the birds. This event happened previous to the ex-

The Familiar Essay

pulsion of the tyrant Christiern the Second from Sweden." The battle which I witnessed took place in the Presidency of Polk,[1] five years before the passage of Webster's Fugitive-Slave Bill. ⊦ Many a village Bose,[2] fit only to course a mud turtle in a victualing cellar, sported his heavy quarters in the woods, without the knowledge of his master, and ineffectually smelled at old fox burrows and woodchucks' holes; led perchance by some slight cur which nimbly threaded the wood, and might still inspire a natural terror in its denizens; now far behind his guide, barking like a canine bull toward some small squirrel which had treed itself for scrutiny, then, cantering off, bending the bushes with his weight, imagining that he is on the track of some stray member of the jerbilla[3] family. Once I was surprised to see a cat walking along the stony shore of the pond, for they rarely wander so far from home. The surprise was mutual. Nevertheless, the most domestic cat, which has lain on a rug all her days, appears quite at home in the woods, and, by her sly and stealthy behavior, proves herself more native there than the regular inhabitants. Once, when berrying, I met with a cat with young kittens in the woods, quite wild, and they all, like their mother, had their backs up and were fiercely spitting at me. A few years before I lived in the woods there was what was called a "winged cat" in one of the farmhouses in Lincoln nearest the pond, Mr. Gilian Baker's. When I called to see her in June, 1842, she was gone a-hunting in the woods, as was her wont (I am not sure whether it was a male or female, and so use the more common pronoun), but her mistress told me that she came into the neighborhood a little more than a year before, in April, and was finally taken into their house; that she was of a dark brownish-gray color, with a white spot on her throat, and white feet, and had a large bushy tail like a fox; that in the winter the fur grew thick and flatted out along her sides, forming strips ten or twelve inches long by

---

[1] The battle of the ants is in part a satire on the war with Mexico, which Thoreau opposed.   [2] A dog.   [3] perhaps jerboa (pocket mouse).

two and a half wide, and under her chin like a muff, the upper side loose, the under matted like felt, and in the spring these appendages dropped off. They gave me a pair of her "wings," which I keep still. There is no appearance of a membrane about them. Some thought it was part flying squirrel or some other wild animal, which is not impossible, for, according to naturalists, prolific hybrids have been produced by the union of the marten and domestic cat. This would have been the right kind of cat for me to keep, if I had kept any; for why should not a poet's cat be winged as well as his horse?

In the fall the loon (*Colymbus glacialis*) came, as usual, to molt and bathe in the pond, making the woods ring with his wild laughter before I had risen. At rumor of his arrival all the Milldam sportsmen are on the alert, in gigs and on foot, two by two and three by three, with patent rifles and conical balls and spyglasses. They come rustling through the woods like autumn leaves, at least ten men to one loon. Some station themselves on this side of the pond, some on that, for the poor bird cannot be omnipresent; if he dive here he must come up there. But now the kind October wind rises, rustling the leaves and rippling the surface of the water, so that no loon can be heard or seen, though his foes sweep the pond with spyglasses and make the woods resound with their discharges. The waves generously rise and dash angrily, taking sides with all waterfowl, and our sportsmen must beat a retreat to town and shop and unfinished jobs. But they were too often successful. When I went to get a pail of water early in the morning I frequently saw this stately bird sailing out of my cove within a few rods. If I endeavored to overtake him in a boat, in order to see how he would maneuver, he would dive and be completely lost, so that I did not discover him again, sometimes, till the latter part of the day. But I was more than a match for him on the surface. He commonly went off in a rain.

As I was paddling along the north shore one very calm October afternoon, for such days especially they settle on to the lakes, like the milkweed down, having looked in vain over the pond for a loon, suddenly one, sailing out from the shore toward the middle a few rods in front of me, set up his wild laugh and betrayed himself. I pursued with a paddle, and he dived, but when he came up I was nearer than before. He dived again, but I miscalculated the direction he would take, and we were fifty rods apart when he came to the surface this time, for I had helped to widen the interval; and again he laughed loud and long, and with more reason than before. He maneuvered so cunningly that I could not get within half a dozen rods of him. Each time, when he came to the surface, turning his head this way and that, he coolly surveyed the water and the land, and apparently chose his course so that he might come up where there was the widest expanse of water and at the greatest distance from the boat. It was surprising how quickly he made up his mind and put his resolve into execution. He led me at once to the widest part of the pond, and could not be driven from it. While he was thinking one thing in his brain, I was endeavoring to divine his thought in mine. It was a pretty game, played on the smooth surface of the pond, a man against a loon. Suddenly your adversary's checker disappears beneath the board, and the problem is to place yours nearest to where his will appear again. Sometimes he would come up unexpectedly on the opposite side of me, having apparently passed directly under the boat. So long-winded was he and so unweariable, that when he had swum farthest he would immediately plunge again, nevertheless; and then no wit could divine where in the deep pond, beneath the smooth surface, he might be speeding his way like a fish, for he had time and ability to visit the bottom of the pond in its deepest part. It is said that loons have been caught in the New York lakes eighty feet beneath the surface, with hooks set for trout, though Walden is deeper than that. How surprised must the fishes be to see this ungainly visitor from another sphere speeding his way amid their schools! Yet he appeared to know his course as surely under water as on the

surface, and swam much faster there. Once or twice I saw a
ripple where he approached the surface, just put his head out to
reconnoiter, and instantly dived again. I found that it was as
well for me to rest on my oars and wait his reappearing as to
endeavor to calculate where he would rise; for again and again,
when I was straining my eyes over the surface one way, I
would suddenly be startled by his unearthly laugh behind me.
But why, after displaying so much cunning, did he invariably
betray himself the moment he came up by that loud laugh?
Did not his white breast enough betray him? He was indeed
a silly loon, I thought. I could commonly hear the plash of the
water when he came up, and so also detected him. But after
an hour he seemed as fresh as ever, dived as willingly, and swam
yet farther than at first. It was surprising to see how serenely
he sailed off with unruffled breast when he came to the surface,
doing all the work with his webbed feet beneath. His usual
note was this demoniac laughter, yet somewhat like that of a
waterfowl; but occasionally, when he had balked me most
successfully and come up a long way off, he uttered a long-
drawn, unearthly howl, probably more like that of a wolf than
any bird; as when a beast puts his muzzle to the ground and
deliberately howls. This was his looning — perhaps the wildest
sound that is ever heard here, making the woods ring far and
wide. I concluded that he laughed in derision of my efforts,
confident of his own resources. Though the sky was by this
time overcast, the pond was so smooth that I could see where
he broke the surface when I did not hear him. His white breast,
the stillness of the air, and the smoothness of the water were
all against him. At length, having come up fifty rods off, he
uttered one of those prolonged howls, as if calling on the god
of loons to aid him, and immediately there came a wind from
the east and rippled the surface, and filled the whole air with
misty rain, and I was impressed as if it were the prayer of the
loon answered, and his god was angry with me; and so I left
him disappearing far away on the tumultuous surface.

SIMEON STRUNSKY

[1879–   ]

NIGHT LIFE

The sun heaves up from its sleeping-place somewhere in the vicinity of Flatbush, an extremely early riser, like most suburban residents, and loses no time in setting out upward and westward to its place of business over Manhattan. But the sun is not the first comer there. Its earliest rays surprise an army at work. Creatures of the night, they cower and dissolve in the oncoming of the light. The yellow glare of their oil torches and the ghastly violet-blue of their vacuum tubes pale, flicker, and go out before the onrush of dawn. It is amazing how a great city can snore with equanimity while entire regiments and squadrons carry on operations in the streets, quietly but with no attempt at concealment, under the very eyes of the police with whom, in fact, they seem to have a complete understanding. No political revolutions in the name of good citizenship, no shifting of commissioners and inspectors and captains, can conceivably destroy the *entente cordiale* between the police and these workers in the dark. If anything, the patrolman will stop in his rounds to watch their maneuvers with an eye of amicable appraisal, and when they begin to scatter with the dawn from their places of congregation he speeds them on their way with a word of cheer.

And the great city sleeps, its pulse scarcely disturbed by the feverish activity of the army of darkness. Or if the city catches a rumble of their movements and stirs in its slumber, it is only

Simeon Strunsky

to turn over and go to sleep again. No hypnotic spell will account for this indifference of a city of five millions to the presence of an army in its gaslit streets. It is merely habit. If here and there in the cubical hives where New York takes its rest an unquiet sleeper tosses in his bed and resents the disturbance, it is not to wish that these prowlers of the night were caught and sent to jail, but only to wish that they went about their business more discreetly — this great host of marketmen, grocers, butchers, milkmen, pushcart engineers, and news vendors who have been engaged since soon after midnight in the enormous task of preparing the city's breakfast.

For this, of course, is the real night life of New York—the life that beats at rapid pace in the great water-front markets, in the newspaper pressrooms around Brooklyn Bridge, under the acetylene glare over excavations for the new subways, and in the thousand bakery shops that line the avenues and streets. This is the underworld of which we speak so little because it is a real underworld. It is not made up of subterranean galleries and shafts inhabited by a race engaged in undermining the upper world. It is a true underworld on which the upper world of the daylight hours is grounded. The foundations of society run down into the night where the city's food, the city's ways of communication, and the city's news are being made ready and garnished for the full roar of the day's life. Compared with these workers of the dark the operations of the housebreaker and his sister of the shadowy sidewalks sink into insignificance. It is but a turn of the hand for the army of the laborious underworld to undo the mischief which the outlaws of the night have performed. Between one and five in the morning they create ten thousand times the wealth which it is in the power of the jailbird to destroy.

The point fascinates me. We need urgently a vindication of the night, and especially of night in the city. Occasionally, it is true, we pay lip service to Night as the kindly nurse that brings rest to the fevered brow and forgetfulness to the uneasy con-

The Familiar Essay

science. But at heart we think of the things of night as of things of evil. It would pay to set to work a commission of moralists, economic experts and statisticians, at striking a balance between the good and evil that are done in the night and the day. Personally I have no doubt at all as to which way the figures would point. It is only a question of how far the day is behind the night in its net contribution to the welfare of humanity. Against night in Greater New York you would have to debit, say, half a hundred burglaries and highway assaults, a handful of fires, a handful of joy-ride fatalities, much gambling and debauchery, and possibly some of the latest plays on Broadway. But from the monetary point of view the wastage and pilferings of the night are trifles compared to what an active quarter of an hour may show in Wall Street after ten in the morning. And as for the moral laxities of the dark it depends on what you call immorality. Greater harm to the fiber of the race may be wrought during the day by the intrigues of unscrupulous business, by factory fire traps, by sweatshops, by the manipulators of our political democracy, than by all the gambling houses and dives in the Tenderloin. After all, the railroad-wrecking financiers, the get-rich-quick promoters, the builders of jerry tenements, the bank looters, bosses, and ward heelers suspend their labors at night.

No; the more you think of it the more you will be persuaded that night is primarily the time of the innocent industries, and for the most part the primitive industries, employing simple, innocent, primitive men — slow-speaking truck farmers, husky red-faced slaughterers in the abattoirs, solid German bakers, and milkmen. The milkman alone is enough to redeem the night from its undeserved evil reputation. A cartload of pasteurized milk for nurslings at four o'clock in the morning represents more service to civilization than a cartful of bullion on its way from the Subtreasury to the vaults of a national bank five hours later.

I am, of course, not thinking now of the early part of the night on Broadway, which is only the bedraggled fringe of day,

Simeon Strunsky

but of the later half of night, which is the fresh anticipation of the dawn. In the still coolness before daybreak the interests of the city come down to human essentials. The commodities dealt in are those that men bought and sold tens of thousands of years before they trafficked in safety razors and Brazilian diamonds. The dealers of the night are concerned with bread, flesh, milk, butter, cheese, fruits, and the green offerings of the fields. Contact with these things cannot but keep the soul clean. There is a fortune for the nerve specialist who will first advise his patients to rise at three in the morning and walk a mile between the rows of wagons and stalls in Gansevoort or Wallabout Market and draw strength from the piles of sweet green produce dewy under the lamplight, and learn patience from the farmer's horses, and observe that even men in their chafferings can be subdued to the innocent medium in which they traffic.

To be sure there are the newspaper men. I have always assumed that it is primarily for them the churches in the lower part of the city offer special services for night workers. If any class of night workers stands in need of prayer it must be the men of my own profession, surely the least innocent of all legitimate trades that are plied after midnight. But as I think of it, even among newspaper men it is the comparatively unspoiled and innocent who work after midnight, members of the lobster squad left on emergency duty, cubs who have not lost all the freshness of the little towns in the Middle West and the South, the men on the linotype machines, the men sweating in the pressrooms, and the short, squat, unshaven men who stagger under enormous bundles of newspapers to the cars and the elevated trains. Here too night has exercised its cleansing selective effect. The big men of the press, the shrewd manipulators of newspaper policy, the editorial pleaders of doubtful causes, the city editors with insistence on the "punch" as against the fact, the Titans of the advertising columns, have all gone home before midnight. As I think of it, the only unrespectable mem-

[143]

The Familiar Essay

bers of the newspaper profession that work at 2 A.M. are the writers of the Extra Special afternoon editions for the next day. Let us hope that they take advantage of the churches' standing offer of special services and prayer for night workers.

When you stroll through the markets, between rows of wagons, stalls, crates, baskets, and squads of perspiring men, you need not force the imagination to call up the solid square miles of brick and stone barracks in which New York's five million, minus some thousands, are asleep, outside the glare of the arc lights and kerosene torches. You can tell Hercules from his foot, and you can tell New York from the size of its maw, of which a single day's filling keeps thousands of men at work. There it sleeps, the big, dark brute, and in another three hours it will yawn and sit up and blink its eyes and roar for its food. The markets are only the spots of highest activity in the business of providing fodder for the creature. Turn out of the crush of Gansevoort Market and walk south through Washington Street and Greenwich Street and Hudson Street, a good mile and a half south through silent warehouses all crammed with food, a solid square mile of provender. The contents of these grim weather-beaten storehouses are open to appraisal by the mere sense of smell as you pass through successive strata of coffee, and sugar, and tea, and spices, and green vegetables, and fruits. If you are sufficiently educated you may detect the individual species within the genus, discern where the pepper merges into cloves, and the heavy odor of banana into the acid aroma of the citrus. It seems almost indecent, this vast debauch of gluttony, this great area given up to the most elemental of the appetites, this Tenderloin of the stomach, until you once more recall the five million individual cells of the animal that will soon have to be fed.

The markets and the warehouses are not the belly of the city, as Zola[1] has called them in his own Paris. The digestive processes of a great city are worked out later and in a million homes.

[1] A naturalistic French novelist (1840–1902).

Simeon Strunsky

The markets are the heart of the city, pumping the life fuel to themselves from across the rivers and the seas, and pumping them out again by drayloads and cartloads through the avenues and streets. In the late afternoon of the day before, everywhere on the circumference of the city, you have come across the driblets and streamlets of nourishment which the markets suck to themselves. In Jersey, in Long Island, and in Westchester you encounter, toward nightfall, heavy farm wagons of exactly the prairie-schooner type that you first met in the school histories, plodding on toward the ferries and the bridges, the drivers nodding over the reins, the horses philosophically conscious of the long hours as well as the long miles ahead of them. Taken one by one these farmers' wagons moving at two miles an hour seem pitifully inadequate to the appetites and imperious demands of a metropolis. But they are only the unquestioning units in the great mobilization of the army of food providers. Their cubic contents and their rate of progress have been accurately estimated by the Von Moltkes[1] of the provision markets. At the appointed time they will drop into their appointed place, forming by companies and squadrons into hollow squares for the daily encounter with humanity's oldest and most indefatigable foe — hunger.

The markets on the water front are the heart of the city's night life, but in all the five boroughs there are local centers of concentrated vitality — the milk depots, the street-railway junctions, the car barns. Where elevated or subway meets with crosstown and longitudinal surface lines you will find at three in the morning as active and garishly illuminated a civic center as many a city of the hinterland would boast of at nine o'clock in the evening. Groups of switchmen, car dispatchers, conductors, motormen, and the casual onlooker whom New York supplies from its inexhaustible womb even at three in the morning, stand in the middle of the road and discuss the most wonder-

[1] The first Von Moltke planned the Prussian campaign against France in 1870-1871; the second was chief of the German General Staff in 1914.

[145]

ful mysteries — so it seems at least in the hush before dawn. And because the cars which they switch and sidetrack and dispatch on their way depart empty of passengers and lose themselves in the shadows, their business too seems one of impressive mystery.

A car conductor at three o'clock in the morning is the most delightful of people to meet. His hands are not yet grimy with the filth of alien nickels and dimes. His temper is as yet unworn with the day's traffic. In the beneficent cool of the night his thwarted social instincts unfold. If you share the rear platform with him, as you will do as a rule, he will accept your fare with a deprecating smile as money passes between gentlemen who stoop to the painful necessity but take no notice of it. Having registered your fare, he will engage you in conversation, and it is amazing how the harassed soul of the car conductor is open to the ideas and forces that rule the great world. If you are timid with conductors and take your way into the car after paying your fare, he will make a pretense of business with the motorman, and, coming back, he will find a remark to draw you out of your surliness or your timidity. He may even sit down next to you, and after five minutes you will be cursing the mechanical necessity of the daylight life which takes this eminently human creature and turns him into a bundle of rasping hurry and incivility. If a visit to the markets is a good cure for neurosis, a trip down Amsterdam Avenue in a surface car at 3 A.M. is a splendid tonic for democracy.

And once more food. For the men who labor in the night, primarily for the city's breakfast, must themselves be fed. Clustered around the markets, and around the railway junctions and car barns, are the brilliantly illuminated Shanleys and Delmonicos of the industrious underworld. What places of warm cheer they are, on a winter night, these long rows of Lunches, whose names are a perpetual lesson in the national geography — Baltimore Lunch, Hartford Lunch, Washington Lunch, New Orleans and Memphis and Utica and Milwaukee

Simeon Strunsky

lunches. They all have tiled floors and white walls and spacious armchairs with a table extension like the chairs in which we used to write examination papers at college. In the rear of the room is the counter supporting the great silver coffee urn. The placards on the walls reek with plenty. You wonder how the resources of an establishment operating on an average level of fifteen cents the meal can supply the promised bounty — sirloins and small steaks, and shellfish out of season, and all the delicacies of the griddle and the casserole; only the prudent consumer will concentrate on the coffee and doughnuts. The rarities are to be had, if you insist, and who would quarrel with the quality of a sirloin steak selling for twenty cents with bread, butter, and coffee, at three in the morning? But it is better to ask for coffee and doughnuts.

An affable humanism permeates the Baltimore Lunch. The proprietor, the chef, the waiter, and the cashier will come forward to meet you and exchange a word or two with you as he wipes up the arm-table. He will take your order and, going behind the counter, will deliver it to himself. If you are extravagant and ask for meats, he will disappear into some sort of cupboard, which is a kitchen, and pleasant pungent odors will precede his reappearance. He will punch your check as a protection against malfeasance by the waiter, and he will ring up your payment on the cash register as a protection against malfeasance on the part of the cashier. If your manners permit, he will come forward and watch you while you eat, not with the affected paternal mien of the head waiter at the Waldorf, but as a brother, a democrat, and a chef who has presided over your food from the first moment till the last and is qualified to take an intimate interest in its ultimate disposal. He is generous with the butter, and as a rule he is indifferent to tips.

Can I do you justice, O Baltimore Lunchman of the Gay White Way in the vicinity of Broadway and Manhattan streets, where the enormous black iron span of the subway viaduct casts its shadow over all the cars that run west to Fort Lee and

E   [147]

The Familiar Essay

north to Fort George and south into the deserted regions of lower Broadway? Your napkins unquestionably were white once upon a time, and your apron is but so-so, but your heart is in the right place, and consequently your manners are perfect. On you too the night has exercised its cleansing effect, wiping out commercialism and leaving behind the instinct for service. You accept my money, but only that you may have the means to go on feeding the useful toilers of the night and occasional castaways like myself. The spirit of profits does not lurk under your flaring arc lights; where is the profit in sirloin steak with bread, butter, and coffee at twenty cents? You are not a trafficker in food, but a minister to human needs; almost as disinterested as the dogs of Saint Bernard, of whom, if you don't mind my saying so, you strongly remind me, with your solid bulk and great shock of hair and the two days' beard and your strangely unmanicured fingers. You do not cater to the pampered palate of the rich, which lusts for strange plants and strange animals and strange liquids to devour. Your sizzling coffee is nectar in the veins of big men who run in on winter nights stamping their feet and smiting their palms stiff from the icy brake handle and switching lever — the simple, innocent toilers of the night. Occasionally your walls resound to the gayety of young voices and your arc lights glow on the shimmer of linen and silks which put your regular customers somewhat out of countenance, as when a troop of young men and girls after loitering wickedly at the dance seek refuge with you while waiting for a car. They taste your coffee and nibble at your doughnuts for a lark. So they say. It is a pretense. They do not nibble, they do not taste; they eat and drink with undeniable relish the rough, unfamiliar fare. After five hours' exercise on the dancing-floor and a ten minutes' wait on a wintry corner, there is an electric spark in your coffee and Titan's food in your doughnuts. Motormen, draymen, what a line of customers is yours! O Youth! O Night! O Baltimore Lunchman!

Simeon Strunsky

The gray of dawn overtakes the armies from the markets, the car barns, and the excavation pits in full retreat. They scatter in every direction, weary, heavy-eyed, but with no sense of defeat in their souls. They throng to the river to lose themselves in the mysterious wilds of Jersey. Their cavalry and train rumble down empty Broadway to South Ferry. They pour eastward toward the bridges or hide themselves in the cellars and ramshackle corner booths of the East Side. They plunge into the subway and, stretched out at full length in the illuminated spaciousness of the Interborough's cars, they pass off into the sleep which falls alike upon the just and the unjust, contrary to general supposition. When the day breaks it finds their haunting-places deserted or given over to small brigades of sweepers and cleaners who make ready for the other kinds of business that are carried on in the full glare of the sun.

Blessed are the meek! While waiting for the inheritance of the earth they are already in full possession of the glory of the sunrise, which we of the comfortable classes know only by hearsay. The tremulous milky gray of the firmament followed by the red flush of daylight is reserved in New York for the truck farmer from the suburbs, the drayman, the food vendors, and the early factory hands. For them only is the beauty of New York as it heaves up out of the shadows. The farmer who has disposed of his wares with expedition and is now on his way back to the Jersey shore, when he looks back, sees the jagged silhouette of our towers and massed brick piles like a host of negroid Titans plodding northward in retreat. Or if his way is by the Municipal boats to Staten Island, he may look back and see a thin shaft of light — ethereal, tremulous, almost faëry, and that pillar of light will be Broadway canyon between its brick walls still clad in shadow. It is given only to the foreign-born ditchers and hewers of the crowded lower Bronx, as they trudge across the bridges over the Harlem, to see before them mighty iron spans flung forward into the shadows or to catch

The Familiar Essay

the mirrored sweep of magic arches lifting up out of the water to link themselves to the arch overhead.

The beauty of New York, rising to meet a new day, is for these lowly workers, and for the unfortunates who stay out in the night not to work but to sleep, because night and the open is their only refuge. When the curtain of night rises on Riverside and reveals Grant's Tomb in frosty vagueness at the end of a green vista, the sight is rarely for those who sleep in the expensive caravansaries along the Drive, and most often for the sleepers on the benches. It is the men who sleep on the benches in Morningside Park that are the first to wonder at the dark line of poplars holding desperate defense against the changing line of daylight, and over the poplars the huge, squat octagon of Saint John's buttressed chapels; unless the sleepers on the benches are anticipated by the angel atop of Saint John's greeting the dawn with his trumpet. Because night loiterers are excluded from Central Park, I suppose that all its awakening loveliness must go for naught. But if the first impingement of the sun on the massed verdure of the park, on its lakes, its Alpine views, its waterfalls, and the fresh, sweet meadows, does find a rare spectator, it must be again one of the homeless who has eluded police regulations to find a night's rest in the great green inclosure. Possibly there may be a poet or two wandering about in Central Park at dawn, but the poets are early risers only in the country. To them the city is only the monstrous, noisy machine of the full day. That on New York City too the sun rises in the morning, working its miracles of beauty, seems to have escaped the poets; or else they have escaped me.

As the sun continues to mount from Flatbush toward the East River bridges, the demoralization of the hosts of night workers grows complete. Either they have disappeared or they straggle on through isolated streets, mere units, like the flotsam of a beaten army. The full light strips them of their dignity. As late even as five o'clock the milkman in the quiet streets is a symbol and a mystery. By six o'clock he is a common purveyor.

Simeon Strunsky

Contact with frowsy elevator boys and gaping grocers' clerks has vulgarized him. His interests are no longer in food, but in commerce. Instead of communing with the night, he is busy with a memorandum book and a lead pencil.

In the full dawn the acetylene flares over the excavation pits have gone out. The dazzling arc lights in the Baltimore and Hartford lunches are out. The street cars, running on shorter schedules, have, taken on their daylight screech and clangor. The conductor is fast sinking into daylight surliness. The huge bundles of newspapers which at night and in bulk have the merit of a really great commodity, the dignity almost of a bag of meal or a crate of eggs, are now resolved into units on the stationers' stands; and if the new day be Sunday the newsman is busy sorting out the twelve different sections of the Sunday paper and putting the comic section on top. Nor can I think of anything in human affairs which can be more futile in the eyes of a Creator than a stationer sorting out comic supplements in the full glory of early sunrise. With its newspaper waiting for it, New York of the ordinary life is ready to get out of bed.

WILLIAM HAZLITT

[1778–1830]

TRAVELLING ABROAD[1]

Ha! here's three of us are sophisticated.[2]

I am one of those who do not think that much is to be gained
in point either of temper or understanding by travelling abroad.
Give me the true, stubborn, unimpaired John Bull feeling, that
keeps fast hold of the good things it fancies in its exclusive
possession, nor ever relaxes in its contempt for foreign frippery
and finery. What is the use of keeping up an everlasting *see-*
saw in the imagination between brown stout[3] and *vin ordi-*
naire,[4] between long and short waists, between English gravity
and French levity? The home-brewed, the home-baked, the
home-spun, "dowlas, filthy dowlas for me!"[5] What, in short,
do we obtain by the contrary method of vain and vexatious
comparison but jealousy of the advantages of others, but dis-
satisfaction with our own? Why is it that the French are so
delighted with themselves? They never quit Paris. Why do
they talk so fast? French is the common language of Europe.
Man was made to stay at home (why else are there so many
millions born who never dreamt of stirring from it?) — to
vegetate, to be rooted to the earth, to cling to his local prejudices, to luxuriate in the follies of his forefathers. At present

[1] Published (unsigned) in the *New Monthly Magazine*, June, 1828. First
assigned to Hazlitt in "New Writings by William Hazlitt," by P. P. Howe,
published by Lincoln MacVeagh, 1925. The essay is unmistakably Hazlitt's.

[2] "King Lear," III, iv, 110. Hazlitt quoted from memory, often inexactly
as here and elsewhere in this essay.   [3] A strong, bitter beer.

[4] Cheap wine served with meals.

[5] Adapted from "1 Henry IV," III, iii, 79.

William Hazlitt

we resemble a set of exotics and fine, sickly plants tossed and tumbled about in flowerpots and rickety cases from shore to shore — not like our native oaks, sturdy, vigorous, gnarled, growing to the soil — "but now a wood is come to Dunsinane"[1]; and clouds of English hover on the steam deck and alight upon the strand. Why, the sun shone just as bright, and this earth of ours rolled round, and the peasant toiled "in the eye of Phœbus, and all night slept in Elysium —"[2]

> next day after dawn,
> Did rise and help Hyperion to his horse:
> And follow'd so the ever-running year
> With profitable labor to his grave —[3]

long before this sailing of steamboats and starting of *diligences*,[4] this cracking of whips and rattling of wheels, this exposing of folly and acquiring of taste was heard of. We now seem to exist only where we are not — to be hurrying on to what is before us, or looking back to what is behind us, never to be fixed to any spot or settled to any employment. We dart like the dragon fly to and fro on the surface of the map, in quest of our insect, glittering prey, and exhibit a picture of impatience, insignificance, and irritability. Formerly an English country gentleman was like the genius of the woods, inclosed in the heart of one of his hereditary oaks; in the present day he approaches nearer to a moody spirit, wandering from one end of Europe to the other, in search of rest and finding none. Enough, enough. Return, ye Absentees — Mr. Macculloch[5] will not prevent you! Break up, ye Traveller's Club, nor longer bestride the world with one foot of the compasses stuck in Pall Mall, and the other at Rome! Your country can do without your straggling ubiquity!

Dr. Johnson remarked long ago how little addition was made

---

[1] "Macbeth," V, v, 45-46.
[2] "Henry V," IV, i, 290-291.
[3] "Henry V," IV, i, 291-294.
[4] public stagecoaches (especially on the Continent).
[5] Author of a book on political economy.

The Familiar Essay

to the conversation of sensible men by foreign travel. Pedants and *petits-maîtres*[1] indeed are always taken up with what they think nobody knows but themselves. It has been proposed as a problem to ascertain whether the slightest trace could be discovered of any impression whatever made on French art by the works of the Italian and other great painters during the fourteen or fifteen years[2] that they remained among them; it is true, the having the Greek statues in their possession seemed to confirm and encourage them in all their faults. They smiled to see the resemblance between a marble statue and their own style of painting; and thought that "if 'twere painted, 'twould be twice as fine." Antique symmetry and elegance only wanted a modern French air added to it to be perfect! Thus we turn away from the lessons afforded to our vanity, or want of taste, and merely attend to what flatters the original disease or superficial bias of our minds. We learn nothing from others, for we see nothing in them but the reflection of our self-love. Not a particle of advance is made, even in our so often boasted candor and liberality. We contrive with all our liberality and candor to *turn the flank* of their virtues and to circumvent their good qualities by some insidious concession or crafty innuendo in such a manner as to convert them into an indirect compliment to ourselves. *Timeo Danaos et dona ferentes.*[3] If we praise them, it is with a lukewarm mental reservation, and we are studying all the time how, with the assistance of a BUT or an IF, we may retract the cowardly donation. Liberality begins and ends at home. It is not a neighborly accomplishment. Or all its professions are verbal, affected, strained, without vital heat or efficacy in them. We make a great gulp to swallow down our prejudices, resolve to be magnanimous, and say: "Come, let

[1] dandies, fops.

[2] Napoleon's spoils from his Italian campaigns were in the Louvre for nearly twenty years. They were restored by order of the Congress of Vienna (1815). French art was at a low ebb at that time.

[3] "I fear the Greeks even when they are bringing gifts" (Virgil, Æneid, II, 49).

William Hazlitt

us acknowledge the plain truth; the French do not get drunk,
they do not rob, nor do they murder people for their money."
We do not think one bit the better of them for this triple cer-
tificate of merit and absolution from moral turpitude, but of
ourselves for our condescension in granting it. We are convinced there must be something in the background, behind the
scenes, to make up for such plausible appearances. We are
twisting the thing about somehow, in some secret corner of our
hearts, to prove that all these negative recommendations show
a want of spirit, of nerve, of hardihood, are effeminate and
sneaking, the virtues of women. Like the patriotic judge in
the time of Queen Elizabeth, who accounted for the compara-
tive honesty of the Scotch in the same way, we say that the
French do not commit so many robberies as we do, because
"they have not such *good hearts*."[1] We pique ourselves, above
all things, on not being a set of milksops. Then as to the mur-
ders abroad, though they are few, they are so strange and unnatural when they do happen, such as husbands killing their
wives, mothers their daughters, etc. A perusal of the *causes
célèbres*[2] fully satisfies the English reader of the total want of
natural affection among the French. As to our drunkenness, as
far as this practice still sticks to us as a national reproach, the
truth is, "we would not change that fault (great as it is) for
their best virtue." All our acknowledgments on this head are
essentially insincere, lip-deep, and at bottom so many ingenious and sidelong compliments to ourselves. The egotism of a
whole people is proof both against conviction and shame.

It is not so, if we can discover any clue, any hint, any loop
hole to find fault. "Oh! most small fault, how ugly in another
dost thou show!"[3] We are then keen enough on the scent, and
"stand like greyhounds on the slips, ready to start away."[4]

[1] bold hearts. The anecdote seems to refer to Sir John Holt, Lord Chief
Justice in the reign of Queen Anne, not of Elizabeth.

[2] "celebrated cases" (famous trials).

[3] Adapted from "King Lear," I, iv, 288–289.

[4] Inexactly quoted from "Henry V," III, i, 31–32.

The Familiar Essay

If a servant inadvertently leaves a door open at night, her defense that there is no danger stands her or her nation in no stead; we are furious at the carelessness of French servants, and forget the implied reproof to ourselves that we come from a place where such carelessness might be fatal. What monstrous injustice! We turn the circumstance over in our minds, and with a little tampering and sophistry it comes out to be owing not to any goodness in the national character, but to the greater security and arbitrariness of the police, which is all in our favor, and we are once more on the right side. This view of the subject is a mighty relief to our feelings, which were beginning to be hurt at there being no chance of our having our throats cut while we slept, even though the doors were left open on purpose. "But then look at our liberty," as Mr. Peel[1] says — charming liberty of being knocked on the head or of knocking others on the head and being hanged for it! The English claim a chartered right to be *blackguards*, and this is all they care for. But if a French marquis filches a tablespoon or pockets a reckoning, then joy to the English! The jubilee and the rejoicing is great. It is clear from thenceforward that the French are a despicable, worthless nation, and the English are "all honorable men."[2] One argues that the titled offender ought to have been pumped upon as "a great moral lesson"; while another traces it to the corruption of the old privileged orders in France, among whom every meanness and profligacy could be practiced with impunity, and consequently all sense of honor and decency was lost. On the same principle we are ready to account for the magnificence of the saloons[3] in Paris, and for the dog holes of kitchens into which they thrust their servants — that is, from the aristocratic pride and pomp of the great, and their utter disregard for the comfort of the lower classes as of an inferior species, according to the old system; but if it is suggested that these same servants may, by the custom of the place, come

[1] An English statesman (1788–1850).   [2] "Julius Cæsar," III, ii, 88.
[3] reception rooms in great houses.

William Hazlitt

into the room with you, or sit in an anteroom through which you have occasion to pass, then *our* aristocratic prejudices take the alarm and begin to be uneasy in their seats. So ill qualified are we to judge of others or ourselves! If things are dirty abroad, there is a great outcry; if they are nice, it is so much the worse. What nonsense! What false refinements! What trifling and effeminacy! Foreign smells are less intolerable than foreign perfumes. I heard it asserted the other day that French snuff was inferior to English, as if this circumstance reëstablished the national character, and all their variety of scents and modes of taking it were mere affectation and pretense. We do not like another's house the better for being finer than our own, nor a country either. It is an insult on our ordinary ideas. The country squires and neighboring dames went away grumbling and sulky from the ostentatious finery of Fonthill Abbey,[1] and no doubt talked a great deal about real comfort when they got home. The French ask, if everything is so disagreeable to us abroad, why do we come? Or, having come, why do we stay? And the plea seems unanswerable. I get into a great many scrapes by maintaining that the mutton is good in Paris — a paradox which is deemed worthy of expatriation. A girl in the *diligence* coming along was very angry the first day because the dinner was bad, there was not a thing she could eat, she was sorry she had ever come to such a country, she would go back again immediately, etc.; the next day the breakfast was admirable; this made her more angry than ever, so many things she did not know which to choose, she hated such a quantity thrown away, and she would touch nothing out of spite and vexation that her former predictions did not continue to be made good. We can forgive anything sooner than a real superiority over us. We would thankfully, joyfully put up with every inconvenience, annoyance, abomination, while from home, to go back with a thorough conviction of our taking

[1] A palatial country house built by William Beckford, the author of "Vathek." Its contents were sold by auction in 1822.

The Familiar Essay

the lead of all the rest of the world in the arts and elegancies of life. Our greatest enemies are those who rob us of our good opinion of ourselves!

An acquaintance of mine is settled in a French boarding house. What scenes we have (fit to make us die with laughter) in going over the messes and manners of the place! How we exult in the *soupe maigre*!¹ How we triumph in the *bouilli*,² as hard as a bullet! If a single thing were good, it would ruin us for the evening. Then the knives will not cut — and what a thing to set down a single fowl before six people, who seem all ready to fall upon it and tear it in pieces! What meanness and wretched economy! Why don't they get a good substantial joint of meat, in which there would be *cut and come again*? If they had common sense they would. And then the lamentable want of decency and propriety is another never-failing and delightful topic. The child is unswaddled before company, and the dirty clothes for the next week's wash are left stewing in the window all dinner time. The master is such a Goth too, a true Frenchman! When carving he flourishes his knife about in such a manner as to endanger those who sit near him, and stops in the middle with the wing of a duck suspended on the point of his fork, to spout a speech out of some play. Dinner is no sooner over than he watches his opportunity, collects all the bottles and glasses on the table, beer, wine, porter, empties them into his own, heaps his plate with the remnants of fricassees, gravy, vegetables, mustard, melted butter, and sops them all up with a large piece of bread, wipes his plate clean as if a dog had licked it, dips his bread in some other dish that in his hurry had escaped him, and finishes off by picking his teeth with a sharp-pointed knife. He then, having satisfied his most urgent wants, amuses himself during the dessert by putting salt in the governess's fruit and giving a pinch of snuff to a cat which is seated in his lap with a string of beads round its neck. What exquisite refinement! Surely the English are a century behind

¹ "thin soup" (soup without meat).   ² "boiled meat" (usually beef).

William Hazlitt

the French in civilization and politeness! Is it not worth while to run the gantlet of a French boarding house, to pay a hundred and sixty francs a month, to be starved, poisoned, talked, stung to death, to arrive at so consoling a reflection? It may be said that this is a vulgar Frenchman in a low rank of life; I answer that there is no such character in any rank of life in London who spouts Shakespeare one moment, the next picks his teeth with his fork, and then sticks it in a potato to help you to it!

There are four charges that I would seriously bring against the French, and that they themselves are not prepared to repel, for they do not expect them: the want of politeness, the want of imagination, the want of liberality, and the want of grace. All this, being contrary to first appearances and received opinion, may seem to require proof, and it may have it thus:

First, as to the want of politeness, the French are deficient in it for this reason, that they have no sense of pain, no nervous or (if you will) morbid sensibility, and consequently can have little delicacy. They aim at the agreeable, I grant, and succeed; but they have no idea of the disagreeable, and therefore take no pains to avoid giving offense. They consider everything of this kind as a whim of the English. A Frenchman coughs in your face and spits on the floor. He runs up against you in the street, not to affront you, for he very politely begs your pardon, but because he thinks of nothing but himself, and never anticipates the shock which he may give you. For myself, English-like, as one whom disagreeable contingencies meet halfway and follow hard upon, if I see a person coming at the other end of a street I am not easy until I have taken my own side of the pavement, lest it should be thought possible I do not mean to take it. At the same time I contradict another bluntly and argue a point tenaciously, which a Frenchman would not do. A French traveller will thrust his body out of a coach window if there is anything he wishes to see, and keep all the air from you as if the coach were his own property, because he has a pleasure in looking out, and it never once enters his head that you have any objection to being stifled. On the same principle he takes his dog into the coach with him — he has not the shadow of a conception how either he or his dog can be offensive to the most delicate organs! French politeness consists in officiousness and complaisance; they are quick in seeing what will please, and ready to oblige when the way is pointed out to them; they do not idly torment themselves, nor knowingly persist in giving pain to others. They incline to make the best of things, are easy-tempered, conciliating, affable, have no stubbornness nor haughty reserve, nor do they gnaw their hearts out, like the English, about what does or does not concern them, and vent their accumulated bile upon their neighbors. A proof of the natural sociability of the French has been taken from this, that they cannot exist as new settlers in the woods of North America, where they can find no one to talk to or admire but themselves. A Frenchman's ideas rise so fast to the surface that unless he can communicate them immediately they strike inward and produce a most uncomfortable kind of melancholy. Flattery and compliments are one ingredient in French manners. You are most secure on the side of their vanity, for this faculty is tolerably alert in them, and they are less apt to wound that of others from being a little sore themselves. Yet this is not always the case, as they are so well fortified in their own good opinion that they do not very well believe how you can be staggered in yours or put out of countenance by trifling mortifications.

Secondly, as to imagination, it must be allowed that they are woefully at a loss in this respect. The French, taken as a nation, have no idea of anything but what is French. They are too well pleased with themselves to be at the trouble of going out of themselves. Vanity and imagination are two incompatible qualities. This is one reason of their dislike to drunkenness. It puts them quite beside themselves, and disturbs that natural intoxication and smooth flow of the animal spirits in which they delight to contemplate their own image as in a glass. A drunken man is no longer a Frenchman. His consciousness of himself

William Hazlitt

and others is gone. I wonder what a Frenchman's dreams are made of? There is no trace of them in his poetry; there is nothing there but *idées nettes*.[1] An instance of their inherent want of imagination was that when they got the Apollo Belvidere[2] in their possession, they declared that it was "to remain there forever." They could not conceive a change in the affairs of the world possible; the present moment, the present object, is with them the whole of time and space. So if you have no money in your pocket they are in despair, and think you never can have any; if you bring out a bag full of crowns they will go away with part of their demand, or even without any of it, as well satisfied as if you had paid the whole. They had no notion how the Russians should burn Moscow. Paris is, in their apprehension, the whole of the universe, and they conceive of those who live out of it as breathing an atmosphere of barbarism. They have a certain respect for the English as having beat them; they think this is owing to some superiority in our jack-tars, and that Paris is not a seaport! When David[3] was looking round at some *chefs-d'œuvres* of Annibale Carracci[4] in the Louvre, he said, "We thought these pictures fine once!" He looked for the traces of his own style in them, and saw that they were farther and farther removed from them.

Thirdly, the French "want grace, who never wanted wit."[5] Grace is not composed of angles. A Frenchwoman walks as if she had tender feet. She does not walk, but fidget and shuffle along like a fantoccini figure[6] on a board. I have heard an excellent judge describe the late queen of France as gliding across an antechamber where he stood to see her, coming in with her large hoop sideways, as if she was borne on a cloud. This was, no doubt, the perfection of the thing, but the ordinary practice

[1] "well-defined ideas."
[2] Under Napoleon; restored to the Vatican in 1816.
[3] A French historical painter (1748–1825).
[4] A Bolognese painter (1560–1609).
[5] Pope, "Satires," V, 289.   [6] A puppet in a puppet show.

The Familiar Essay

is deficient. I deny that a wriggle, however quick or light or erect, is grace. At the same time I allow that the English women in Paris (even those of quality) look like country people in London. Yet the French women look well in London. They have not the same vacant stare, the same improgressiveness, or want of quicksilver in their heels. The French have too sudden a jerk in their movements, and keep their muscles too tight and too incessantly at work, while the English seem as if their bodies were a burden to them, and only move their joints to get forward. They have no elasticity or firmness. *There are faults on both sides.* Anyone may mimic the common French walk by twisting and tripping and ambling on tiptoe; but real grace is not to be caricatured. If I want to know what real grace is, I ask myself, How the Venus de Medicis would move from her pedestal? Not like a Frenchwoman, but like —. The glide of a serpent is graceful; that is, voluminous and expansive. French grace is a dexterous, artificial substitute for the real thing, taught by walking along the dirty, slippery streets of Paris. Grace is made up of curved lines, of continuous, undulating movements; but with the French all is discontinuous, pointed, angular. They are light and airy, it is true; and are borne along by their good spirits, with apparent ease and confidence in themselves, which is so far better than our lumpish, clodhopping, slouching gait. We are in all respects a contradiction to each other; but it does not follow that either is perfect. The English seem made of pure earth; the French have more air mixed with their clay, the Italians more fire, the Germans more water. Yet the heavy, phlegmatic Germans have invented clocks, gunpowder, the art of printing, and the art of oil-painting. What have the other nations of the modern world to bring against these four things? The French pretend to set the fashions to their neighbors. They laugh at us for our caps and bonnets as *outré*[1] and *d'un mauvais goût,*[2] though we borrowed this bad taste from them a year or two before!

[1] "extravagant" (exaggerated).   [2] "in bad taste."

William Hazlitt

Fourthly, to complete this tissue of charges against French manners, they are full of *tracasserie*, of trick and low cunning; they are a thorough "nation of shopkeepers."[1] All their *bonhomie*[2] and complaisance are at an end as soon as their interest is concerned. They are rude or polite, just as they think they can make most by it. A French gentleman travelling in company with others gets a cup of coffee at a little shop for three halfpence, and laughs at you for paying two francs for a bad breakfast at the inn. They demand payment for board and lodging beforehand, which shows either a grasping disposition or a want of confidence. Besides, you cannot depend on them for a moment. A restless inconsequentiality runs through all they do. They seem naturally desirous of escaping from obligations of every kind. If they cut a throat, it is that of some relation from being *ennuyé*[3] with a repetition of the same intercourse — *toujours perdrix*.[4] If you make a bargain with them and someone else comes and offers them a *sou*[5] more, they take it, and smile at your disappointment or pretend not to have understood you. If they can impose on you for once, they think it a wonderful achievement, and consider the loss of your custom nothing. This would be looking too far forward. Therefore they can never be a commercial people; for commerce has a long memory and long hands.[6]

[1] A satirical description of England by Barère (1755–1841) but usually attributed to Napoleon. Hazlitt applies it to the French.

[2] "good nature."   [3] "bored."

[4] "always partridge" (always the same).

[5] A sou is the twentieth part of a franc.

[6] French rogues are cheats, not thieves. French honesty arises not perhaps from the love of justice, but from a repugnance to violence or force. They are a complaisant people, and would not rob you without first asking your consent and making you an accomplice in your own wrong. There is no rudeness done to the will in this, when it is previously won over to their side, and you are the ready dupe of their artifice and *finesse*. There is a vanity as well as love of gain concerned in this. The French will make a fool of you for nothing, and will hardly be prevailed upon to take your goods except by stratagem. Besides, they have a less rude grasp of

The Familiar Essay

To return to our own good folks. Really, it is not surprising that they meet with the sort of *accueil*[1] they do, that they are surrounded and stared at and made a prize of like some outlandish beast cast upon hostile shores. Instead of having arrived by the usual conveyances, they might be supposed to have been thrown out of a balloon or to have dropped from the clouds, they are so stunned, and shocked, and stupefied, and jammed all together, without any variety of character or appearance. There is no perceptible difference between the lord and the commoner, the lady and her maid. A pert French *soubrette*[2] going along laughs at them both alike. Travelling, like Death, levels all distinctions. "The toe of the citizen treads on the courtier's heel, and galls his kibe."[3] We are all *hail fellow well met*. The difference is not worth the counting. It is as if one great personification of John Bull had been suspended over the Continent, and had been dashed to the ground in a thousand fragments, all bruised and senseless alike. A galvanic process is necessary to restore us to life. The national character is fastened to our shoulders like a peddler's pack. It is in vain for anyone to think of holding up his head, of straightening his back, of quickening his step, or unloosing his tongue; we are still outdone in all these particulars by the French, who appear a forward antithesis to us, and we turn back to join the *awkward squad* of our countrymen, and make common cause with them. What signify our poor individual pretensions if we see a whole nation having the start of us, and determined to keep it? No! no one professes to be any better than his neighbors; or if he does step forward to distinguish himself with a vapid air of

external objects, less tenaciousness of property and substantial comforts than the English: they live more upon air. They make consummate sharpers from their quickness and indifference. Farther south the natives rob out of laziness and impudence united, and are very alert in this respect. "Know, Signor Santillane," says the bravo in "Gil Blas," "that when the question is to carry off the goods of another, I have the strength of Hercules." [Hazlitt's note]   [1] "reception" (welcome).

[2] "lady's maid."   [3] Adapted from "Hamlet," V, i, 152–153.

William Hazlitt

assurance, he is soon put back. Like a clown in company, who forgets all his jokes, one would suppose there had been no such thing as wit or humor in England because a French barber is unacquainted with it; we veil our proud pretensions to the genius of French grimace — in pure sheepishness and *mauvaise honte*[1] we give up Fielding and Congreve as dull Englishmen or raw beginners; Prior's Chloe[2] was a dowdy, and Waller's Sacharissa[3] a mistake! But to make some amends, we have a *corps de réserve* to retire upon in our wisdom and our courage, in our Newton and our Locke (Shakespeare we are shy of bringing forward), in our trade and commerce, our religion and government; and everyone on these acknowledged premises struts a hero and a sage. Then all our men are honest and all our women virtuous, and not like the French. In London there are no rogues, prostitutes, sharpers, or the rest of it. We persuade ourselves that we are just the reverse of all that we would be thought to hate or despise in others. We mix up our foibles and our virtues, our dullness and our vanity, our wisdom and our valor, very kindly in the same dish, and, like people out at sea in a boat in the last extremity, each fancies himself entitled to an equal share in the common lot! Can anything be more unfriendly than this state of the exacerbation of our private and public prejudices, in which everything is transposed and distorted, in the mere spirit of contradiction, to a just estimate either of ourselves or others?

We feel at a loss abroad, or (in the common phrase) like fish out of water, because nobody takes much notice of or knows anything about us. But is it not the same in going into any country town in England? Does a deputation wait upon us from the principal inhabitants when we arrive by the coach at Birmingham[4] or Coventry? An Englishman has so far more honor out of his own country, where he is (as Cowley expresses

[1] "bashfulness."   [2] In the poems of Matthew Prior (1664–1721).
[3] Lady Dorothy Sidney, addressed in the love lyrics of Edmund Waller (1606–1687).   [4] Birmingham was not yet a great city.

[165]

The Familiar Essay

it) "a species by himself," and entitled to some distinction as a novelty or nondescript. But in the one case we feel at home, and do not care about the people in a provincial town taking no notice of us, because we know they are no better than we; in a foreign country we are not quite so sure of this, and the indifference of others becomes connected with a dread of insignificance on our part. In London we have common topics and common amusements, as inhabitants of the same great city; and the *esprit de cocagne*[1] in some measure qualifies and carries off petty chagrins and individual slights. What adds to the feeling of littleness, dissipation, and vulgarity in Paris, is that you are taken up only with the present, passing objects — the shops, the houses, the dirt, the finery, the walks, the people, dogs, and monkeys; in London, that is, at home, you have unavoidably certain associations with the past, and the metropolis gradually grows and emerges out of its original obscurity in the "mind's eye."[2] The house here in the Rue de Chantereine, where Bonaparte alighted after the battle of Marengo, is hardly known. It is the order of the day to efface the memory of their short-lived greatness. There is a tendency in the mind to know causes and consequences — without which it grows restive and impatient. The immediate object torn out of its place in the order of events at least does not satisfy the mind of an Englishman. We have not faith, we have not interest in it. This is the reason of the sense of listlessness, of fretfulness, and disgust whenever we are thrown into a crowd, particularly at a distance from home. We are then more at fault than ever. Yet why must we be in the secret, in the cabinet council of passing events? Are they not to go on without us? Must our desire to interfere, or curiosity to know the exact truth, stop their progress? Can we not look at the frontispiece and be pleased with it, without reading the book? Cannot a French milliner sit in a shop gracefully, and with every attention to propriety, without asking our leave or first satisfying us

[1] "spirit of feast" (or plenty).   [2] "Hamlet," I, ii, 185.

William Hazlitt

whether the change from slatternliness to neatness, from coquetry to modesty, is real or apparent? Oh! it is wretched, this importunate humor of making ourselves the pivot on which the whole world turns round. Strain and swell out our self-importance as we will, it is but a point in comparison with the sum of things. How do foreigners get on in our absence? We find them just the same when we return. The English are not the sun that shines on France. How did they manage before we were born, in the times of Madame de Pompadour and Madame La Vallière[1]? Were the court beauties to wait to know our pleasure before they gave their answers to Louis XIV or Louis XV? Madame de Sévigné[2] wrote very pretty letters, though the *New Monthly Magazine* was not then in existence! One would think at first that reading and reflection would cure this teasing disposition; and yet, by giving us a kind of factitious interest and omnipresence in such cases, it mixes us up with everything again, and confirms our original egotism, as if we had a right to be consulted and to give our opinion on what thus passes in review before us. Nature is incorrigible — there is no crevice so small or intricate at which our self-love will not contrive to creep in. *Naturam expellas furca, usque recurret!*[3] The only alternative to be pursued in these circumstances is to visit Paris with all the ignorance, simplicity, and disposition to admire with which Sir Francis Wronghead[4] and his family came up to London; or to go abroad spitting our spite at every stage, and determined to condemn in the lump, like Matthew Bramble[5] — the halfway course between of questioning and criticizing and accounting for everything is intolerable.

[1] Referred to below as the mistresses of Louis XIV and Louis XV.
[2] A French letter writer (1626–1696).
[3] Horace, "Epistles," I, x, 24. Translated by Francis as follows:
> For Nature, driven out with proud disdain,
> All-powerful goddess, will return again."

[4] In "The Provoked Husband," by Vanbrugh and Cibber.
[5] In Smollett's "Humphrey Clinker."

The Familiar Essay

Come then, and let us away from all this cabal and impertinence, and let us cross the Alps. Pictures, ruins, mountains, defy this petty personality and painful jealousy. They are abstractions of the mind. With the first sight of Mont Blanc you leave yourself behind, and travel through a romance — in a waking dream of the distant and the past. Who, in crossing Mount Cenis, thinks of Tottenham Court Road? Who, in the Louvre or the Vatican, is jealous of the claims of native art? Who, in the streets of Turin or Ferrara, does not find himself at home — in the home of early imagination, in the palaces and porticoes of high-sounding thought? Here the whole impression tells for itself — simple, entire, majestic — and has no drawback of invidious, cowardly comparison. What we have read of in books or had glimpses of in fancy; "those brave, sublunary[1] things," handed down from age to age and wrought into our memory, these form part of ourselves, and we have no uneasiness on that head. Here fame triumphs over envy, the great over the little. There is here nothing that can be connected with upstart pretension or personal competition or the fashion of the hour: all speaks of the past, of glory departed, of the races that are gone, and between whom and us the grave has placed a lofty barrier. Their cities are the cities of the dead — from their moldering battlements the faces of the rugged warriors still look out. Sometimes, as I gaze upon the dying embers in my room, the ruddy streaks and nodding fragments shape themselves into an Italian landscape, and Radicofani[2] rises in the distance, receding into the light of setting suns, that seem bidding the world farewell forever from their splendor, their pomp, and the surrounding gloom! Or Perugia opens its cloistered gates, and I look down upon the world beneath, and Foligno and Spoleto stretch out their dark groves and shining walls behind me! You seem walking in the valley of the shadow

[1] Usually so quoted, but properly "translunary"; from Drayton's "Elegy to Henry Reynolds, Esq."

[2] Radicofani, Perugia, Foligno, and Spoleto are all in central Italy.

William Hazlitt

of life; *ideal* palaces, groves, and cities (realized to the bodily sense) everywhere rise up before you — "The earth hath bubbles as the water hath, and these are of them!"[1] You scale the heavens or descend into the tomb; but you are always taken out of yourself, and view objects by the twilight of history. You have no more to do with the present race of people than perusing an old book; you and they are alike spectators of the mighty scene — their country is the inheritance of the imagination! In Switzerland, on the other hand, the magnitude of the objects, as well as the quiet and seclusion of the customary modes of life, annihilates all personal reflections. If you fall from the top of one of those crags, you will break your neck whether you are a Frenchman or an Englishman; in the valley below, you may exclaim without much affectation, "Vain pomp and glory of the world, I hate ye!"[2] Again, in Holland you gain an accession to your ideas of civilization by recognizing large tracts of mud and water as the dwellings of men, and are happy to find that a Dutchman is not a boor. You draw no parallel between yourself and him; and clap him on the back, and praise the neatness of his houses and windows without envying the owner. Our intercourse is as friendly, and as free from rivalry, as the notice we take of a great shock-dog. Our petty national prejudices do not bristle up at every turn "like quills upon the fretful porcupine."[3] So far it is well. In other places I forget myself, but in France I am always an Englishman. The *black ox*[4] there treads upon my forehead. In a town in Italy some prisoners from behind the bars of a jail window called out "Francese" as we passed, meaning thereby that *they* were gentlemen and that we were French. I was not displeased to have got so far south as to have worn out the traces of my personal identity in this manner. Anything to leave the sense of self behind us, and not to aggravate it by foreign travel and national antipathies! It is well to be a citizen of the

[1] "Macbeth," I, iii, 79–80.   [3] "Hamlet," I, v, 20.
[2] "Henry VIII," III, ii, 365.   [4] proverbial for misfortune.

The Familiar Essay

world, to fall in, as nearly as we can, with the ways and feelings of others and make oneself at home wherever one comes; or it is better still to live in an *ideal* world, superior to the ordinary one, to carry in one's breast "that peace which passeth understanding,"[1] that no accident of time or place, irritation or disappointment, can assail, except for the moment, that neither debts nor duns annoy, that reconciles itself to all situations and smooths all difficulties; not to be calm in solitude and agitated in the assemblies of men, but in the midst of a great city to retain possession of one's faculties as in a perfect solitude, and in a wilderness to be surrounded with the gorgeousness of art; to owe no allegiance to the elements, not to be the creature of circumstances, dependent on a gust of wind, a bad smell, a dinner, or a waiter at an inn, the good or bad state of the roads, but to make the best of our goings and comings, and of all circumstances, as only passages of that longer yet brief journey, that by fitful stages and various *ups* and *downs* conducts us to "our native dust and final home!"[2]

[1] Philippians iv, 7.
[2] A double quotation freely adapted from "Paradise Lost," X, 1084–1085 and XI, 462–463.

Robert Louis Stevenson

[1850–1894]

ÆS TRIPLEX

The changes wrought by death are in themselves so sharp
and final, and so terrible and melancholy in their consequences,
that the thing stands alone in man's experience, and has no
parallel upon earth. It outdoes all other accidents because it is
the last of them. Sometimes it leaps suddenly upon its victims,
like a Thug.[1]; sometimes it lays a regular siege and creeps upon
their citadel during a score of years. And when the business is
done, there is sore havoc made in other people's lives, and a
pin knocked out by which many subsidiary friendships hung
together. There are empty chairs, solitary walks, and single
beds at night. Again, in taking away our friends, death does not
take them away utterly, but leaves behind a mocking, tragical,
and soon intolerable residue, which must be hurriedly concealed.
Hence a whole chapter of sights and customs striking to the
mind, from the pyramids of Egypt to the gibbets and dule trees[3]
of medieval Europe. The poorest persons have a bit of pageant
going toward the tomb; memorial stones are set up over the
least memorable; and, in order to preserve some show of respect
for what remains of our old loves and friendships, we must
accompany it with much grimly ludicrous ceremonial, and the

[1] One of an organization of religious assassins in India, serving the goddess of destruction.   [3] trees on which condemned persons were hanged.

[171]

The Familiar Essay

hired undertaker parades before the door. All this, and much more of the same sort, accompanied by the eloquence of poets, has gone a great way to put humanity in error; nay, in many philosophies the error has been embodied and laid down with every circumstance of logic; although in real life the bustle and swiftness, in leaving people little time to think, have not left them time enough to go dangerously wrong in practice.

As a matter of fact, although few things are spoken of with more fearful whisperings than this prospect of death, few have less influence on conduct under healthy circumstances. We have all heard of cities in South America built upon the side of fiery mountains, and how, even in this tremendous neighborhood, the inhabitants are not a jot more impressed by the solemnity of mortal conditions than if they were delving gardens in the greenest corner of England. There are serenades and suppers and much gallantry among the myrtles overhead; and meanwhile the foundation shudders underfoot, the bowels of the mountain growl, and at any moment living ruin may leap sky-high into the moonlight, and tumble man and his merry-making in the dust. In the eyes of very young people and very dull old ones there is something indescribably reckless and desperate in such a picture. It seems not credible that respectable married people, with umbrellas, should find appetite for a bit of supper within quite a long distance of a fiery mountain; ordinary life begins to smell of high-handed debauch when it is carried on so close to a catastrophe; and even cheese and salad, it seems, could hardly be relished in such circumstances without something like a defiance of the Creator. It should be a place for nobody but hermits dwelling in prayer and maceration, or mere born devils drowning care in a perpetual carouse.

And yet, when one comes to think upon it calmly, the situation of these South American citizens forms only a very pale figure for the state of ordinary mankind. This world itself, traveling blindly and swiftly in overcrowded space, among a

[172]

Robert Louis Stevenson

million other worlds traveling blindly and swiftly in contrary directions, may very well come by a knock that would set it into explosion like a penny squib. And what, pathologically looked at, is the human body with all its organs, but a mere bagful of petards[1]? The least of these is as dangerous to the whole economy as the ship's powder magazine to the ship; and with every breath we breathe, and every meal we eat, we are putting one or more of them in peril. If we clung as devotedly as some philosophers pretend we do to the abstract idea of life, or were half as frightened as they make out we are, for the subversive accident that ends it all, the trumpets might sound by the hour and no one would follow them into battle — the blue peter[2] might fly at the truck,[3] but who would climb into a seagoing ship? Think (if these philosophers were right) with what a preparation of spirit we should affront the daily peril of the dinner table; a deadlier spot than any battlefield in history, where the far greater proportion of our ancestors have miserably left their bones! What woman would ever be lured into marriage, so much more dangerous than the wildest sea? And what would it be to grow old? For, after a certain distance, every step we take in life we find the ice growing thinner below our feet, and all around us and behind us we see our contemporaries going through. By the time a man gets well into the seventies, his continued existence is a mere miracle; and when he lays his old bones in bed for the night, there is an overwhelming probability that he will never see the day. Do the old men mind it, as a matter of fact? Why, no. They were never merrier; they have their grog at night, and tell the raciest stories; they hear of the death of people about their own age, or even younger, not as if it was a grisly warning, but with a simple childlike pleasure at having outlived someone else; and when a draft might puff them out like a guttering candle, or a bit of a stumble shatter them like so much glass, their old

[1] firecrackers. [2] A blue flag with a white square, hoisted before sailing.
[3] A wooden cap at the top of a mast, with holes for ropes.

The Familiar Essay

hearts keep sound and unaffrighted, and they go on, bubbling with laughter, through years of man's age compared to which the valley at Balaclava[1] was as safe and peaceful as a village cricket green on Sunday. It may fairly be questioned (if we look to the peril only) whether it was a much more daring feat for Curtius[2] to plunge into the gulf, than for any old gentleman of ninety to doff his clothes and clamber into bed.

Indeed, it is a memorable subject for consideration, with what unconcern and gayety mankind pricks on along the Valley of the Shadow of Death. The whole way is one wilderness of snares, and the end of it, for those who fear the last pinch, is irrevocable ruin. And yet we go spinning through it all, like a party for the Derby. Perhaps the reader remembers one of the humorous devices of the deified Caligula[3]: how he encouraged a vast concourse of holiday-makers on to his bridge over Baiæ bay; and when they were in the height of their enjoyment, turned loose the Prætorian Guards among the company and had them tossed into the sea. This is no bad miniature of the dealings of nature with the transitory race of man. Only, what a checkered picnic we have of it, even while it lasts! and into what great waters, not to be crossed by any swimmer, God's pale Prætorian throws us over in the end!

We live the time that a match flickers; we pop the cork of a ginger-beer bottle, and the earthquake swallows us on the instant. Is it not odd, is it not incongruous, is it not, in the highest sense of human speech, incredible, that we should think so highly of the ginger beer and regard so little the devouring earthquake? The love of Life and the fear of Death are two famous phrases that grow harder to understand the more we think about them. It is a well-known fact that an immense proportion of boat accidents would never happen if people held the sheet in their hands instead of making it fast; and yet,

[1] Where the charge of the Light Brigade was made (Crimean War, 1854).
[2] A legendary Roman youth who leaped into a chasm to appease the wrath of the gods against the city.   [3] Emperor of Rome, 37–41.

Robert Louis Stevenson

unless it be some martinet of a professional mariner or some landsman with shattered nerves, every one of God's creatures makes it fast. A strange instance of man's unconcern and brazen boldness in the face of death!

We confound ourselves with metaphysical phrases, which we import into daily talk with noble inappropriateness. We have no idea of what death is, apart from its circumstances and some of its consequences to others; and although we have some experience of living, there is not a man on earth who has flown so high into abstraction as to have any practical guess at the meaning of the word "life." All literature, from Job and Omar Khayyám to Thomas Carlyle or Walt Whitman, is but an attempt to look upon the human state with such largeness of view as shall enable us to rise from the consideration of living to the Definition of Life. And our sages give us about the best satisfaction in their power when they say that it is a vapor, or a show, or made out of the same stuff with dreams. Philosophy, in its more rigid sense, has been at the same work for ages; and after a myriad bald heads have wagged over the problem, and piles of words have been heaped one upon another into dry and cloudy volumes without end, philosophy has the honor of laying before us, with modest pride, her contribution toward the subject: that life is a Permanent Possibility of Sensation. Truly a fine result! A man may very well love beef, or hunting, or a woman; but surely, surely, not a Permanent Possibility of Sensation! He may be afraid of a precipice, or a dentist, or a large enemy with a club, or even an undertaker's man; but not certainly of abstract death. We may trick with the word "life" in its dozen senses until we are weary of tricking; we may argue in terms of all the philosophies on earth, but one fact remains true throughout — that we do not love life, in the sense that we are greatly preoccupied about its conservation; that we do not, properly speaking, love life at all, but living. Into the views of the least careful there will enter some degree of providence; no man's eyes are fixed entirely on the passing

The Familiar Essay

hour; but although we have some anticipation of good health, good weather, wine, active employment, love, and self-approval, the sum of these anticipations does not amount to anything like a general view of life's possibilities and issues; nor are those who cherish them most vividly at all the most scrupulous of their personal safety. To be deeply interested in the accidents of our existence, to enjoy keenly the mixed texture of human experience, rather leads a man to disregard precautions, and risk his neck against a straw. For surely the love of living is stronger in an Alpine climber roping over a peril, or a hunter riding merrily at a stiff fence, than in a creature who lives upon a diet and walks a measured distance in the interest of his constitution.

There is a great deal of very vile nonsense talked upon both sides of the matter: tearing divines reducing life to the dimensions of a mere funeral procession, so short as to be hardly decent; and melancholy unbelievers yearning for the tomb as if it were a world too far away. Both sides must feel a little ashamed of their performances now and again when they draw in their chairs to dinner. Indeed, a good meal and a bottle of wine is an answer to most standard works upon the question. When a man's heart warms to his viands, he forgets a great deal of sophistry, and soars into a rosy zone of contemplation. Death may be knocking at the door, like the Commander's statue[1]; we have something else in hand, thank God, and let him knock. Passing bells are ringing all the world over. All the world over, and every hour, someone is parting company with all his aches and ecstasies. For us also the trap is laid. But we are so fond of life that we have no leisure to entertain the terror of death. It is a honeymoon with us all through, and none of the longest. Small blame to us if we give our whole hearts to this glowing bride of ours, to the appetites, to honor, to the hungry curiosity of the mind, to the pleasure of the eyes in nature, and the pride of our own nimble bodies.

[1] In the stories of Don Juan the statue of the Commander comes to avenge his death on Don Juan.

Robert Louis Stevenson

that set him upon his dictionary, and carried him through tri-
umphantly until the end! Who, if he were wisely considerate
of things at large, would ever embark upon any work much
more considerable than a halfpenny post card? Who would
project a serial novel, after Thackeray and Dickens had each
fallen in mid-course? Who would find heart enough to begin
to live, if he dallied with the consideration of death?

And, after all, what sorry and pitiful quibbling all this is!
To forego all the issues of living in a parlor with a regulated
temperature — as if that were not to die a hundred times over,
and for ten years at a stretch! As if it were not to die in one's
own lifetime, and without even the sad immunities of death!
As if it were not to die, and yet be the patient spectators of our
own pitiable change! The Permanent Possibility is preserved,
but the sensations carefully held at arm's length, as if one kept
a photographic plate in a dark chamber. It is better to lose
health like a spendthrift than to waste it like a miser. It is
better to live and be done with it than to die daily in the sick-
room. By all means begin your folio; even if the doctor does
not give you a year, even if he hesitates about a month, make
one brave push and see what can be accomplished in a week.
It is not only in finished undertakings that we ought to honor
useful labor. A spirit goes out of the man who means execution,
which outlives the most untimely ending. All who have meant
good work with their whole hearts have done good work, although they may die before they have the time to sign it. Every
heart that has beat strong and cheerfully has left a hopeful
impulse behind it in the world and bettered the tradition of
mankind. And even if death catch people, like an open pitfall,
and in mid-career, laying out vast projects and planning monstrous foundations, flushed with hope, and their mouths full of
boastful language, they should be at once tripped up and
silenced: is there not something brave and spirited in such a
termination? and does not life go down with a better grace,
foaming in full body over a precipice, than miserably straggling

E   [179]

The Familiar Essay

to an end in sandy deltas? When the Greeks made their fine saying that those whom the gods love die young, I cannot help believing they had this sort of death also in their eye. For surely, at whatever age it overtake the man, this is to die young. Death has not been suffered to take so much as an illusion from his heart. In the hot-fit of life, a-tiptoe on the highest point of being, he passes at a bound on to the other side. The noise of the mallet and chisel is scarcely quenched, the trumpets are hardly done blowing, when, trailing with him clouds of glory, this happy-starred, full-blooded spirit shoots into the spiritual land.

The Formal Essay

A formal essay may seem to be almost a contradiction in terms; for an essential quality of the essay is its intimacy and its freedom of form.

However, the difference is one of degree rather than of kind; the formal essay is not an opposite kind of writing, but an essay which is less subjective, less informal, more purely expository. It is concerned less with a man's personal reaction to life than with his critical examination of it. It is perhaps best illustrated in the critical essay, with its careful examination of literature; the biographical or historical essay, with its judicial appraisal of human character and action; the philosophical or didactic essay, with its weighing of ideas and of social institutions; and the editorial essay, with its commentary on the course of events.

The formal essayist may be writing of his favorite poet, but he speaks as a careful critic and not as a mere enthusiast. He may be addressing his close personal friend who has threatened him with imprisonment for violation of a repressive law, but his interest is in the larger issue of the freedom of speech.

Forerunners of the formal essay are to be found in the more elaborate critical and philosophical passages in the *Spectator* and in the *Rambler*. In the nineteenth century the critical reviews gave rise to a fuller development of the type. The middle of the nineteenth century was a time of religious questioning, and this found expression in the theological writings of Newman and Arnold; it was a time of scientific advancement, and this gave rise to the essays of Huxley; it was a time of literary unrest, following the violent revolt of the Romantic writers

[181]

The Formal Essay

against the eighteenth-century orthodoxy, and this gave rise to a new appraisal of literary standards. It was filled with social and economic changes, with new theories of government and education, of social institutions and public morality; all this found expression in the formal essay.

If one were to ask for the consciously "modern" note in literature, he might find it most quickly in the formal essays of our own time. It occurs also in the social novel, the problem play, the poem of the slums or the factory. Even in the great revival of the personal essay which has taken place during the present generation, there is a frequent suggestion of a spirit of doubt, of questioning, of disillusionment, or of a cynical outlook on life. Democracy has not proved a panacea for all political ills; the World War has not ended cruelty and greed; the equality of the sexes has not made all homes ideally happy.

In regard to this discontent two very different replies have been offered. One is that of the many popular scientific writers of our own time who hold that the millennium is to be reached by way of the laboratory and the factory. Further experimentation, further invention, and further external aids will right all the ills of mankind. We are told by these writers that the world has made more progress in the past century than in all the long era which went before.

An opposing theory is represented by the essay on "President Eliot and Liberal Education in America." According to this view human nature has shown no such amazing betterment. A man cannot lift himself up by his boot straps; mechanical aids to progress are of less value than the cultivation of "an humble and a contrite heart."

In our own time, as in Bacon's, the peculiar appeal of essays is in their interest in human concerns. Whether they are familiar or formal in style, they "come home to men's business and bosoms."

WILLIAM HAZLITT

[1778–1830]

ON FAMILIAR STYLE[1]

It is not easy to write a familiar style. Many people mistake
a familiar for a vulgar style, and suppose that to write without
affectation is to write at random. On the contrary, there is
nothing that requires more precision, and, if I may so say,
purity of expression, than the style I am speaking of. It utterly
rejects not only all unmeaning pomp, but all low, cant phrases,
and loose, unconnected, *slipshod* allusions. It is not to take the
first word that offers, but the best word in common use; it
is not to throw words together in any combinations we please,
but to follow and avail ourselves of the true idiom of the language. To write a genuine familiar or truly English style is to
write as any one would speak in common conversation who had
a thorough command and choice of words, or who could discourse with ease, force, and perspicuity, setting aside all pedantic
and oratorical flourishes. Or, to give another illustration, to
write naturally is the same thing in regard to common conversation as to read naturally is in regard to common speech. It
does not follow that it is an easy thing to give the true accent
and inflection to the words you utter, because you do not
attempt to rise above the level of ordinary life and colloquial
speaking. You do not assume, indeed, the solemnity of the
pulpit, or the tone of stage declamation; neither are you at
liberty to gabble on at a venture, without emphasis or discretion, or to resort to vulgar dialect or clownish pronunciation.
You must steer a middle course. You are tied down to a given

[1] The twenty-fourth essay of "Table Talk" (1821–1822).

The Formal Essay

and appropriate articulation, which is determined by the habitual associations between sense and sound, and which you can only hit by entering into the author's meaning, as you must find the proper words and style to express yourself by fixing your thoughts on the subject you have to write about. Any one may mouth out a passage with a theatrical cadence, or get upon stilts to tell his thoughts; but to write or speak with propriety and simplicity is a more difficult task. Thus it is easy to affect a pompous style, to use a word twice as big as the thing you want to express: it is not so easy to pitch upon the very word that exactly fits it. Out of eight or ten words equally common, equally intelligible, with nearly equal pretensions, it is a matter of some nicety and discrimination to pick out the very one the preferableness of which is scarcely perceptible, but decisive. The reason why I object to Dr. Johnson's style is that there is no discrimination, no selection, no variety in it. He uses none but "tall, opaque words,"[1] taken from the "first row of the rubric"[2] — words with the greatest number of syllables, or Latin phrases with merely English terminations. If a fine style depended on this sort of arbitrary pretension, it would be fair to judge of an author's elegance by the measurement of his words and the substitution of foreign circumlocutions (with no precise associations) for the mother tongue.[3] How simple it is to be dignified without ease, to be pompous without meaning! Surely, it is but a mechanical rule for avoiding what is low to be always pedantic and affected. It is clear you cannot use a vulgar English word if you never use a common English word at all. A fine tact is shown in adhering to those which are perfectly common, and yet never falling into any expressions which are debased by disgusting circumstances,

[1] Sterne, "Tristram Shandy," III, xx ("The Author's Preface").

[2] Adapted from "Hamlet," II, ii, 437.

[3] I have heard of such a thing as an author who makes it a rule never to admit a monosyllable into his vapid verse. Yet the charm and sweetness of Marlowe's lines depended often on their being made up almost entirely of monosyllables. [Hazlitt's note]

William Hazlitt

or which owe their signification and point to technical or professional allusions. A truly natural or familiar style can never
be quaint or vulgar, for this reason, that it is of universal force
and applicability, and that quaintness and vulgarity arise out
of the immediate connection of certain words with coarse and
disagreeable or with confined ideas. The last form what we
understand by *cant* or *slang* phrases. To give an example of
what is not very clear in the general statement : I should say
that the phrase *To cut with a knife* or *To cut a piece of wood* is
perfectly free from vulgarity, because it is perfectly common;
but *To cut an acquaintance* is not quite unexceptionable, because it is not perfectly common or intelligible, and has hardly
yet escaped out of the limits of slang phraseology. I should
hardly, therefore, use the word in this sense without putting it
in italics as a license of expression, to be received *cum grano
salis*.[1] All provincial or by-phrases come under the same mark
of reprobation — all such as the writer transfers to the page
from his fireside or a particular *coterie*, or that he invents for
his own sole use and convenience. I conceive that words are
like money, not the worse for being common, but that it is the
stamp of custom alone that gives them circulation or value. I
am fastidious in this respect, and would almost as soon coin
the currency of the realm as counterfeit the king's English. I
never invented or gave a new and unauthorized meaning to
any word but one single one (the term "impersonal" applied
to feelings), and that was in an abstruse metaphysical discussion to express a very difficult distinction. I have been (I
know) loudly accused of reveling in vulgarisms and broken
English. I cannot speak to that point; but so far I plead
guilty to the determined use of acknowledged idioms and common elliptical expressions. I am not sure that the critics in
question know the one from the other; that is, can distinguish
any medium between formal pedantry and the most barbarous
solecism. As an author I endeavor to employ plain words and

[1] "with a grain of salt" (with due allowances).

[185]

The Formal Essay

popular modes of construction, as, were I a chapman[1] and dealer, I should common weights and measures.

The proper force of words lies not in the words themselves, but in their application. A word may be a fine-sounding word, of an unusual length, and very imposing from its learning and novelty, and yet in the connection in which it is introduced may be quite pointless and irrelevant. It is not pomp or pretension, but the adaptation of the expression to the idea, that clenches a writer's meaning — as it is not the size or glossiness of the materials, but their being fitted each to its place, that gives strength to the arch; or as the pegs and nails are as necessary to the support of the building as the larger timbers, and more so than the mere showy, unsubstantial ornaments. I hate anything that occupies more space than it is worth. I hate to see a load of bandboxes go along the street, and I hate to see a parcel of big words without anything in them. A person who does not deliberately dispose of all his thoughts alike in cumbrous draperies and flimsy disguises may strike out twenty varieties of familiar everyday language, each coming somewhat nearer to the feeling he wants to convey, and at last not hit upon that particular and only one which may be said to be identical with the exact impression in his mind. This would seem to show that Mr. Cobbett[2] is hardly right in saying that the first word that occurs is always the best. It may be a very good one; and yet a better may present itself on reflection or from time to time. It should be suggested naturally, however, and spontaneously, from a fresh and lively conception of the subject. We seldom succeed by trying at improvement, or by merely substituting one word for another that we are not satisfied with, as we cannot recollect the name of a place or person by merely plaguing ourselves about it. We wander farther from the point by persisting in a wrong scent; but it

[1] a peddler or merchant.
[2] An English political economist (1763–1835) noted for his forceful style. He at one time lived in the United States.

William Hazlitt

starts up accidentally in the memory when we least expected it, by touching some link in the chain of previous association.

There are those who hoard up and make a cautious display of nothing but rich and rare phraseology — ancient medals, obscure coins, and Spanish pieces of eight.[1] They are very curious to inspect, but I myself would neither offer nor take them in the course of exchange. A sprinkling of archaisms is not amiss, but a tissue of obsolete expressions is more fit *for keep than wear*. I do not say I would not use any phrase that had been brought into fashion before the middle or the end of the last century; but I should be shy of using any that had not been employed by any approved author during the whole of that time. Words, like clothes, get old-fashioned or mean and ridiculous when they have been for some time laid aside. Mr. Lamb is the only imitator of old English style I can read with pleasure; and he is so thoroughly imbued with the spirit of his authors that the idea of imitation is almost done away. There is an inward unction, a marrowy vein both in the thought and feeling, an intuition, deep and lively, of his subject, that carries off any quaintness or awkwardness arising from an antiquated style and dress. The matter is completely his own, though the manner is assumed. Perhaps his ideas are altogether so marked and individual as to require their point and pungency to be neutralized by the affectation of a singular but traditional form of conveyance. Tricked out in the prevailing costume, they would probably seem more startling and out of the way. The old English authors, Burton, Fuller, Coryat, Sir Thomas Browne,[2] are a kind of mediators between us and the more eccentric and whimsical modern, reconciling us to his peculiarities. I do not, however, know how far this is the case or not, till he condescends to write like one of us. I must confess that what I like best of his papers under the signature of Elia (still I do not presume, amidst such excellence, to decide what is

[1] Spanish dollars.
[2] Four seventeenth-century writers who influenced Lamb greatly.

The Formal Essay

most excellent) is the account of "Mrs. Battle's Opinions on Whist," which is also the most free from obsolete allusions and turns of expression — "A well of native English undefiled."[1] To those acquainted with his admired prototypes, these "Essays" of the ingenious and highly gifted author have the same sort of charm and relish that Erasmus's "Colloquies"[2] or a fine piece of modern Latin have to the classical scholar. Certainly I do not know any borrowed pencil that has more power or felicity of execution than the one of which I have here been speaking.

It is as easy to write a gaudy style without ideas as it is to spread a pallet of showy colors or to smear in a flaunting transparency. "What do you read?" "Words, words, words." "What is the matter?"[3] "*Nothing*," it might be answered. The florid style is the reverse of the familiar. The last is employed as an unvarnished medium to convey ideas; the first is resorted to as a spangled veil to conceal the want of them. When there is nothing to be set down but words, it costs little to have them fine. Look through the dictionary, and cull out a *florilegium*,[4] rival the *tulippomania*.[5] *Rouge* high enough, and never mind the natural complexion. The vulgar, who are not in the secret, will admire the look of preternatural health and vigor; and the fashionable, who regard only appearances, will be delighted with the imposition. Keep to your sounding generalities, your tinkling phrases, and all will be well. Swell out an unmeaning truism to a perfect tympany of style. A thought, a distinction, is the rock on which all this brittle cargo of verbiage splits at once. Such writers have merely *verbal* imaginations, that retain nothing but words. Or their puny thoughts have dragon wings all green and gold. They soar far

[1] Adapted from Spenser's praise of Chaucer: "well of English undefyled" ("The Faerie Queene," IV, ii, 32).

[2] The "Colloquies" (1524) were written in Latin.

[3] "Hamlet," II, ii, 192–195.

[4] "a culling of flowers" (a bouquet).

[5] The "tulip craze" (in Holland).

William Hazlitt

above the vulgar failing of the *sermo humi obrepens*[1] — their most ordinary speech is never short of an hyperbole, splendid, imposing, vague, incomprehensible, magniloquent, a cento of sounding commonplaces. If some of us, whose "ambition is more lowly,"[2] pry a little too narrowly into nooks and corners to pick up a number of "unconsidered trifles,"[3] they never once direct their eyes or lift their hands to seize on any but the most gorgeous, tarnished, threadbare, patchwork set of phrases, the left-off finery of poetic extravagance, transmitted down through successive generations of barren pretenders. If they criticize actors and actresses, a huddled phantasmagoria of feathers, spangles, floods of light, and oceans of sound float before their morbid sense, which they paint in the style of Ancient Pistol.[4] Not a glimpse can you get of the merits or defects of the performers: they are hidden in a profusion of barbarous epithets and willful rhodomontade. Our hyper-critics are not thinking of these little fantoccini beings "that strut and fret their hour upon the stage,"[5] but of tall phantoms of words, abstractions, *genera* and *species*, sweeping clauses, periods that unite the Poles, forced alliterations, astounding antitheses — "And on their pens *Fustian* sits plumed."[6] If they describe kings and queens, it is an Eastern pageant. The coronation at either House is nothing to it. We get at four repeated images — a curtain, a throne, a scepter, and a footstool. These are with them the wardrobe of a lofty imagination; and they turn their servile strains to servile uses. Do

---

[1] "prose crawling along the ground." The Latin phrase is adapted from Horace's "Epistles," II, i, 250–251.

[2] Adapted from "The Tempest," I, ii, 482–483.

[3] "The Winter's Tale," IV, iii, 26.

[4] A bombastic character in "Henry IV," "Henry V," and "The Merry Wives of Windsor."

[5] "Macbeth," V, v, 25. Hazlitt quotes inexactly, as he often does.

[6] Apparently adapted from Milton's "Paradise Lost," IV, 988–989:

> "His stature reach'd the sky, and on his crest
> Sat horror plumed."

The Formal Essay

we read a description of pictures? It is not a reflection of tones and hues which "nature's own sweet and cunning hand laid on,"[1] but piles of precious stones, rubies, pearls, emeralds, Golconda's[2] mines, and all the blazonry of art. Such persons are in fact besotted with words, and their brains are turned with the glittering but empty and sterile phantoms of things. Personifications, capital letters, seas of sunbeams, visions of glory, shining inscriptions, the figures of a transparency, Britannia with her shield, or Hope leaning on an anchor, make up their stock in trade. They may be considered as *hieroglyphical* writers. Images stand out in their minds isolated and important merely in themselves, without any groundwork of feeling — there is no context in their imaginations. Words affect them in the same way, by the mere sound; that is, by their possible, not by their actual, application to the subject in hand. They are fascinated by first appearances, and have no sense of consequences. Nothing more is meant by them than meets the ear: they understand or feel nothing more than meets their eye. The web and texture of the universe, and of the heart of man, is a mystery to them: they have no faculty that strikes a chord in unison with it. They cannot get beyond the daubings of fancy, the varnish of sentiment. Objects are not linked to feelings, words to things, but images revolve in splendid mockery, words represent themselves in their strange rhapsodies. The categories of such a mind are pride and ignorance — pride in outside show, to which they sacrifice everything, and ignorance of the true worth and hidden structure both of words and things. With a sovereign contempt for what is familiar and natural, they are the slaves of vulgar affectation, of a routine of high-flown phrases. Scorning to imitate realities, they are unable to invent anything, to strike out one original idea. They are not copyists of nature, it is true; but they are the poorest of all plagiarists, the plagiarists of words. All is

[1] "Twelfth Night," I, v, 258.
[2] Golconda, in India, was once famous for diamonds.

[190]

William Hazlitt

far-fetched, dear-bought, artificial, Oriental in subject and allusion; all is mechanical, conventional, vapid, formal, pedantic in style and execution. They startle and confound the understanding of the reader by the remoteness and obscurity of their illustrations; they soothe the ear by the monotony of the same everlasting round of circuitous metaphors. They are the *mock school* in poetry and prose. They flounder about between fustian in expression and bathos in sentiment. They tantalize the fancy, but never reach the head nor touch the heart. Their Temple of Fame is like a shadowy structure raised by Dullness to Vanity, or like Cowper's description of the Empress of Russia's palace of ice, "as worthless as in show 'twas glittering":

It smiled, and it was cold![1]

[1] Cowper, "The Task," V, 176.

THOMAS BABINGTON MACAULAY

[1800–1859]

JOHN BUNYAN[1]

This is an eminently beautiful and splendid edition of a book
which well deserves all that the printer and the engraver can
do for it. "The Life of Bunyan" is, of course, not a performance
which can add much to the literary reputation of such a writer
as Mr. Southey. But it is written in excellent English and, for
the most part, in an excellent spirit. Mr. Southey propounds,
we need not say, many opinions from which we altogether
dissent; and his attempts to excuse the odious persecution to
which Bunyan was subjected have sometimes moved our indignation. But we will avoid this topic. We are at present
much more inclined to join in paying homage to the genius of
a great man than to engage in a controversy concerning church
government and toleration.

We must not pass without notice the engravings with which
this beautiful volume is decorated. Some of Mr. Heath's wood-
cuts are admirably designed and executed. Mr. Martin's
illustrations do not please us quite so well. His Valley of
the Shadow of Death is not that Valley of the Shadow of
Death which Bunyan imagined. At all events, it is not that
dark and horrible glen which has from childhood been in our
mind's eye. The valley is a cavern; the quagmire is a lake;
the straight path runs zigzag; and Christian appears like a
speck in the darkness of the immense vault. We miss, too,
those hideous forms which make so striking a part of the

[1] This was originally published as a review of Robert Southey's edition
of "The Pilgrim's Progress" (1830).

Thomas Babington Macaulay

description of Bunyan, and which Salvator Rosa[1] would have loved to draw. . . .[2]

The characteristic peculiarity of "The Pilgrim's Progress" is that it is the only work of its kind which possesses a strong human interest. Other allegories only amuse the fancy. The allegory of Bunyan has been read by many thousands with tears. There are some good allegories in Johnson's works, and some of still higher merit by Addison. In these performances there is, perhaps, as much wit and ingenuity as in "The Pilgrim's Progress." But the pleasure which is produced by the Vision of Mirza, the Vision of Theodore, the genealogy of Wit, or the contest between Rest and Labor, is exactly similar to the pleasure which we derive from one of Cowley's[3] odes or from a canto of "Hudibras."[4] It is a pleasure which belongs wholly to the understanding, and in which the feelings have no part whatever. Nay, even Spenser himself, though assuredly one of the greatest poets that ever lived, could not succeed in the attempt to make allegory interesting. It was in vain that he lavished the riches of his mind on the House of Pride and the House of Temperance. One unpardonable fault — the fault of tediousness — pervades the whole of the "Fairy Queen." We become sick of Cardinal Virtues and Deadly Sins, and long for the society of plain men and women. Of the persons who read the first canto, not one in ten reaches the end of the first book and not one in a hundred perseveres to the end of the poem. Very few and very weary are those who are in at the death of the Blatant Beast. If the last six books, which are said to have been destroyed in Ireland, had been preserved, we doubt whether any heart less stout than that of a commentator would have held out to the end.

[1] An Italian painter (1615–1673), especially known for his violent and somber landscapes.

[2] A passage in which Macaulay criticizes the illustrations of Mr. Martin has been omitted here.

[3] Cowley (1618–1667) was one of the "metaphysical" poets.

[4] A satirical poem by Samuel Butler (1612–1680).

The Formal Essay

It is not so with "The Pilgrim's Progress." That wonderful book, while it obtains admiration from the most fastidious critics, is loved by those who are too simple to admire it. Doctor Johnson, all whose studies were desultory, and who hated, as he said, to read books through, made an exception in favor of "The Pilgrim's Progress." That work, he said, was one of the two or three works which he wished longer. It was by no common merit that the illiterate sectary extracted praise like this from the most pedantic of critics and the most bigoted of Tories. In the wildest parts of Scotland "The Pilgrim's Progress" is the delight of the peasantry. In every nursery "The Pilgrim's Progress" is a greater favorite than "Jack the Giant Killer." Every reader knows the straight and narrow path, as well as he knows a road in which he has gone backward and forward a hundred times. This is the highest miracle of genius — that things which are not should be as though they were; that the imaginations of one mind should become the personal recollections of another. And this miracle the tinker has wrought. There is no ascent, no declivity, no resting place, no turnstile, with which we are not perfectly acquainted. The wicket gate, and the desolate swamp which separates it from the City of Destruction; the long line of road, as straight as a rule can make it; the Interpreter's house, and all its fair shows; the prisoner in the iron cage; the palace, at the doors of which armed men kept guard, and on the battlements of which walked persons clothed all in gold; the cross and the sepulcher; the steep hill and the pleasant arbor; the stately front of the House Beautiful by the wayside; the low green valley of Humiliation, rich with grass and covered with flocks, all are as well known to us as the sights of our own street. Then we come to the narrow place where Apollyon strode right across the whole breadth of the way to stop the journey of Christian, and where afterwards the pillar was set up to testify how bravely the pilgrim had fought the good fight. As we advance the valley becomes deeper and deeper. The shade of the precipices on both sides

Thomas Babington Macaulay

falls blacker and blacker. The clouds gather overhead. Doleful voices, the clanking of chains, and the rushing of many feet to and fro are heard through the darkness. The way, hardly discernible in gloom, runs close by the mouth of the burning pit, which sends forth its flames, its noisome smoke, and its hideous shapes, to terrify the adventurer. Thence he goes on, amidst the snares and pitfalls, with the mangled bodies of those who have perished lying in the ditch by his side. At the end of the long dark valley he passes the dens in which the old giants dwelt, amidst the bones of those whom they had slain.

Then the road passes straight on through a waste moor, till at length the towers of a distant city appear before the traveler; and soon he is in the midst of the innumerable multitudes of Vanity Fair. There are the jugglers and the apes, the shops and the puppet shows. There are Italian Row, and French Row, and Spanish Row, and Britain Row, with their crowds of buyers, sellers, and loungers, jabbering all the languages of the earth.

Thence we go on by the little hill of the silver-mine, and through the meadow of lilies, along the bank of that pleasant river which is bordered on both sides by fruit trees. On the left branches off the path leading to the horrible castle, the courtyard of which is paved with the skulls of pilgrims; and right onward are the sheepfolds and orchards of the Delectable Mountains.

From the Delectable Mountains, the way lies through the fogs and briers of the Enchanted Ground, with here and there a bed of soft cushions spread under a green arbor. And beyond is the land of Beulah, where the flowers, the grapes, and the songs of birds never cease and where the sun shines night and day. Thence are plainly seen the golden pavements and streets of pearl on the other side of that black and cold river over which there is no bridge.

All the stages of the journey, all the forms which cross or overtake the pilgrims, giants and hobgoblins, ill-favored ones and shining ones, the tall, comely, swarthy Madam Bubble, with her great purse by her side, and her fingers playing with the money, the black man in the bright vesture, Mr. Worldly Wiseman and my Lord Hategood, Mr. Talkative, and Mrs. Timorous, all are actually existing beings to us. We follow the travelers through their allegorical progress with interest not inferior to that with which we follow Elizabeth[1] from Siberia to Moscow, or Jeanie Deans[2] from Edinburgh to London. Bunyan is almost the only writer who ever gave to the abstract the interest of the concrete. In the works of many celebrated authors, men are mere personifications. We have not an Othello, but jealousy; not an Iago, but perfidy; not a Brutus, but patriotism. The mind of Bunyan, on the contrary, was so imaginative that personifications, when he dealt with them, became men. A dialogue between two qualities, in his dream, has more dramatic effect than a dialogue between two human beings in most plays. . . .[3]

"The Pilgrim's Progress" undoubtedly is not a perfect allegory. The types are often inconsistent with each other; and sometimes the allegorical disguise is altogether thrown off. The river, for example, is emblematic of death; and we are told that every human being must pass through the river. But Faithful does not pass through it. He is martyred, not in shadow, but in reality, at Vanity Fair. Hopeful talks to Christian about Esau's birthright and about his own convictions of sin as Bunyan might have talked with one of his own congregation. The damsels at the House Beautiful catechize Christiana's boys, as any good ladies might catechize any boys at a Sunday school. But we do not believe that any man, whatever might be his genius, and whatever his good luck, could long continue a figurative history without falling into many inconsistencies. We are

[1] The heroine of a popular romance, "Elizabeth, or the Exiles in Siberia," by a French writer, Madame Cottin (1770–1807).

[2] The heroine of Scott's "Heart of Midlothian."

[3] A digression in which Macaulay criticizes the poetry of Shelley has been omitted here.

[196]

Thomas Babington Macaulay

sure that inconsistencies, scarcely less gross than the worst
into which Bunyan has fallen, may be found in the shortest
and most elaborate allegories of the *Spectator* and the *Rambler*. "The Tale of a Tub" and "The History of John Bull"
swarm with similar errors, if the name of error can be properly
applied to that which is unavoidable. It is not easy to make a
simile go on all fours. But we believe that no human ingenuity
could produce such a centipede as a long allegory, in which
the correspondence between the outward sign and the thing
signified should be exactly preserved. Certainly no writer,
ancient or modern, has yet achieved the adventure. The best
thing, on the whole, that an allegorist can do, is to present to
his readers a succession of analogies, each of which may separately be striking and happy, without looking very nicely to
see whether they harmonize with each other. This Bunyan
has done; and, though a minute scrutiny may detect inconsistencies in every page of his tale, the general effect which the
tale produces on all persons, learned and unlearned, proves that
he has done well. The passages which it is most difficult to
defend are those in which he altogether drops the allegory, and
puts into the mouth of his pilgrims religious ejaculations and
disquisitions better suited to his own pulpit at Bedford or Reading than to the Enchanted Ground or to the Interpreter's Garden. Yet even these passages, though we will not undertake to
defend them against the objections of critics, we feel that we
could ill spare. We feel that the story owes much of its charm
to these occasional glimpses of solemn and affecting subjects
which will not be hidden, which force themselves through the
veil and appear before us in their native aspect. The effect is
not unlike that which is said to have been produced on the
ancient stage, when the eyes of the actor were seen flaming
through his mask and giving life and expression to what would
else have been an inanimate and uninteresting disguise.

It is very amusing and very instructive to compare "The
Pilgrim's Progress" with the "Grace Abounding." The latter

The Formal Essay

work is indeed one of the most remarkable pieces of autobiography in the world. It is a full and open confession of the fancies which passed through the mind of an illiterate man whose affections were warm, whose nerves were irritable, whose imagination was ungovernable, and who was under the influence of the strongest religious excitement. In whatever age Bunyan had lived, the history of his feelings would, in all probability, have been very curious. But the time in which his lot was cast was the time of a great stirring of the human mind. A tremendous burst of public feeling, produced by the tyranny of the hierarchy, menaced the old ecclesiastical institutions with destruction. To the gloomy regularity of one intolerant church had succeeded the license of innumerable sects, drunk with the sweet and heady must of their new liberty. Fanaticism, engendered by persecution and destined to engender persecution in turn, spread rapidly through society. Even the strongest and most commanding minds were not proof against this strange taint. Any time might have produced George Fox and James Naylor.[1] But to one time alone belong the frantic delusions of such a statesman as Vane, and the hysterical tears of such a soldier as Cromwell.

The history of Bunyan is the history of a most excitable mind in an age of excitement. By most of his biographers he has been treated with gross injustice. They have understood in a popular sense all those strong terms of self-condemnation which he employed in a theological sense. They have, therefore, represented him as an abandoned wretch, reclaimed by means almost miraculous; or, to use their favorite metaphor, "as a brand plucked from the burning." Mr. Ivimey calls him the depraved Bunyan and the wicked tinker of Elstow. Surely Mr. Ivimey ought to have been too familiar with the bitter accusations which the most pious people are in the habit of

---

[1] George Fox and James Nayler (or Naylor) were early Quakers. They represent the mystical and religious life of the age, as Sir Harry Vane represents the political life and Oliver Cromwell the military life.

Thomas Babington Macaulay

bringing against themselves, to understand literally all the strong expressions which are to be found in the "Grace Abounding." It is quite clear, as Mr. Southey most justly remarks, that Mr. Bunyan never was a vicious man. He married very early; and he solemnly declares that he was strictly faithful to his wife. He does not appear to have been a drunkard. He owns, indeed, that when a boy he never spoke without an oath. But a single admonition cured him of this bad habit for life; and the cure must have been wrought early, for at eighteen he was in the army of the Parliament, and if he had carried the vice of profaneness into that service he would doubtless have received something more than an admonition from Sergeant Bind-their-kings-in-chains or Captain Hew-Agag-in-pieces-before-the-Lord. Bell-ringing and playing at hockey on Sundays seem to have been the worst vices of this depraved tinker. They would have passed for virtues with Archbishop Laud. It is quite clear that from a very early age Bunyan was a man of a strict life and of a tender conscience. "He had been," says Mr. Southey, "a blackguard." Even this we think too hard a censure. Bunyan was not, we admit, so fine a gentleman as Lord Digby[1]; yet he was a blackguard no otherwise than as every tinker that ever lived has been a blackguard. Indeed, Mr. Southey acknowledges this. "Such he might have been expected to be by his birth, breeding, and vocation. Scarcely, indeed, by possibility, could he have been otherwise." A man whose manners and sentiments are decidedly below those of his class deserves to be called a blackguard; but it is surely unfair to apply so strong a word of reproach to one who is only what the great mass of every community must inevitably be.

Those horrible internal conflicts which Bunyan has described with so much power of language prove, not that he was a worse man than his neighbors, but that his mind was constantly occupied by religious considerations, that his fervor exceeded his

[1] George, Lord Digby (1612–1677), a Royalist leader, was a soldier, courtier, poet, and strikingly handsome man of fashion.

The Formal Essay

knowledge, and that his imagination exercised despotic power over his body and mind. He heard voices from heaven. He saw strange visions of distant hills, pleasant and sunny as his own Delectable Mountains. From those abodes he was shut out, and placed in a dark and horrible wilderness, where he wandered through ice and snow, striving to make his way into the happy region of light. At one time he was seized with an inclination to work miracles. At another time he thought himself actually possessed by the devil. He could distinguish the blasphemous whispers. He felt his infernal enemy pulling at his clothes behind him. He spurned with his feet and struck with his hands at the destroyer. Sometimes he was tempted to sell his part in the salvation of mankind. Sometimes a violent impulse urged him to start up from his food, to fall on his knees, and to break forth into prayer. At length he fancied that he had committed the unpardonable sin. His agony convulsed his robust frame. It was, he says, as if his breastbone would split; and this he took for a sign that he was destined to burst asunder like Judas. The agitation of his nerves made all his movements tremulous; and this trembling he supposed was a visible mark of his reprobation, like that which had been set on Cain. At one time, indeed, an encouraging voice seemed to rush in at the window, like the noise of wind, but very pleasant, and commanded, as he says, a great calm in his soul. At another time a word of comfort "was spoke loud unto him; it showed a great word; it seemed to be writ in great letters." But these intervals of ease were short. His state during two years and a half was generally the most horrible that the human mind can imagine. "I walked," says he, with his own peculiar eloquence, "to a neighboring town, and sat down upon a settle in the street, and fell into a very deep pause about the most fearful state my sin had brought me to; and after long musing, I lifted up my head; but methought I saw as if the sun that shineth in the heavens did grudge to give me light; and as if the very stones in the streets and tiles upon the houses did band themselves against me. Methought that they all combined together to banish me out of the world! I was abhorred of them, and unfit to dwell among them, because I had sinned against the Savior. Oh, how happy now was every creature over I! for they stood fast and kept their station; but I was gone and lost." Scarcely any madhouse could produce an instance of delusion so strong or of misery so acute.

It was through this Valley of the Shadow of Death, overhung by darkness, peopled with devils, resounding with blasphemy and lamentation, and passing amidst quagmires, snares, and pitfalls, close by the very mouth of hell, that Bunyan journeyed to that bright and fruitful land of Beulah, in which he sojourned during the latter days of his pilgrimage. The only trace which his cruel sufferings and temptations seem to have left behind them was an affectionate compassion for those who were still in the state in which he had once been. Religion has scarcely ever worn a form so calm and soothing as in his allegory. The feeling which predominates through the whole book is a feeling of tenderness for weak, timid, and harassed minds. The character of Mr. Fearing, of Mr. Feeble-Mind, of Mr. Despondency and his daughter Miss Muchafraid; the account of poor Littlefaith, who was robbed by the three thieves of his spending money; the description of Christian's terror in the dungeons of Giant Despair and in his passage through the river, all clearly show how strong a sympathy Bunyan felt, after his own mind had become clear and cheerful, for persons afflicted with religious melancholy.

Mr. Southey, who has no love for the Calvinists, admits that if Calvinism had never worn a blacker appearance than in Bunyan's works, it would never have become a term of reproach. In fact, those works of Bunyan with which we are acquainted are by no means more Calvinistic than the homilies of the Church of England. The moderation of his opinions

The Formal Essay

on the subject of predestination gave offense to some zealous persons. We have seen an absurd allegory, the heroine of which is named Hephzibah, written by some raving supralapsarian[1] preacher who was dissatisfied with the mild theology of "The Pilgrim's Progress." In this foolish book, if we recollect rightly, the Interpreter is called the Enlightener, and the House Beautiful is Castle Strength. Mr. Southey tells us that the Catholics had also their "Pilgrim's Progress" without a Giant Pope, in which the Interpreter is the Director, and the House Beautiful Grace's Hall. It is surely a remarkable proof of the power of Bunyan's genius that two religious parties, both of which regarded his opinions as heterodox, should have had recourse to him for assistance.

There are, we think, some characters and scenes in "The Pilgrim's Progress" which can be fully comprehended and enjoyed only by persons familiar with the history of the times through which Bunyan lived. The character of Mr. Greatheart, the guide, is an example. His fighting is, of course, allegorical; but the allegory is not strictly preserved. He delivers a sermon on imputed righteousness to his companions; and, soon after, he gives battle to Giant Grim, who had taken upon him to back the lions. He expounds the fifty-third chapter of Isaiah to the household and guests of Gaius; and then he sallies out to attack Slaygood, who was of the nature of flesh-eaters, in his den. These are inconsistencies; but they are inconsistencies which add, we think, to the interest of the narrative. We have not the least doubt that Bunyan had in view some stout old Greatheart of Naseby and Worcester,[2] who prayed with his men before he drilled them, who knew the spiritual state of every dragoon in his troop, and who, with the praises of God in his mouth and a two-edged sword in his hand, had turned to flight,

[1] One who believes that before men were created God had determined which were to be saved and which damned.
[2] Naseby (1645) and Worcester (1651), decisive victories for the Parliamentary forces against the Royalists.

Thomas Babington Macaulay

on many fields of battle, the swearing, drunken bravoes of
Rupert and Lunsford.[1]

Every age produces such men as By-ends. But the middle
of the seventeenth century was eminently prolific of such men.
Mr. Southey thinks that the satire was aimed at some particular
individual, and this seems by no means improbable. At all
events, Bunyan must have known many of those hypocrites
who followed religion only when religion walked in silver
slippers, when the sun shone, and when the people applauded.
Indeed, he might have easily found all the kindred of By-ends
among the public men of his time. He might have found among
the peers my Lord Turn-about, my Lord Time-server, and my
Lord Fair-speech; in the House of Commons, Mr. Smooth-
man, Mr. Any-thing, and Mr. Facing-both-ways; nor would
"the parson of the parish, Mr. Two-tongues," have been wanting. The town of Bedford probably contained more than one
politician who, after contriving to raise an estate by seeking
the Lord during the reign of the saints,[2] contrived to keep what
he had got by persecuting the saints during the reign of the
strumpets,[3] and more than one priest who, during repeated
changes in the discipline and doctrines of the church, had remained constant to nothing but his benefice.

One of the most remarkable passages in "The Pilgrim's
Progress" is that in which the proceedings against Faithful
are described. It is impossible to doubt that Bunyan intended
to satirize the mode in which state trials were conducted under
Charles the Second. The license given to the witnesses for the
prosecution, the shameless partiality and ferocious insolence
of the judge, the precipitancy and the blind rancor of the jury,
remind us of those odious mummeries which, from the Restoration to the Revolution, were merely forms preliminary to
hanging, drawing, and quartering. Lord Hategood performs

---

[1] Prince Rupert (1619–1682) and Sir Thomas Lunsford (1610?–1653?)
were leaders of the Royalist forces.

[2] Under Cromwell.   [3] Under Charles II and James II.

The Formal Essay

the office of counsel for the prisoners as well as Scroggs[1] himself could have performed it.

JUDGE. Thou runagate, heretic, and traitor, hast thou heard what these honest gentlemen have witnessed against thee?

FAITHFUL. May I speak a few words in my own defense?

JUDGE. Sirrah, sirrah! thou deservest to live no longer, but to be slain immediately upon the place; yet, that all men may see our gentleness to thee, let us hear what thou, vile runagate, hast to say.

No person who knows the state trials can be at a loss for parallel cases. Indeed, write what Bunyan would, the baseness and cruelty of the lawyers of those times "sinned up to it still," and even went beyond it. The imaginary trial of Faithful before a jury composed of personified vices was just and merciful when compared with the real trial of Lady Alice Lisle[2] before that tribunal where all the vices sat in the person of Jeffries.[3]

The style of Bunyan is delightful to every reader, and invaluable as a study to every person who wishes to obtain a wide command over the English language. The vocabulary is the vocabulary of the common people. There is not an expression, if we except a few technical terms of theology, which would puzzle the rudest peasant. We have observed several pages which do not contain a single word of more than two syllables; yet no writer has said more exactly what he meant to say. For magnificence, for pathos, for vehement exhortation, for subtle disquisition, for every purpose of the poet, the orator, and the divine, this homely dialect, the dialect of plain workingmen, was perfectly sufficient. There is no book in our literature on which we could so readily stake the fame of the old

[1] Sir William Scroggs (1623?–1683), a notorious Lord Chief Justice during the trials for the Popish Plot.

[2] Alice Lisle (1614?–1685) was judicially murdered by Jeffreys on a charge of sheltering a supporter of Monmouth.

[3] Lord George Jeffreys (1648–1689), a judge remembered for his brutality in the trial of the followers of Monmouth in 1685. In recent years there has been some effort to palliate his offenses.

Thomas Babington Macaulay

unpolluted English language; no book which shows so well how rich that language is in its own proper wealth, and how little it has been improved by all that it has borrowed.

Cowper said, forty or fifty years ago, that he dared not name John Bunyan in his verse for fear of moving a sneer. To our refined forefathers we suppose Lord Roscommon's "Essay on Translated Verse" and the Duke of Buckinghamshire's "Essay on Poetry" appeared to be compositions infinitely superior to the allegory of the preaching tinker. We live in better times; and we are not afraid to say that, though there were many clever men in England during the latter half of the seventeenth century, there were only two great creative minds. One of those minds produced the "Paradise Lost," the other "The Pilgrim's Progress."

Thomas De Quincey

[1785–1859]

LITERATURE OF KNOWLEDGE AND LITERATURE OF POWER [1]

What is it that we mean by *literature*? Popularly, and amongst the thoughtless, it is held to include everything that is printed in a book. Little logic is required to disturb *that* definition. The most thoughtless person is easily made aware that in the idea of *literature* one essential element is some relation to the general and common interest of man — so that which applies to a local, or professional, or merely personal interest, even though presenting itself in the shape of a book, will not belong to literature. So far the definition is easily narrowed; and it is as easily expanded. For not only is much that takes a station in books not literature, but, inversely, much that really *is* literature never reaches a station in books. The weekly sermons of Christendom, that vast pulpit literature which acts so extensively upon the popular mind, — to warn, to uphold, to renew, to comfort, to alarm, — does not attain the sanctuary of libraries in the ten-thousandth part of its extent. The drama, again, — as, for instance, the finest part of Shakespeare's plays in England, and all leading Athenian plays in the noontide of the Attic stage, — operated as a literature on the public mind, and were (according to the strictest letter of that term), *published* through the audiences that witnessed their representation some time before they were published as things to be

---

[1] From De Quincey's essay "Alexander Pope." Another statement of the same idea occurs in Letter III of De Quincey's "Letters to a Young Man."

Thomas De Quincey

read; and they were published in this scenical mode of publication with much more effect than they could have had as books during ages of costly copying or of costly printing.

Books, therefore, do not suggest an idea coextensive and interchangeable with the idea of literature; since much literature, scenic, forensic, or didactic (as from lecturers and public orators), may never come into books, and much that does come into books may connect itself with no literary interest. But a far more important correction, applicable to the common vague idea of literature, is to be sought not so much in a better definition of literature as in a sharper distinction of the two functions which it fulfills. In that great social organ which, collectively, we call literature, there may be distinguished two separate offices that may blend, and often *do* so, but capable, severally, of a severe insulation, and naturally fitted for reciprocal repulsion. There is, first, the literature of *knowledge*, and, secondly, the literature of *power*. The function of the first is — to *teach*; the function of the second is — to *move* : the first is a rudder, the second an oar or a sail. The first speaks to the *mere* discursive understanding; the second speaks ultimately, it may happen, to the higher understanding or reason, but always *through* affections of pleasure and sympathy. Remotely, it may travel toward an object seated in what Lord Bacon[1] calls "dry light"; but proximately it does and must operate — else it ceases to be a literature of *power* — on and through that *humid* light which clothes itself in the mists and glittering *iris* of human passions, desires, and genial emotions. Men have so little reflected on the higher functions of literature as to find it a paradox if one should describe it as a mean or subordinate purpose of books to give information. But this is a paradox only in the sense which makes it honorable to be paradoxical. Whenever we talk in ordinary language of seeking information or gaining knowledge, we understand the words as connected with something of absolute novelty. But it is the grandeur of all

[1] Properly, Sir Francis Bacon or Lord Verulam.

The Formal Essay

truth which *can* occupy a very high place in human interests
that it is never absolutely novel to the meanest of minds; it
exists eternally by way of germ or latent principle in the lowest
as in the highest, needing to be developed, but never to be
planted. To be capable of transplantation is the immediate
criterion of a truth that ranges on a lower scale.

Besides which, there is a rarer thing than truth; namely,
power, or deep sympathy with truth. What is the effect, for
instance, upon society, of children? By the pity, by the tenderness, and by the peculiar modes of admiration which connect
themselves with the helplessness, with the innocence, and with
the simplicity of children, not only are the primal affections
strengthened and continually renewed, but the qualities which
are dearest in the sight of heaven — the frailty, for instance,
which appeals to forbearance, the innocence which symbolizes
the heavenly, and the simplicity which is most alien from the
worldly — are kept up in perpetual remembrance, and their
ideals are continually refreshed. A purpose of the same nature
is answered by the higher literature; namely, the literature of
power. What do you learn from "Paradise Lost"? Nothing
at all. What do you learn from a cookery book? Something
new, something that you did not know before, in every para-
graph. But would you therefore put the wretched cookery book
on a higher level of estimation than the divine poem? What
you owe to Milton is not any knowledge, of which a million
separate items are still but a million of advancing steps on the
same earthly level; what you owe is *power* — that is, exercise
and expansion to your own latent capacity of sympathy with
the infinite, where every pulse and each separate influx is a
step upward, a step ascending as upon a Jacob's ladder[1] from
earth to mysterious altitudes above the earth. All the steps
of knowledge, from first to last, carry you further on the
same plane, but could never raise you one foot above your
ancient level of earth; whereas the very *first* step in power

[1] Genesis xxviii, 12.

[208]

Thomas De Quincey

is a flight — is an ascending movement into another element where earth is forgotten.

Were it not that human sensibilities are ventilated and continually called out into exercise by the great phenomena of infancy, or of real life as it moves through chance and change, or of literature as it recombines these elements in the mimicries of poetry, romance, etc., it is certain that, like any animal power or muscular energy falling into disuse, all such sensibilities would gradually droop and dwindle. It is in relation to these great *moral* capacities of man that the literature of power, as contradistinguished from that of knowledge, lives and has its field of action. It is concerned with what is highest in man; for the Scriptures themselves never condescended to deal by suggestion or coöperation with the mere discursive understanding. When speaking of man in his intellectual capacity, the Scriptures speak not of the understanding, but of "the understanding heart" — making the heart, that is, the great *intuitive* (or nondiscursive) organ, to be the interchangeable formula for man in his highest state of capacity for the infinite. Tragedy, romance, fairy tale, or epopee,[1] all alike restore to man's mind the ideals of justice, of hope, of truth, of mercy, of retribution, which else (left to the support of daily life in its realities) would languish for want of sufficient illustration.

What is meant, for instance, by "poetic justice"? It does not mean a justice that differs by its object from the ordinary justice of human jurisprudence, for then it must be confessedly a very bad kind of justice; but it means a justice that differs from common forensic justice by the degree in which it attains its object — a justice that is more omnipotent over its own ends, as dealing, not with the refractory elements of earthly life, but with the elements of its own creation and with materials flexible to its own purest preconceptions. It is certain that, were it not for the literature of power, these ideals would often remain amongst us as mere arid notional forms; whereas, by the

[1] An epic poem.

The Formal Essay

creative forces of man put forth in literature, they gain a vernal life of restoration and germinate into vital activities. The commonest novel, by moving in alliance with human fears and hopes, with human instincts of wrong and right, sustains and quickens those affections. Calling them into action, it rescues them from torpor. And hence the preëminency over all authors that merely *teach* of the meanest that *moves*, or that teaches, if at all, indirectly *by* moving. The very highest work that has ever existed in the literature of knowledge is but a *provisional* work — a book upon trial and sufferance and *quamdiu bene se gesserit.*[1] Let its teaching be even partially revised, let it be but expanded, — nay, even let its teaching be but placed in a better order, — and instantly it is superseded. Whereas the feeblest works in the literature of power, surviving at all, survive as finished and unalterable amongst men. For instance, the "Principia"[2] of Sir Isaac Newton was a book *militant* on earth from the first. In all stages of its progress it would have to fight for its existence: first, as regards absolute truth; secondly, when that combat was over, as regards its form or mode of presenting the truth. And as soon as a Laplace,[3] or anybody else, builds higher upon the foundations laid by this book, effectually he throws it out of the sunshine into decay and darkness; by weapons won from this book he superannuates and destroys this book, so that soon the name of Newton remains as a mere *nominis umbra,*[4] but his book, as a living power, has transmigrated into other forms. Now, on the contrary, the Iliad, the "Prometheus" of Æschylus, the "Othello" or "King Lear," the "Hamlet" or "Macbeth," and the "Paradise Lost," are not militant, but triumphant forever, as long as the languages exist in which they speak or can be taught to speak. They never *can* transmigrate into new incarnations. To reproduce

[1] "during good behavior."
[2] Newton's "Principia" (1687) was a landmark in scientific thought.
[3] A French mathematician and astronomer (1749–1827).
[4] "shadow of a name."

Thomas De Quincey

these in new forms or variations, even if in some things they should be improved, would be to plagiarize. A good steam engine is properly superseded by a better. But one lovely pastoral valley is not superseded by another, nor a statue of Praxiteles[1] by a statue of Michael Angelo.[2] These things are separated not by imparity, but by disparity. They are not thought of as unequal under the same standard, but as different in *kind*, and, if otherwise equal, as equal under a different standard. Human works of immortal beauty and works of nature in one respect stand on the same footing; they never absolutely repeat each other, never approach so near as not to differ, and they differ not as better and worse, or simply by more and less: they differ by undecipherable and incommunicable differences, that cannot be caught by mimicries, that cannot be reflected in the mirror of copies, that cannot become ponderable in the scales of vulgar comparison. . . . At this hour, five hundred years since their creation, the tales of Chaucer, never equaled on this earth for their tenderness and for life of picturesqueness, are read familiarly by many in the charming language of their natal day, and by others in the modernizations of Dryden, of Pope, and Wordsworth. At this hour, one thousand eight hundred years since their creation, the pagan tales of Ovid, never equaled on this earth for the gayety of their movement and the capricious graces of their narrative, are read by all Christendom. This man's people and their monuments are dust, but *he* is alive; he has survived them, as he told us that he had it in his commission to do, by a thousand years, "and shall a thousand more."

All the literature of knowledge builds only ground nests, that are swept away by floods or confounded by the plow; but the literature of power builds nests in aërial altitudes of temples sacred from violation, or of forests inaccessible to fraud. *This*

[1] A Greek sculptor of the fourth century B. C.
[2] Michelangelo Buonarroti, a Florentine sculptor, painter, and poet (1475–1564).

The Formal Essay

is a great prerogative of the *power* literature, and it is a greater which lies in the mode of its influence. The *knowledge* literature, like the fashion of this world, passeth away. An encyclopedia is its abstract, and in this respect it may be taken for its speaking symbol — that before one generation has passed, an encyclopedia is superannuated; for it speaks through the dead memory and unimpassioned understanding, which have not the repose of higher faculties, but are continually enlarging and varying their phylacteries. But all literature properly so called, — literature κατ' ἐξοχήν,[1] — for the very reason that it is so much more durable than the literature of knowledge, is (and by the very same proportion it is) more intense and electrically searching in its impressions. The directions in which the tragedy of this planet has trained our human feelings to play, and the combinations into which the poetry of this planet has thrown our human passions of love and hatred, of admiration and contempt, exercise a power for bad or good over human life that cannot be contemplated, when stretching through many generations, without a sentiment allied to awe. And of this let everyone be assured: that he owes to the impassioned books which he has read many a thousand more of emotions than he can consciously trace back to them. Dim by their origination, these emotions yet arise in him and mold him through life like forgotten incidents of his childhood.

[1] "preëminently."

MATTHEW ARNOLD

[1822–1888]

MILTON

The most eloquent voice [1] of our century uttered, shortly before leaving the world, a warning cry against "the Anglo-Saxon contagion." The tendencies and aims, the view of life and the social economy of the ever-multiplying and spreading Anglo-Saxon race, would be found congenial, this prophet feared, by all the prose, all the vulgarity amongst mankind, and would invade and overpower all nations. The true ideal would be lost; a general sterility of mind and heart would set in.

The prophet had in view, no doubt, in the warning thus given, us and our colonies, but the United States still more. There the Anglo-Saxon race is already most numerous, there it increases fastest; there material interests are most absorbing and pursued with most energy; there the ideal, the saving ideal, of a high and rare excellence, seems perhaps to suffer most danger of being obscured and lost. Whatever one may think of the general danger to the world from the Anglo-Saxon contagion, it appears to me difficult to deny that the growing greatness and influence of the United States does bring with it some danger to the ideal of a high and rare excellence. The *average man* is too much a religion there; his performance is unduly magnified, his shortcomings are not duly seen and admitted.

[1] Perhaps Victor Hugo (1802–1885), the leading French literary influence of the nineteenth century.

The Formal Essay

A lady in the state of Ohio sent to me only the other day a volume on American authors; the praise given throughout was of such high pitch that in thanking her I could not forbear saying that for only one or two of the authors named was such a strain of praise admissible, and that we lost all real standard of excellence by praising so uniformly and immoderately. She answered me with charming good temper, that very likely I was quite right, but it was pleasant to her to think that excellence was common and abundant. But excellence is not common and abundant; on the contrary, as the Greek poet[1] long ago said, excellence dwells among rocks hardly accessible, and a man must almost wear his heart out before he can reach her. Whoever talks of excellence as common and abundant is on the way to lose all right standard of excellence. And when the right standard of excellence is lost, it is not likely that much which is excellent will be produced.

To habituate ourselves, therefore, to approve, as the Bible says, things that are really excellent is of the highest importance. And some apprehension may justly be caused by a tendency in Americans to take, or, at any rate, attempt to take, profess to take, the average man and his performances too seriously, to overrate and overpraise what is not really superior.

But we have met here today to witness the unveiling of a gift in Milton's honor, and a gift bestowed by an American, Mr. Childs of Philadelphia; whose cordial hospitality so many Englishmen, I myself among the number, have experienced in America. It was only last autumn that Stratford-upon-Avon celebrated the reception of a gift from the same generous donor in honor of Shakespeare. Shakespeare and Milton — he who wishes to keep his standard of excellence high cannot choose two better objects of regard and honor. And it is an American who has chosen them, and whose beautiful gift in honor of one of them, Milton, with Mr. Whittier's simple and true

[1] Simonides of Ceos (Hiller's "Poetae Lyrici Graeci," No. 41). A similar idea is expressed by Hesiod ("Works and Days," ll. 289 ff.).

Matthew Arnold

lines[1] inscribed upon it, is unveiled today. Perhaps this gift in honor of Milton, of which I am asked to speak, is, even more than the gift in honor of Shakespeare, one to suggest edifying reflections to us.

Like Mr. Whittier, I treat the gift of Mr. Childs as a gift in honor of Milton, although the window given is in memory of his second wife, Catherine Woodcock, the "late espousèd saint" of the famous sonnet, who died in childbed at the end of the first year of her marriage with Milton, and who lies buried here with her infant. Milton is buried in Cripplegate; but he lived for a good while in this parish of St. Margaret's, Westminster, and here he composed part of "Paradise Lost" and the whole of "Paradise Regained" and "Samson Agonistes." When death deprived him of the Catherine whom the new window commemorates, Milton had still some eighteen years to live, and Cromwell, his "chief of men," was yet ruling England. But the Restoration, with its "sons of Belial," was not far off, and in the meantime Milton's heavy affliction had laid fast hold upon him — his eyesight had failed totally; he was blind. In what remained to him of life he had the consolation of producing the "Paradise Lost" and the "Samson Agonistes," and such a consolation we may indeed count as no slight one. But the daily life of happiness in common things and in domestic affections — a life of which, to Milton as to Dante, too small a share was given — he seems to have known most, if not only, in his one married year with the wife who is here buried. Her form "vested all in white," as in his sonnet he relates that after her death she appeared to him; her face veiled, but with "love, sweetness, and goodness" shining in her person, — this fair and gentle daughter of the rigid sectarist of Hackney, this lovable companion with whom Milton had rest and happiness

[1] The new world honors him whose lofty plea
For England's freedom made her own more sure,
Whose song, immortal as its theme, shall be
Their common freehold while both worlds endure.

one year, is a part of Milton indeed, and in calling up her memory we call up his.

And in calling up Milton's memory we call up, let me say, a memory upon which, in prospect of the Anglo-Saxon contagion and of its dangers supposed and real, it may be well to lay stress even more than upon Shakespeare's. If to our English race an inadequate sense for perfection of work is a real danger, if the discipline of respect for a high and flawless excellence is peculiarly needed by us, Milton is of all our gifted men the best lesson, the most salutary influence. In the sure and flawless perfection of his rhythm and diction he is as admirable as Virgil or Dante, and in this respect he is unique amongst us. No one else in English literature and art possesses the like distinction.

Thomson, Cowper, Wordsworth, all of them good poets who have studied Milton, followed Milton, adopted his form, fail in their diction and rhythm if we try them by that high standard of excellence maintained by Milton constantly. From style really high and pure Milton never departs; their departures from it are frequent.

Shakespeare is divinely strong, rich, and attractive. But sureness of perfect style Shakespeare himself does not possess. I have heard a politician express wonder at the treasures of political wisdom in a certain celebrated scene of "Troilus and Cressida"; for my part I am at least equally moved to wonder at the fantastic and false diction in which Shakespeare has in that scene clothed them. Milton, from one end of "Paradise Lost" to the other, is in his diction and rhythm constantly a great artist in the great style. Whatever may be said as to the subject of his poem, as to the conditions under which he received his subject and treated it, that praise, at any rate, is assured to him.

For the rest, justice is not at present done, in my opinion, to Milton's management of the inevitable matter of a Puritan epic, a matter full of difficulties for a poet. Justice is not done to the *architectonics*, as Goethe would have called them, of "Paradise Lost"; in these too the power of Milton's art is

Matthew Arnold

remarkable. But this may be a proposition which requires discussion and development for establishing it, and they are impossible on an occasion like the present.

That Milton, of all our English race, is by his diction and rhythm the one artist of the highest rank in the great style whom we have, this I take as requiring no discussion; this I take as certain.

The mighty power of poetry and art is generally admitted. But where the soul of this power, of this power at its best, chiefly resides, very many of us fail to see. It resides chiefly in the refining and elevation wrought in us by the high and rare excellence of the great style. We may feel the effect without being able to give ourselves clear account of its cause, but the thing is so. Now, no race needs the influences mentioned, the influences of refining and elevation, more than ours; and in poetry and art our grand source for them is Milton.

To what does he owe this supreme distinction? To nature first and foremost; to that bent of nature for inequality which to the worshipers of the average man is so unacceptable; to a gift, a divine favor. "The older one grows," says Goethe, "the more one prizes natural gifts, because by no possibility can they be procured and stuck on." Nature formed Milton to be a great poet. But what other poet has shown so sincere a sense of the grandeur of his vocation and a moral effort so constant and sublime to make and keep himself worthy of it? The Milton of religious and political controversy, and perhaps of domestic life also, is not seldom disfigured by want of amenity, by acerbity. The Milton of poetry, on the other hand, is one of those great men "who are modest," — to quote a fine remark of Leopardi,[1] that gifted and stricken young Italian, who in his sense for poetic style is worthy to be named with Dante and Milton, — "who are modest, because they continually compare themselves, not with other men, but with that idea of the perfect which they have before their mind." The Milton

[1] Giacomo Leopardi (1798-1837), an Italian lyric poet.

of poetry is the man, in his own magnificent phrase, of "devout prayer to that Eternal Spirit that can enrich with all utterance and knowledge, and sends out his Seraphim with the hallowed fire of his altar, to touch and purify the lips of whom he pleases." And finally, the Milton of poetry is, in his own words again, the man of "industrious and select reading." Continually he lived in companionship with high and rare excellence — with the great Hebrew poets and prophets, with the great poets of Greece and Rome. The Hebrew compositions were not in verse, and can be not inadequately represented by the grand, measured prose of our English Bible. The verse of the poets of Greece and Rome no translation can adequately reproduce. Prose cannot have the power of verse; verse translation may give whatever of charm is in the soul and talent of the translator himself, but never the specific charm of the verse and poet translated. In our race are thousands of readers, presently there will be millions, who know not a word of Greek and Latin and will never learn those languages. If this host of readers are ever to gain any sense of the power and charm of the great poets of antiquity, their way to gain it is not through translations of the ancients, but through the original poetry of Milton, who has the like power and charm because he has the like great style.

Through Milton they may gain it, for, in conclusion, Milton is English; this master in the great style of the ancients is English. Virgil, whom Milton loved and honored, has at the end of the Æneid a noble passage, where Juno, seeing the defeat of Turnus and the Italians imminent, the victory of the Trojan invaders assured, entreats Jupiter that Italy may nevertheless survive and be herself still; may retain her own mind, manners, and language, and not adopt those of the conqueror.

Sit Latium, sint Albani per secula reges![1]

Jupiter grants the prayer; he promises perpetuity and the future to Italy — Italy reënforced by whatever virtue the

[1] "Let there be Latium; let there be Alban kings for centuries."

Matthew Arnold

Trojan race has, but Italy, not Troy. This we may take as a
sort of parable suiting ourselves. All the Anglo-Saxon contagion,
all the flood of Anglo-Saxon commonness, beats vainly against
the great style but cannot shake it, and has to accept its
triumph. But it triumphs in Milton, in one of our own race,
tongue, faith, and morals. Milton has made the great style no
longer an exotic here; he has made it an inmate amongst us, a
leaven, and a power. Nevertheless he and his hearers on both
sides of the Atlantic are English, and will remain English —

> Sermonem Ausonii patrium moresque tenebunt.[1]

The English race overspreads the world, and at the same time
the ideal of an excellence the most high and the most rare abides
a possession with it forever.

[1] " The Ausonians shall keep their native language and customs."

ROBERT LOUIS STEVENSON

[1850–1894]

A GOSSIP ON ROMANCE

In anything fit to be called by the name of reading, the process itself should be absorbing and voluptuous; we should gloat over a book, be rapt clean out of ourselves, and rise from the perusal, our mind filled with the busiest, kaleidoscopic dance of images, incapable of sleep or of continuous thought. The words, if the book be eloquent, should run thenceforward in our ears like the noise of breakers, and the story, if it be a story, repeat itself in a thousand colored pictures to the eye. It was for this last pleasure that we read so closely, and loved our books so dearly, in the bright, troubled period of boyhood. Eloquence and thought, character and conversation, were but obstacles to brush aside as we dug blithely after a certain sort of incident, like a pig for truffles. For my part, I liked a story to begin with an old wayside inn where, "towards the close of the year 17—," several gentlemen in three-cocked hats were playing bowls. A friend of mine preferred the Malabar coast in a storm, with a ship beating to windward, and a scowling fellow of herculean proportions striding along the beach; he, to be sure, was a pirate. This was further afield than my home-keeping fancy loved to travel, and designed altogether for a larger canvas than the tales that I affected. Give me a highwayman and I was full to the brim; a Jacobite would do, but the highwayman was my favorite dish. I can still hear that merry clatter of the hoofs along the moonlit lane; night and the coming of the day are still related in my mind with the

Robert Louis Stevenson

doings of John Rann or Jerry Abershaw [1]; and the words "postchaise," the "great North road," "ostler," and "nag" still sound in my ears like poetry.[2] One and all, at least, and each with his particular fancy, we read storybooks in childhood, not for eloquence or character or thought, but for some quality of the brute incident. That quality was not mere bloodshed or wonder. Although each of these was welcome in its place, the charm for the sake of which we read depended on something different from either. My elders used to read novels aloud; and I can still remember four different passages which I heard before I was ten, with the same keen and lasting pleasure. One I discovered long afterwards to be the admirable opening of "What will he Do with It?"[3]; it was no wonder I was pleased with that. The other three still remain unidentified. One is a little vague; it was about a dark, tall house at night, and people groping on the stairs by the light that escaped from the open door of a sick-room. In another a lover left a ball and went walking in a cool, dewy park, whence he could watch the lighted windows and the figures of the dancers as they moved. This was the most sentimental impression I think I had yet received, for a child is somewhat deaf to the sentimental. In the last a poet, who had been tragically wrangling with his wife, walked forth on the sea beach on a tempestuous night and witnessed the horrors of a wreck.[4] Different as they are, all these early favorites have a common note; they have all a touch of the romantic.

Drama is the poetry of conduct; romance, the poetry of circumstance. The pleasure that we take in life is of two sorts — the active and the passive. Now we are conscious of a great

[1] highwaymen.

[2] Stevenson planned an ambitious story called "The Great North Road," but it remained unfinished and was published as a fragment after his death.

[3] A novel by Bulwer-Lytton, published in 1858.

[4] Since traced by many obliging correspondents to the gallery of Charles Kingsley. [Stevenson's note]

The Formal Essay

command over our destiny; anon we are lifted up by circumstance, as by a breaking wave, and dashed we know not how into the future. Now we are pleased by our conduct, anon merely pleased by our surroundings. It would be hard to say which of these modes of satisfaction is the more effective, but the latter is surely the more constant. Conduct is three parts of life, they say; but I think they put it high. There is a vast deal in life and letters both which is not immoral, but simply a-moral; which either does not regard the human will at all, or deals with it in obvious and healthy relations; where the interest turns, not upon what a man shall choose to do, but on how he manages to do it; not on the passionate slips and hesitations of the conscience, but on the problems of the body and of the practical intelligence, in clean, open-air adventure, the shock of arms, or the diplomacy of life. With such material as this it is impossible to build a play, for the serious theater exists solely on moral grounds and is a standing proof of the dissemination of the human conscience. But it is possible to build upon this ground the most joyous of verses and the most lively, beautiful, and buoyant tales.

One thing in life calls for another; there is a fitness in events and places. The sight of a pleasant arbor puts it in our mind to sit there. One place suggests work, another idleness, a third early rising and long rambles in the dew. The effect of night, of any flowing water, of lighted cities, of the peep of day, of ships, of the open ocean, calls up in the mind an army of anonymous desires and pleasures. Something, we feel, should happen; we know not what, yet we proceed in quest of it. And many of the happiest hours of life fleet by us in this vain attendance on the genius of the place and moment. It is thus that tracts of young fir, and low rocks that reach into deep soundings, particularly torture and delight me. Something must have happened in such places, and perhaps ages back, to members of my race; and when I was a child I tried in vain to invent appropriate games for them, as I still try, just as vainly, to fit

Robert Louis Stevenson

them with the proper story. Some places speak distinctly. Certain dank gardens cry aloud for a murder; certain old houses demand to be haunted; certain coasts are set apart for shipwreck. Other spots again seem to abide their destiny, suggestive and impenetrable, "miching mallecho."[1] The inn at Burford Bridge,[2] with its arbors and green garden and silent, eddying river, — though it is known already as the place where Keats wrote some of his "Endymion" and Nelson parted from his Emma,[3] — still seems to wait the coming of the appropriate legend. Within these ivied walls, behind these old green shutters, some further business smolders, waiting for its hour. The old Hawes Inn at the Queen's Ferry [4] makes a similar call upon my fancy. There it stands, apart from the town, beside the pier, in a climate of its own, half inland, half marine — in front, the ferry bubbling with the tide and the guardship swinging to her anchor; behind, the old garden with the trees. Americans seek it already for the sake of Lovel and Oldbuck, who dined there at the beginning of "The Antiquary." But you need not tell me — that is not all; there is some story, unrecorded or not yet complete, which must express the meaning of that inn more fully. So it is with names and faces; so it is with incidents that are idle and inconclusive in themselves, and yet seem like the beginning of some quaint romance, which the all-careless author leaves untold. How many of these romances have we not seen determine at their birth; how many people have met us with a look of meaning in their eye, and sunk at once into trivial acquaintances; to how many places have we not drawn near, with express intimations, — "here my destiny awaits me," — and we have but dined there and passed on! I have lived both at the Hawes and Burford in a perpetual flutter — on the heels,

[1] sneaking mischief ("Hamlet," III, ii, 147).
[2] Twenty-five miles southwest of London, in one of the most lovely parts of England.   [3] Lady Hamilton (1765?-1815), Lord Nelson's mistress.
[4] On the Firth of Forth, north of Edinburgh. "The Antiquary," by Scott, opens there.

The Formal Essay

as it seemed, of some adventure that should justify the place; but though the feeling had me to bed at night and called me again at morning in one unbroken round of pleasure and suspense, nothing befell me in either worth remark. The man or the hour had not yet come; but some day, I think, a boat shall put off from the Queen's Ferry, fraught with a dear cargo, and some frosty night a horseman, on a tragic errand, rattle with his whip upon the green shutters of the inn at Burford.[1]

Now, this is one of the natural appetites with which any lively literature has to count. The desire for knowledge, I had almost added the desire for meat, is not more deeply seated than this demand for fit and striking incident. The dullest of clowns tells, or tries to tell, himself a story, as the feeblest of children uses inventions in his play; and even as the imaginative grown person, joining in the game, at once enriches it with many delightful circumstances, the great creative writer shows us the realization and the apotheosis of the daydreams of common men. His stories may be nourished with the realities of life, but their true mark is to satisfy the nameless longings of the reader and to obey the ideal laws of the daydream. The right kind of thing should fall out in the right kind of place; the right kind of thing should follow; and not only the characters talk aptly and think naturally, but all the circumstances in a tale answer one to another like notes in music. The threads of a story come from time to time together and make a picture in the web; the characters fall from time to time into some attitude to each other or to nature, which stamps the story home like an illustration. Crusoe recoiling from the footprint; Achilles shouting over against the Trojans; Ulysses bending the great bow; Christian running with his fingers in his ears[2] —

[1] Since the above was written I have tried to launch the boat with my own hands in "Kidnapped." Some day, perhaps, I may try a rattle at the shutters. [Stevenson's note]

[2] Central incidents in four great narratives: "Robinson Crusoe," the Iliad, the Odyssey, and "The Pilgrim's Progress."

Robert Louis Stevenson

these are each culminating moments in the legend, and each
has been printed on the mind's eye for ever. Other things we
may forget: we may forget the words, although they are beautiful; we may forget the author's comment, although perhaps it
was ingenious and true; but these epoch-making scenes, which
put the last mark of truth upon a story and fill up, at one blow,
our capacity for sympathetic pleasure, we so adopt into the
very bosom of our mind that neither time nor tide can efface
or weaken the impression. This, then, is the plastic part of
literature: to embody character, thought, or emotion in some
act or attitude that shall be remarkably striking to the mind's
eye. This is the highest and hardest thing to do in words; the
thing which, once accomplished, equally delights the schoolboy
and the sage, and makes, in its own right, the quality of epics.
Compared with this, all other purposes in literature, except the
purely lyrical or the purely philosophic, are bastard in nature,
facile of execution, and feeble in result. It is one thing to write
about the inn at Burford, or to describe scenery with the word-
painters; it is quite another to seize on the heart of the suggestion and make a country famous with a legend. It is one thing
to remark and to dissect, with the most cutting logic, the com-
plications of life and of the human spirit; it is quite another to
give them body and blood in the story of Ajax[1] or of Hamlet.
The first is literature, but the second is something besides, for
it is likewise art.

English people of the present day are apt, I know not why,
to look somewhat down on incident, and reserve their admiration for the clink of teaspoons and the accents of the curate.
It is thought clever to write a novel with no story at all, or at
least with a very dull one. Reduced even to the lowest terms,
a certain interest can be communicated by the art of narrative;
a sense of human kinship stirred; and a kind of monotonous
fitness, comparable to the words and air of "Sandy's Mull,"
preserved among the infinitesimal occurrences recorded. Some

[1] In the tragedy "Ajax," by Sophocles (496–406 B.C.).

The Formal Essay

people work in this manner with even a strong touch. Mr. Trollope's inimitable clergymen naturally arise to the mind in this connection. But even Mr. Trollope does not confine himself to chronicling small beer. Mr. Crawley's collision with the Bishop's wife,[1] Mr. Melnette dallying in the deserted banquet room,[2] are typical incidents, epically conceived, fitly embodying a crisis. Or again look at Thackeray. If Rawdon Crawley's blow were not delivered, "Vanity Fair" would cease to be a work of art. That scene is the chief ganglion of the tale; and the discharge of energy from Rawdon's fist is the reward and consolation of the reader. The end of "Esmond" is a yet wider excursion from the author's customary fields: the scene at Castlewood is pure Dumas; the great and wily English borrower has here borrowed from the great unblushing French thief; as usual he has borrowed admirably well, and the breaking of the sword rounds off the best of all his books with a manly, martial note. But perhaps nothing can more strongly illustrate the necessity for marking incident than to compare the living fame of "Robinson Crusoe" with the discredit of "Clarissa Harlowe."[3] "Clarissa" is a book of a far more startling import, worked out on a great canvas with inimitable courage and unflagging art. It contains wit, character, passion, plot, conversations full of spirit and insight, letters sparkling with unstrained humanity; and if the death of the heroine be somewhat frigid and artificial, the last days of the hero strike the only note of what we now call Byronism, between the Elizabethans and Byron himself. And yet a little story of a shipwrecked sailor, with not a tenth part of the style nor a thousandth part of the wisdom, exploring none of the arcana of humanity and deprived of the perennial interest of love, goes on from edition to edition, ever young, while "Clarissa" lies upon the shelves unread. A friend of mine, a Welsh blacksmith, was twenty-five years old and could neither read

[1] In "The Last Chronicle of Barset."   [2] In "The Way we Live Now."
[3] By Samuel Richardson (1689–1761). It was published in 1747–1748 and greatly influenced the development of the novel.

nor write, when he heard a chapter of "Robinson" read aloud in a farm kitchen. Up to that moment he had sat content, huddled in his ignorance, but he left that farm another man. There were daydreams, it appeared, divine daydreams, written and printed and bound, and to be bought for money and enjoyed at pleasure. Down he sat that day, painfully learned to read Welsh, and returned to borrow the book. It had been lost, nor could he find another copy but one that was in English. Down he sat once more, learned English, and at length, and with entire delight, read "Robinson." It was like the story of a love chase. If he had heard a letter from "Clarissa," would he have been fired with the same chivalrous ardor? I wonder. Yet "Clarissa" has every quality that can be shown in prose, one alone excepted — pictorial, or picture-making, romance; while "Robinson" depends, for the most part and with the overwhelming majority of its readers, on the charm of circumstance.

In the highest achievements of the art of words, the dramatic and the pictorial, the moral and romantic interest, rise and fall together by a common and organic law. Situation is animated with passion, passion clothed upon with situation. Neither exists for itself, but each inheres indissolubly with the other. This is high art; and not only the highest art possible in words, but the highest art of all, since it combines the greatest mass and diversity of the elements of truth and pleasure. Such are epics, and the few prose tales that have the epic weight. But as from a school of works, aping the creative, incident and romance are ruthlessly discarded, so may character and drama be omitted or subordinated to romance. There is one book, for example, more generally loved than Shakespeare, that captivates in childhood, and still delights in age, — I mean the "Arabian Nights," — where you shall look in vain for moral or for intellectual interest. No human face or voice greets us among that wooden crowd of kings and genies, sorcerers and beggarmen. Adventure, on the most naked terms, furnishes

E

The Formal Essay

forth the entertainment and is found enough. Dumas approaches perhaps nearest of any modern to these Arabian authors in the purely material charm of some of his romances. The early part of "Monte Cristo," down to the finding of the treasure, is a piece of perfect story-telling; the man never breathed who shared these moving incidents without a tremor; and yet Faria is a thing of packthread and Dantès little more than a name. The sequel is one long-drawn error, gloomy, bloody, unnatural, and dull; but as for these early chapters, I do not believe there is another volume extant where you can breathe the same unmingled atmosphere of romance. It is very thin and light, to be sure, as on a high mountain; but it is brisk and clear and sunny in proportion. I saw the other day, with envy, an old and a very clever lady setting forth on a second or third voyage into "Monte Cristo." Here are stories which powerfully affect the reader, which can be perused at any age, and where the characters are no more than puppets. The bony fist of the showman visibly propels them; their springs are an open secret; their faces are of wood, their bellies filled with bran; and yet we thrillingly partake of their adventures. And the point may be illustrated still further. The last interview between Lucy and Richard Feverel[1] is pure drama; more than that, it is the strongest scene, since Shakespeare, in the English tongue. Their first meeting by the river, on the other hand, is pure romance: it has nothing to do with character; it might happen to any other boy and maiden, and be none the less delightful for the change. And yet I think he would be a bold man who should choose between these passages. Thus, in the same book, we may have two scenes, each capital in its order: in the one, human passion, deep calling unto deep, shall utter its genuine voice; in the second, according circumstances, like instruments in tune, shall build up a trivial but desirable incident, such as we love to prefigure for ourselves; and in the end, in spite of the critics, we may hesitate to give the

[1] In "The Ordeal of Richard Feverel," by George Meredith (1828–1909).

preference to either. The one may ask more genius—-I do not say it does; but at least the other dwells as clearly in the memory.

True romantic art, again, makes a romance of all things. It reaches into the highest abstraction of the ideal; it does not refuse the most pedestrian realism. "Robinson Crusoe" is as realistic as it is romantic: both qualities are pushed to an extreme, and neither suffers. Nor does romance depend upon the material importance of the incidents. To deal with strong and deadly elements, banditti, pirates, war and murder, is to conjure with great names, and, in the event of failure, to double the disgrace. The arrival of Haydn and Consuelo at the Canon's villa[1] is a very trifling incident; yet we may read a dozen boisterous stories from beginning to end and not receive so fresh and stirring an impression of adventure. It was the scene of Crusoe at the wreck, if I remember rightly, that so bewitched my blacksmith. Nor is the fact surprising. Every single article the castaway recovers from the hulk is "a joy forever"[2] to the man who reads of them. They are the things that should be found, and the bare enumeration stirs the blood. I found a glimmer of the same interest the other day in a new book, "The Sailor's Sweetheart," by Mr. Clark Russell.[3] The whole business of the brig *Morning Star* is very rightly felt and spiritedly written; but the clothes, the books, and the money satisfy the reader's mind like things to eat. We are dealing here with the old cut-and-dry, legitimate interest of treasure trove. But even treasure trove can be made dull. There are few people who have not groaned under the plethora of goods that fell to the lot of the "Swiss Family Robinson," that dreary family. They found article after article, creature after creature, from milk kine to pieces of ordnance, a whole consignment; but no informing taste had presided over the selection, there was no smack or relish in the invoice, and these riches left the fancy

---

[1] In "Consuelo," by George Sand (1804–1876).
[2] From the first line of "Endymion," by Keats (1795–1821).
[3] William Clark Russell (1844–1911), a writer of popular sea tales.

The Formal Essay

cold. The box of goods in Verne's "Mysterious Island" is another case in point: there was no gusto and no glamour about that; it might have come from a shop. But the two hundred and seventy-eight Australian sovereigns on board the *Morning Star* fell upon me like a surprise that I had expected; whole vistas of secondary stories, besides the one in hand, radiated forth from that discovery, as they radiate from a striking particular in life; and I was made for the moment as happy as a reader has the right to be.

To come at all at the nature of this quality of romance, we must bear in mind the peculiarity of our attitude to any art. No art produces illusion; in the theater we never forget that we are in the theater; and while we read a story we sit wavering between two minds, now merely clapping our hands at the merit of the performance, now condescending to take an active part in fancy with the characters. This last is the triumph of romantic story-telling: when the reader consciously plays at being the hero, the scene is a good scene. Now, in character studies the pleasure that we take is critical: we watch, we approve, we smile at incongruities, we are moved to sudden heats of sympathy with courage, suffering, or virtue. But the characters are still themselves, they are not us; the more clearly they are depicted, the more widely do they stand away from us, the more imperiously do they thrust us back into our place as a spectator. I cannot identify myself with Rawdon Crawley[1] or with Eugène de Rastignac,[2] for I have scarce a hope or fear in common with them. It is not character but incident that woos us out of our reserve. Something happens as we desire to have it happen to ourselves; some situation, that we have long dallied with in fancy, is realized in the story with enticing and appropriate details. Then we forget the characters; then we push the hero aside; then we plunge into the tale in our own person and bathe in fresh experience; and then, and then

---

[1] A character in "Vanity Fair," already mentioned on page 226.
[2] A young man who occurs in a number of stories by Balzac (1799–1850).

Robert Louis Stevenson

only, do we say we have been reading a romance. It is not only pleasurable things that we imagine in our daydreams: there are lights in which we are willing to contemplate even the idea of our own death; ways in which it seems as if it would amuse us to be cheated, wounded, or calumniated. It is thus possible to construct a story, even of tragic import, in which every incident, detail, and trick of circumstance shall be welcome to the reader's thoughts. Fiction is to the grown man what play is to the child; it is there that he changes the atmosphere and tenor of his life; and when the game so chimes with his fancy that he can join in it with all his heart, when it pleases him with every turn, when he loves to recall it and dwells upon its recollection with entire delight, fiction is called romance.

Walter Scott is out and away the king of the romantics. "The Lady of the Lake" has no indisputable claim to be a poem beyond the inherent fitness and desirability of the tale. It is just such a story as a man would make up for himself, walking, in the best health and temper, through just such scenes as it is laid in. Hence it is that a charm dwells undefinable among these slovenly verses, as the unseen cuckoo fills the mountains with his note; hence, even after we have flung the book aside, the scenery and adventures remain present to the mind, a new and green possession, not unworthy of that beautiful name, "The Lady of the Lake," or that direct, romantic opening, — one of the most spirited and poetical in literature, — "The stag at eve had drunk his fill." The same strength and the same weaknesses adorn and disfigure the novels. In that ill-written, ragged book, "The Pirate," the figure of Cleveland — cast up by the sea on the resounding foreland of Dunrossness — moving, with the blood on his hands and the Spanish words on his tongue, among the simple islanders — singing a serenade under the window of his Shetland mistress — is conceived in the very highest manner of romantic invention. The words of his song, "Through groves of palm," sung in such a scene and by such a lover, clench, as in a nutshell, the emphatic contrast upon which

The Formal Essay

the tale is built. In "Guy Mannering," again, every incident is delightful to the imagination; and the scene when Harry Bertram lands at Ellangowan is a model instance of romantic method.

"I remember the tune well," he says, "though I cannot guess what should at present so strongly recall it to my memory." He took his flageolet from his pocket and played a simple melody. Apparently the tune awoke the corresponding associations of a damsel. . . . She immediately took up the song —

> "Are these the links of Forth, she said;
> Or are they the crooks of Dee,
> Or the bonny woods of Warroch Head
> That I so fain would see?"

"By heaven!" said Bertram, "it is the very ballad."

On this quotation two remarks fall to be made. First, as an instance of modern feeling for romance, this famous touch of the flageolet and the old song is selected by Miss Braddon[1] for omission. Miss Braddon's idea of a story, like Mrs. Todgers's[2] idea of a wooden leg, were something strange to have expounded. As a matter of personal experience Meg's appearance to old Mr. Bertram on the road, the ruins of Derncleugh, the scene of the flageolet, and the Dominie's recognition of Harry are the four strong notes that continue to ring in the mind after the book is laid aside. The second point is still more curious. The reader will observe a mark of excision in the passage as quoted by me. Well, here is how it runs in the original: "a damsel who, close behind a fine spring about halfway down the descent, and which had once supplied the castle with water, was engaged in bleaching linen."[3] A man who gave in such copy would be discharged from the staff of a daily paper. Scott has forgotten to prepare the reader for the presence of the "damsel"; he has

---

[1] Mary Elizabeth Braddon (Mrs. John Maxwell) (1837–1915), a minor novelist.   [2] In Dickens's "Martin Chuzzlewit."

[3] This passage is as bad as the one above is fine; but Stevenson, who left three of his principal stories unfinished, forgets the pressure under which Scott worked.

Robert Louis Stevenson

forgotten to mention the spring and its relation to the ruin; and now, face to face with his omission, instead of trying back and starting fair, crams all this matter, tail foremost, into a single shambling sentence. It is not merely bad English or bad style; it is abominably bad narrative besides.

Certainly the contrast is remarkable, and it is one that throws a strong light upon the subject of this paper. For here we have a man of the finest creative instinct touching with perfect certainty and charm the romantic junctures of his story; and we find him utterly careless, almost, it would seem, incapable, in the technical matter of style, and not only frequently weak but frequently wrong in points of drama. In character parts, indeed, and particularly in the Scotch, he was delicate, strong, and truthful; but the trite, obliterated features of too many of his heroes have already wearied two generations of readers. At times his characters will speak with something far beyond propriety with a true heroic note; but on the next page they will be wading wearily forward with an ungrammatical and undramatic rigmarole of words. The man who could conceive and write the character of Elspeth of the Craigburnfoot,[1] as Scott has conceived and written it, had not only splendid romantic but splendid tragic gifts. How comes it, then, that he could so often fob us off with languid, inarticulate twaddle?

It seems to me that the explanation is to be found in the very quality of his surprising merits. As his books are play to the reader, so were they play to him. He conjured up the romantic with delight, but he had hardly patience to describe it. He was a great daydreamer, a seer of fit and beautiful and humorous visions, but hardly a great artist — hardly, in the manful sense, an artist at all. He pleased himself, and so he pleases us. Of the pleasures of his art he tasted fully; but of its toils and vigils and distresses never man knew less.[2] A great romantic—an idle child.

[1] In "The Antiquary."
[2] G. K. Chesterton, in his essay on "Sir Walter Scott," contends very forcibly that the absence of straining for effect is a source of Scott's power.

STUART PRATT SHERMAN

[1881–1926]

TRADITION

To lengthen the childhood of the individual, at the same time bringing to bear upon it the influences of tradition, is the obvious way to shorten the childhood of races, nations, classes, and so to quicken the general processes of civilization. Yet in the busy hum of self-approbation which accompanies the critical activities of our young people, perhaps the dominant note is their satisfaction at having emancipated themselves from the fetters of tradition, the oppression of classical precedent, the burden of an inherited culture. By detaching the new literature from its learned past they are confident that they are assuring it a popular future. Turn to any one of half a dozen books which discuss the present movement, and you will learn that people are now discovering, for example, "often to their own surprise," that they can read and enjoy poetry. That is because poetry has been subjected to "democratization." The elder writers, such as Shakespeare, Milton, Emerson, and Longfellow, constantly graveled them with strange and obsolete phrases, like "multitudinous seas incarnadine" and like "tumultuous privacy of storm." The ancient writers sent them to out-of-the-way reference books to look up obscure legends about Troy (not the city where collars are made), and old stuff about war in heaven, and the landing at Plymouth Rock. It is therefore a relief to countless eager young souls that Mr. Mencken has dismissed all this as "the fossil literature taught in col-

Stuart Pratt Sherman

leges," and that Mary Austin insists that native verse rhythms must be "within the capacity of the democratically bred." It is a joy to hear from Mr. Untermeyer that modern readers of poetry may now come out from the "lifeless and literary storehouse" and use life itself for their glossary, as indeed they may — or the morning's newspaper.

Those who encourage us to hope for crops without tillage, learning without study, and literary birth without gestation or travail are doubtless animated by a desire to augment the sum of human felicity; but one recalls Burke's passionate ejaculation: "Oh! no, sir, no. Those things which are not practicable are not desirable." To the new mode of procuring a literary renascence there may be raised one objection, which, to minds of a certain temper, will seem rather grave: all experience is against it. Such is the thesis recently argued by an English critic, Mr. H. J. Massingham, who reviews with mingled amusement and alarm the present "self-conscious rebellion against tradition." In the eyes of our excited young "cosmopolitans," whose culture has a geographic rather than an historical extension, Mr. Massingham's opinions will of course appear to be hopelessly prejudiced by his Oxford breeding, his acquaintance with the classics, his saturation in Elizabethan literature, and his avowed passion for old books in early editions, drilled by the bibliomaniac worm, "prehistoric" things, like Nares' "Glossary" and Camden's "Remains." But it is not merely the opinion of our critic that is formidable: "The restoration of the traditional link with the art of the past is a conservative and revolutionary necessity." It is not the supporting opinion of Sir Joshua Reynolds: "The only food and nourishment of the mind of an artist is the great works of his predecessors." Sir Joshua, too, was prejudiced by his position as a pillar of the robust English classicism of George III's time. It is not even the opinion of Henry James, whom Mr. Massingham proclaims the profoundest critic since Coleridge and who even our own irreverent youth seem to suspect should be mentioned respect-

The Formal Essay

fully: "It takes an endless amount of history to make even a little tradition and an endless amount of tradition to make even a little taste and an endless amount of taste, by the same token, to make even a little tranquillity."

The formidable arguments against the radical engineers of renascence are just the notorious facts of literary history. The fact that a bit of the "fossil literature taught in colleges," the story of Arthur, written in Latin by a Welsh monk in the twelfth century, has flowered and fruited in poetry, painting, and music generation after generation pretty much over the civilized world. The fact that Chaucer and his contemporaries, in whom poetry had a glorious rebirth, had previously devoured everything in what Mr. Untermeyer would call the "lifeless and literary storehouse" of the Middle Ages. The fact that the Elizabethans, to quote Mr. Massingham's vigorous phrase, flung themselves on tradition "like a hungry wolf, not only upon the classics but upon all the tradition open to them." The fact that Restoration comedy is simply a revival of late Caroline in the hands of men who had studied Molière. The fact that the leaders of the new movement in the eighteenth century, when they wished to break from the stereotyped classicism, did not urge young people to slam the door on the past, but, on the contrary, harked back over the heads of Pope and Dryden to the elder and more central tradition of Milton, Shakespeare, and Spenser, and sluiced into the arid fields of common sense, grown platitudinous, the long-dammed or subterranean currents of medieval romance. The fact that "Childe Harold," "Adonais," "The Eve of St. Agnes," "The Cotter's Saturday Night," and "The Castle of Indolence" were all written by imitators of Spenser or by imitators of his imitators. The fact, to omit the Victorians, that Mr. W. B. Yeats, the most skillful living engineer of literary renascence, set all his collaborators to digging around the roots of the ancient Celtic tree before we enjoyed the blossoming of the new spring in Ireland. The fact that John Masefield, freshest and most tuneful voice in England, is obviously steeped to the lips in the poetry of Byron, Shakespeare, Spenser, and Chaucer.

Why is it that the great poets, novelists, and critics, with few exceptions, have been, in the more liberal sense of the word, scholars — masters of several languages, students of history and philosophy, antiquarians? First of all because the great writer conceives of his vocation as the most magnificent and the most complex of crafts. He is to be his own architect, master builder, carpenter, painter, singer, orator, poet, and dramatist. His materials, his tools, his methods, are, or may be, infinite. To him, then, the written tradition is a school and a museum in which, if he has a critical and inventive mind, he learns, from both the successes and the failures of his predecessors, how to set to work upon his own problems of expression. As Mr. Yeats is fond of pointing out, the young poet may find Herbert and Vaughan more helpful to him than the work of his own contemporaries, because the faults in the elder poets, the purple patches that failed to hold their color, will not attract and mislead him.

But tradition is more than a school of crafts. It is a school of mood and manners. The artist who is also a scholar cannot fail to discover that what distinguishes all the golden periods of art, what constitutes the perpetual appeal of the masters, is a kind of innermost poise and serenity, tragic in Sophocles, heroic in Michelangelo, skeptical in Montaigne, idyllic in Sidney, ironic in Fielding. This enviable tranquillity reigns only in a mind that, looking before and after, feels itself the representative of something outlasting time, some national ideal, some religious faith, some permanent human experience, some endless human quest. Nothing begets this mood and manner, the sovereign mark of good breeding in letters, like habitual association with those who have it, the majority of whom are, in the vulgar sense of the word, dead. Izaak Walton, a minor writer in whose work there is a golden afterglow of the great age, calls, in one of his Angler's Dialogues, for "that

The Formal Essay

smooth song which was made by Kit Marlowe, now at least fifty years ago," and for the answer to it "which was made by Sir Walter Raleigh in his younger days." If some of our modern imitators of the auctioneer and the steam calliope would now and then, instead of reading one another, step into the "lifeless and literary storehouse" and compare these "fossils" conscientiously with their own recent efforts to make verse popular! "They were old-fashioned poetry," says Piscator, apologetically, "but choicely good, I think much better than the strong lines that are now in fashion in this critical age."

Out of the tranquillity induced by working in a good literary tradition develops form. The clever theorists who insist that form alone matters, that form is the only preservative element in literature, forget that form is not "self-begotten" but a product of the formative spirit. Mr. Massingham is a bit fastidious in his use of this word. He denies form, for example, to Pope and to Swinburne. Though both have technique, that is another matter. "Form," he declares, "is a vision contained and made manifest." He attributes the unproductiveness of our age in the field of satire to a vision without a traditional base, reeling and shifting in the choppy waters of contemporary opinion. His remarks on the deficiencies of Gilbert Cannan as a satirist and novelist further elucidate his idea; and they may serve also as a comment upon many of the younger writers in America:

The works of Mr. Cannan seem to say, "That is what life is — a surge of base and beautiful forces, intensified in the consciousness of man." But that is a fallacy. Life is like that to the layman, but it is the business of the artist to see a clue in it, to give it shape and order, to weld its particles into congruity. Here is where his lack of a constructive or satiric purpose growing out of and controlling the material tells to his hurt. He knows life in the raw, but the satirist would put it in the oven and dish it up. So he wanders in the dark, and we blunder after him. But we want light, if it be only from a tallow candle.

Stuart Pratt Sherman

Now, many of the young writers in America are disposed to reject the English tradition as unserviceable lumber. They scorn equally the greater part of the American tradition as puritanical, effeminate, or over-intellectualized. If they seek foreign allies, it is with those who help them forget our national characteristics, our native bent and purposes, our discovered special American "genius." In what measure is the revolt due to the conduct of the movement by writers whose blood and breeding are as hostile to the English strain as a cat to water? Whatever the answer, I suspect that the young people who are being congratulated right and left on their emancipation from tradition are rather open to condolence than to felicitation. They have broken away from so much that was formative, and they suffer so obviously in consequence of the break. Their poets have lost a skill which Poe had : though they paint a little, and chant a little, and speak a great deal of faintly rhythmical prose, they have not learned how to sing. Their novelists have lost a vision which Howells had : though they have shaken off the "moralistic incubus" and have released their "suppressed desires," they have not learned how to conceive or to present a coherent picture of civilized society. Their leaders have lost a constructiveness which a critic so laden with explosives as Emerson exhibited : though they have blown up the old highways they have not made new roads.

Am I doing the "young people" an injustice? I turn from their anthologies of verse, where I keep searching in vain for such music as the angler's milkmaid sang ; and from the novels of Mr. Cabell, in whom I have not discovered that ascending sun heralded by the lookouts ; to "A Modern Book of Criticism," recently collected and put forth by Mr. Ludwig Lewisohn. The editor's desire is to show us that "a group of critics, young men or men who do not grow old, are at work upon the creation of a civilized cultural atmosphere in America." The idea resembles that, does it not? of Mr. Waldo Frank, who recently informed us that literature began in America in 1900 —

The Formal Essay

or was it 1910? — at Mr. Stieglitz's place in New York. It is related also to that recent comprehensive indictment edited by Mr. Harold Stearns and ironically entitled "Civilization in the United States." The implication is clearly that the country which developed Bradford, Franklin, Emerson, Lincoln, Thoreau, Whitman, Mark Twain, here and there in villages and backwoods, had no "civilized cultural atmosphere" worth mentioning. It does not seem quite plausible.

But let us proceed with Mr. Lewisohn. His critics: "Like a group of shivering young Davids — slim and frail but with a glimpse of morning sunshine on their foreheads — they face an army of Goliaths." The slim and shivering young Davids turn out on investigation to be Mr. Huneker, Mr. Spingarn, Mr. Mencken, Mr. Lewisohn, Mr. Hackett, Mr. Van Wyck Brooks, and Randolph Bourne. It is not a group, taken as a whole, however it may be connected with the house of Jesse, which should be expected to hear any profound murmuring of ancestral voices or to experience any mysterious inflowing of national experience in meditating on the names of Mark Twain, Whitman, Thoreau, Lincoln, Emerson, Franklin, and Bradford. One doesn't blame our Davids for their inability to connect themselves vitally with this line of Americans, for their inability to receive its tradition or to carry it on. But one cannot help asking whether this inability does not largely account for the fact that Mr. Lewisohn's group of critics are restless impressionists, almost destitute of doctrine, and with no discoverable unifying tendency except to let themselves out into a homeless happy land where they may enjoy the "colorful" cosmic weather, untroubled by business men, or middle-class Americans, or congressmen, or moralists, or humanists, or philosophers, or professors, or Victorians, or Puritans, or New Englanders, or Messrs. Tarkington and Churchill. A jolly lot of Goliaths to slay before we get that "civilized cultural atmosphere."

By faithfully studying the writings of Mr. Mencken, Mr. Lewisohn, and other "shivering young Davids," I have obtained

Stuart Pratt Sherman

a fairly clear conception of what a "civilized cultural atmosphere" is not. It consists of none of those heart-remembered things — our own revenue officers probing our old shoes for diamond necklaces, our own New York newspapers, and Maryland chicken on the Albany boat — which cause a native American returning from a year in Europe to exclaim as he sails up the tranquil bosom of the Hudson and rushes by a standard steel Pullman, back to the great warm embrace of his own land, "Thank Heaven, we are home again." No, it is none of these things. If, without going to Munich, you wish to know what a "civilized cultural atmosphere" really is, you must let Mr. Lewisohn describe it for you as it existed, till the passage of the Volstead act, in one or two odd corners of old New York : "The lamps of the tavern had orange-colored shades, the wainscoting was black with age. The place was filled with a soothing dusk and the blended odor of beer and tobacco and Wiener Schnitzel. *I was, at least, back in civilization.* That tavern is gone now, swept away by the barbarism of the Neo-Puritans."

To the book from which this quotation is made, Mr. Lewisohn's recently published autobiographical record, "Up Stream," students of contemporary critical currents and eddies are much indebted. The author, like many of the other belligerent young writers who have shown in recent years a grave concern for the state of civilization in America, has ostensibly been directing his attack against our national culture from a very elevated position. He has professed himself one of the enlightened spirits who from time to time rise above the narrowing prejudices of nationality into the free air of the republic of letters, the grand cosmopolis of the true humanist. From his watchtower — apparently "in the skies" — he has launched lightnings of derision at those who still weave garlands for their Lares and Penates, at the nationalist with his "selective sympathies," at the traditionalist with his sentimental fondness for folkways. Those who feel strongly attracted, as I do myself, to the Ciceronian and Stoic conception of a universal humanity

[241]

The Formal Essay

and by the Christian and Augustinian vision of a universal City of God, may easily have mistaken Mr. Lewisohn for a "sharpshooter" of the next age, an outpost from the land of their heart's desire. But in "Up Stream" Mr. Lewisohn drops the mask and reveals himself, for all his Jewish radicalism,[1] as essentially a sentimental and homesick German, longing in exile for a Germany which exists only in his imagination.

Even the purified and liberated mind of a Child of Light, living according to nature and reason, is unable to rid itself wholly of "selective sympathies." It betrays under provocation a merely "traditional emotion" for a cultural atmosphere compounded of the odors of beer, tobacco, and Wiener Schnitzel, with perhaps a whiff of Kant and a strain of Hungarian music floating through it, while two or three high philosophical spirits discuss what a poet can do when his wife grows old and stringy. I do not think it necessary to remonstrate with a man merely because his effective nature responds powerfully to a vision of felicity thus composed; but I think it a bit impractical to ask "a nation of prohibitionists and Puritans" to accept this vision as the goal of cultural efforts in America. It is a help to fruitful controversy, however, when a man abandons his absurdly insincere professions of "universal sympathy" — his purring protestation that he desires "neither to judge nor to condemn" — and frankly admits that he likes the German life,

[1] In a notably competent article on "The Case of Mr. Lewisohn," which appeared in *The Menorah Journal* of June, 1922, Professor Jacob Zeitlin writes: "Whether entirely just or strongly colored, it is evident that Mr. Lewisohn's criticism of state universities has little relevance to his character as a Jew. It indicates nothing more than that his sensitive æsthetic organism recoiled in pain from an environment that was uncongenial. And the same observation holds concerning his reaction toward American life in general. He but adds his voice to a chorus of growing volume, reiterating the now familiar burden of the crudeness and narrowness of our political and social ideas. There is ample ground for such a protest as he makes, but it is not a protest that can be identified with any recognizably Jewish outlook." [Sherman's note]

Stuart Pratt Sherman

what he knows of it, and that he regards American life, what he knows of it, as "ugly and mean."

The militant hostility of alien-minded critics toward what they conceive to be the dominant traits of the national character is, on the whole, to be welcomed as provocative of reflection and as a corrective to national conceit. But the amendment of that which is really ugly and mean and basely repressive in our contemporary society is less likely to be achieved by listening to the counsels of exiled emancipators from Munich than by harking back to our own liberative tradition, which long antedates the efforts of these bewildered impressionists.

When we grow dull and inadventurous and slothfully content with our present conditions and our old habits, it is not because we are "traditionalists"; it is, on the contrary, because we have ceased to feel the formative spirit of our own traditions. It is not much in the American vein, to be sure, to construct private little anarchies in the haze of a smoking-room; but practical revolt, on a large scale and sagaciously conducted, is an American tradition, which we should continue to view with courage and the tranquillity which is related to courage. America was born because it revolted. It revolted because it condemned. It condemned because its sympathies were not universal but selective. Its sympathies were selective because it had a vision of a better life, pressing for fulfillment. That vision, and not a conception of life as a meaningless "surge of base and beautiful forces," liberated its chief men of letters. Thence their serenity, in place of that "gentle but chronic dizziness" which a critic of Young Germany, Hugo von Hofmannsthal, says "vibrates among us." Thence, too, their freedom from ancestor worship and bondage to the letter. Listen to Emerson:

> Ask not me, as Muftis can,
> To recite the Alcoran;
> Well I love the meaning sweet;
> I tread the book beneath my feet.

E

[243]

The Formal Essay

Thence, too, the traditional bent of the American spirit toward modernity, toward realism. It was nearly a hundred years ago that our then-leading critic[1] wrote in his journal: "You must exercise your genius in some form that has essential life now; do something which is proper to the hour and cannot but be done."[2] Did he not recognize what was to be done? I quote once more from him a finer sentence than any of our impressionists has ever written: "A wife, a babe, a brother, poverty, and a country, which the Greeks had, I have."[3] The grip and the beauty of that simple sentence are due to a union in it of an Athenian vision with Yankee self-reliance. It is the kind of feeling that comes to a man who has lived in a great tradition.

[1] Ralph Waldo Emerson (1803–1882).
[2] In the entry for May 4, 1836 (Emerson's "Journals," IV, 38–39).
[3] In the entry for November 8, 1836 (Emerson's "Journals," IV, 145).

John Richard Green

[1837–1883]

JEANNE D'ARC[1]

Jeanne D'Arc was the child of a laborer of Domremy, a little
village in the neighborhood of Vaucouleurs on the borders of
Lorraine and Champagne. Just without the cottage where she
was born began the great woods of the Vosges, where the children of Domremy drank in poetry and legend from fairy ring
and haunted well, hung their flower garlands on the sacred trees,
and sang songs to the "good people"[2] who might not drink of
the fountain because of their sins. Jeanne loved the forest; its
birds and beasts came lovingly to her at her childish call. But
at home men saw nothing in her but "a good girl, simple and
pleasant in her ways," spinning and sewing by her mother's side
while the other girls went to the fields, tender to the poor and
sick, fond of church, and listening to the church bell with a
dreamy passion of delight which never left her. This quiet life
was broken by the storm of war as it at last came home to
Domremy. As the outcasts and wounded passed by the little
village, the young peasant girl gave them her bed and nursed
them in their sickness. Her whole nature summed itself up in
one absorbing passion: she "had pity," to use the phrase forever on her lip, "on the fair realm of France." As her passion
grew she recalled old prophecies that a maid from the Lorraine
border should save the land; she saw visions; St. Michael appeared to her in a flood of blinding light, and bade her go to the
help of the king and restore to him his realm. "Messire,"
answered the girl, "I am but a poor maiden; I know not how

[1] From "History of the English People."   [2] The fairies.

[245]

to ride to the wars, or to lead men at arms." The archangel returned to give her courage and to tell her of "the pity" that there was in heaven for the fair realm of France. The girl wept, and longed that the angels who appeared to her would carry her away, but her mission was clear. It was in vain that her father when he heard her purpose swore to drown her ere she should go to the field with men at arms. It was in vain that the priest, the wise people of the village, the captain of Vaucouleurs, doubted and refused to aid her. "I must go to the king," persisted the peasant girl, "even if I wear my limbs to the very knees." "I had far rather rest and spin by my mother's side," she pleaded with a touching pathos, "for this is no work of my choosing, but I must go and do it, for my Lord wills it." "And who," they asked, "is your Lord?" "He is God." Words such as these touched the rough captain at last; he took Jeanne by the hand and swore to lead her to the king. She reached Chinon in the opening of March, but here too she found hesitation and doubt. The theologians proved from their books that they ought not to believe her. "There is more in God's books than in yours," Jeanne answered simply. At last Charles himself received her in the midst of a throng of nobles and soldiers. "Gentle Dauphin," said the girl, "my name is Jeanne the Maid. The Heavenly King sends me to tell you that you shall be anointed and crowned in the town of Rheims, and you shall be lieutenant of the Heavenly King who is the King of France."

Orleans had already been driven by famine to offers of surrender when Jeanne appeared in the French court, and a force was gathering under the Count of Dunois at Blois for a final effort at its relief. It was at the head of this force that Jeanne placed herself. The girl was in her eighteenth year — tall, finely formed, with all the vigor and activity of her peasant rearing, able to stay from dawn to nightfall on horseback without meat or drink. As she mounted her charger, clad in white armor from head to foot, with a great white banner studded with fleur-de-lys waving over her head, she seemed "a thing

John Richard Green

divine, whether to see or hear." The ten thousand men at arms who followed her from Blois, rough plunderers whose only prayer was that of La Hire, "Sire Dieu, I pray you to do for La Hire what La Hire would do for you, were you captain at arms and he God," left off their oaths and foul living at her word and gathered round the altars on their march. Her shrewd peasant humor helped her to manage the wild soldiery, and her followers laughed over their camp fires at an old warrior who had been so puzzled by her prohibition of oaths that she suffered him still to swear by his baton. For in the midst of her enthusiasm her good sense never left her. The people crowded round her as she rode along, praying her to work miracles and bringing crosses and chaplets to be blessed by her touch. "Touch them yourself," she said to an old Dame Margaret; "your touch will be just as good as mine." But her faith in her mission remained as firm as ever. "The Maid prays and requires you," she wrote to Bedford, "to work no more distraction in France, but to come in her company to rescue the Holy Sepulcher from the Turk." "I bring you," she told Dunois when he sallied out of Orleans to meet her after her two days' march from Blois, "I bring you the best aid ever sent to anyone, the aid of the King of Heaven." The besiegers looked down overawed as she entered Orleans and, riding round the walls, bade the people shake off their fear of the forts which surrounded them. Her enthusiasm drove the hesitating generals to engage the handful of besiegers, and the enormous disproportion of forces at once made itself felt. Fort after fort was taken until only the strongest remained, and then the council of war resolved to adjourn the attack. "You have taken your counsel," replied Jeanne, "and I take mine." Placing herself at the head of the men at arms, she ordered the gates to be thrown open, and led them against the fort. Few as they were, the English fought desperately, and the Maid, who had fallen wounded while endeavoring to scale its walls, was borne into a vineyard, while Dunois sounded the retreat. "Wait a while!"

The Formal Essay

the girl imperiously pleaded, "eat and drink! so soon as my standard touches the wall you shall enter the fort." It touched, and the assailants burst in. On the next day the siege was abandoned, and on the eighth of May the force which had conducted it withdrew in good order to the north.

In the midst of her triumph Jeanne still remained the pure, tender-hearted peasant girl of the Vosges. Her first visit as she entered Orleans was to the great church, and there, as she knelt at mass, she wept in such a passion of devotion that "all the people wept with her." Her tears burst forth afresh at her first sight of bloodshed and of the corpses strewn over the battle-field. She grew frightened at her first wound, and only threw off the touch of womanly fear when she heard the signal for retreat. Yet more womanly was the purity with which she passed through the brutal warriors of a medieval camp. It was her care for her honor which led her to clothe herself in a soldier's dress. She wept hot tears when told of the foul taunts of the English, and called passionately to God to witness her chastity. "Yield thee, yield thee, Glasdale," she cried to the English warrior whose insults had been foulest, as he fell wounded at her feet; "you called me harlot! I have great pity on your soul." But all thought of herself was lost in the thought of her mission. It was in vain that the French generals strove to remain on the Loire. Jeanne was resolute to complete her task, and while the English remained panic-stricken around Paris she brought Charles to march upon Rheims, the old crowning place of the kings of France. Troyes and Châlons submitted as she reached them; Rheims drove out the English garrison and threw open her gates to the king.

With his coronation the Maid felt her errand to be over. "O gentle king, the pleasure of God is done," she cried, as she flung herself at the feet of Charles and asked leave to go home. "Would it were His good will," she pleaded with the archbishop, as he forced her to remain, "that I might go and keep sheep once more with my sisters and my brothers; they would be so glad to see me again!" But the policy of the French court detained her while the cities of the north of France opened their gates to the newly consecrated king. Bedford, however, who had been left without money or men, had now received reën-forcements. Excluded as Cardinal Beaufort had been from the council by Gloucester's intrigues, he poured his wealth without stint into the exhausted treasury till his loans to the Crown reached the sum of half a million; and at this crisis he un-scrupulously diverted an army which he had levied at his own cost for a crusade against the Hussites in Bohemia to his nephew's aid. The tide of success turned again. Charles, after a repulse before the walls of Paris, fell back behind the Loire; while the towns on the Oise submitted anew to the Duke of Burgundy, whose more active aid Bedford had bought by the cession of Champagne. In the struggle against Duke Philip, Jeanne fought with her usual bravery but with the fatal con-sciousness that her mission was at an end; and during the de-fense of Compiègne in the May of 1430 she fell into the power of the Bastard of Vendôme, to be sold by her captor into the hands of the Duke of Burgundy and by the duke into the hands of the English. To the English her triumphs were victories of sorcery; and after a year's imprisonment she was brought to trial on a charge of heresy before an ecclesiastical court with the Bishop of Beauvais at its head.

Throughout the long process which followed every art was used to entangle her in her talk. But the simple shrewdness of the peasant girl foiled the efforts of her judges. "Do you be-lieve," they asked, "that you are in a state of grace?" "If I am not," she replied, "God will put me in it. If I am, God will keep me in it." Her capture, they argued, showed that God had forsaken her. "Since it has pleased God that I should be taken," she answered meekly, "it is for the best." "Will you submit," they demanded at last, "to the judgment of the Church Militant?" "I have come to the King of France," Jeanne replied, "by commission from God and from the Church

The Formal Essay

Triumphant above; to that church I submit." "I had far rather die," she ended passionately, "than renounce what I have done by my Lord's command." They deprived her of mass. "Our Lord can make me hear it without your aid," she said, weeping. "Do your voices," asked the judges, "forbid you to submit to the Church and the Pope?" "Ah, no! our Lord first served." Sick, and deprived of all religious aid, it was no wonder that as the long trial dragged on and question followed question, Jeanne's firmness wavered. On the charge of sorcery and diabolical possession she still appealed firmly to God. "I hold to my Judge," she said, as her earthly judges gave sentence against her, "to the King of Heaven and Earth. God has always been my Lord in all that I have done. The devil has never had power over me." It was only with a view to be delivered from the military prison and transferred to the prisons of the Church that she consented to a formal abjuration of heresy. She feared, in fact, among the soldiery those outrages to her honor, on guard against which she had from the first assumed the dress of a man. In the eyes of the Church her dress was a crime, and she abandoned it; but a renewed affront forced her to resume the one safeguard left her, and the return to it was treated as a relapse into heresy which doomed her to death. At the close of May, 1431, a great pile was raised in the market place of Rouen, where her statue now stands. Even the brutal soldiers who snatched the hated "witch" from the hands of the clergy and hurried her to her doom were hushed as she reached the stake. One, indeed, passed to her a rough cross he had made from a stick he held, and she clasped it to her bosom. As her eyes ranged over the city from the lofty scaffold she was heard to murmur, "O Rouen, Rouen, I have great fear lest you suffer for my death." "Yes! my voices were of God!" she suddenly cried as the last moment came; "they have never deceived me!" Soon the flames reached her; the girl's head sank on her breast; there was one cry of "Jesus!" "We are lost," an English soldier muttered as the crowd broke up; "we have burned a saint."

RALPH WALDO EMERSON

[1803–1882]

GIFTS

Gifts of one who loved me, —
'Twas high time they came;
When he ceased to love me,
Time they stopped for shame.

It is said that the world is in a state of bankruptcy; that the world owes the world more than the world can pay, and ought to go into chancery and be sold. I do not think this general insolvency, which involves in some sort all the population, to be the reason of the difficulty experienced at Christmas and New Year and other times, in bestowing gifts; since it is always so pleasant to be generous, though very vexatious to pay debts. But the impediment lies in the choosing. If at any time it comes into my head that a present is due from me to somebody, I am puzzled what to give, until the opportunity is gone. Flowers and fruits are always fit presents — flowers, because they are a proud assertion that a ray of beauty outvalues all the utilities of the world. These gay natures contrast with the somewhat stern countenance of ordinary nature; they are like music heard out of a workhouse. Nature does not cocker us; we are children, not pets; she is not fond; everything is dealt to us without fear or favor, after severe universal laws. Yet these delicate flowers look like the frolic and interference of love and beauty. Men use[1] to tell us that we love

[1] are accustomed.

The Formal Essay

flattery even though we are not deceived by it, because it shows that we are of importance enough to be courted. Something like that pleasure, the flowers give us; what am I to whom these sweet hints are addressed? Fruits are acceptable gifts, because they are the flower of commodities, and admit of fantastic values being attached to them. If a man should send to me to come a hundred miles to visit him and should set before me a basket of fine summer fruit, I should think there was some proportion between the labor and the reward.

For common gifts necessity makes pertinences and beauty every day, and one is glad when an imperative leaves him no option; since if the man at the door has no shoes, you have not to consider whether you could procure him a paint box. And as it is always pleasing to see a man eat bread or drink water, in the house or out of doors, so it is always a great satisfaction to supply these first wants. Necessity does everything well. In our condition of universal dependence it seems heroic to let the petitioner be the judge of his necessity and to give all that is asked, though at great inconvenience. If it be a fantastic desire, it is better to leave to others the office of punishing him. I can think of many parts I should prefer playing to that of the Furies. Next to things of necessity, the rule for a gift, which one of my friends prescribed, is that we might convey to some person that which properly belonged to his character and was easily associated with him in thought. But our tokens of compliment and love are for the most part barbarous. Rings and other jewels are not gifts, but apologies for gifts. The only gift is a portion of thyself. Thou must bleed for me. Therefore the poet brings his poem; the shepherd, his lamb; the farmer, corn; the miner, a gem; the sailor, coral and shells; the painter, his picture; the girl, a handkerchief of her own sewing. This is right and pleasing, for it restores society in so far to the primary basis, when a man's biography is conveyed in his gift, and every man's wealth is an index of his merit. But it is a cold, lifeless business when you go to the shops to buy me

Ralph Waldo Emerson

something which does not represent your life and talent, but a goldsmith's. This is fit for kings, and rich men who represent kings, and a false state of property, to make presents of gold and silver stuffs as a kind of symbolical sin-offering or payment of blackmail.

The law of benefits is a difficult channel, which requires careful sailing or rude boats. It is not the office of a man to receive gifts. How dare you give them? We wish to be self-sustained. We do not quite forgive a giver. The hand that feeds us is in some danger of being bitten. We can receive anything from love, for that is a way of receiving it from ourselves; but not from anyone who assumes to bestow. We sometimes hate the meat which we eat, because there seems something of degrading dependence in living by it:

> Brother, if Jove to thee a present make,
> Take heed that from his hands thou nothing take.

We ask the whole. Nothing less will content us. We arraign society if it do not give us, besides earth and fire and water, opportunity, love, reverence, and objects of veneration.

He is a good man who can receive a gift well. We are either glad or sorry at a gift, and both emotions are unbecoming. Some violence I think is done, some degradation borne, when I rejoice or grieve at a gift. I am sorry when my independence is invaded, or when a gift comes from such as do not know my spirit, and so the act is not supported; and if the gift pleases me overmuch, then I should be ashamed that the donor should read my heart and see that I love his commodity and not him. The gift, to be true, must be the flowing of the giver unto me, correspondent to my flowing unto him. When the waters are at level, then my goods pass to him, and his to me. All his are mine, all mine his. I say to him, "How can you give me this pot of oil, or this flagon of wine, when all your oil and wine is mine," which belief of mine this gift seems to deny? Hence the fitness of beautiful, not useful things, for gifts. This giving is flat

[253]

The Formal Essay

usurpation; and therefore when the beneficiary is ungrateful, as all beneficiaries hate all Timons,[1] not at all considering the value of the gift but looking back to the greater store it was taken from, I rather sympathize with the beneficiary than with the anger of my lord Timon. For the expectation of gratitude is mean, and is continually punished by the total insensibility of the obliged person. It is a great happiness to get off without injury and heartburning from one who has had the ill luck to be served by you. It is a very onerous business, this of being served, and the debtor naturally wishes to give you a slap. A golden text for these gentlemen is that which I so admire in the Buddhist, who never thanks, and who says, "Do not flatter your benefactors."

The reason of these discords I conceive to be that there is no commensurability between a man and any gift. You cannot give anything to a magnanimous person. After you have served him he at once puts you in debt by his magnanimity. The service a man renders his friend is trivial and selfish compared with the service he knows his friend stood in readiness to yield him, alike before he had begun to serve his friend and now also. Compared with that good will I bear my friend, the benefit it is in my power to render him seems small. Besides, our action on each other, good as well as evil, is so incidental and at random that we can seldom hear the acknowledgments of any person who would thank us for a benefit, without some shame and humiliation. We can rarely strike a direct stroke, but must be content with an oblique one; we seldom have the satisfaction of yielding a direct benefit which is directly received. But rectitude scatters favors on every side without knowing it, and receives with wonder the thanks of all people.

I fear to breathe any treason against the majesty of love, which is the genius and god of gifts and to whom we must not affect to prescribe. Let him give kingdoms or flower leaves in-

[1] An Athenian of the fifth century B.C. whose friends deserted him after he had spent his fortune in entertaining them.

Ralph Waldo Emerson

differently. There are persons from whom we always expect
fairy tokens; let us not cease to expect them. This is prerogative, and not to be limited by our municipal rules. For the rest,
I like to see that we cannot be bought and sold. The best of
hospitality and of generosity is also not in the will, but in fate.
I find that I am not much to you; you do not need me; you
do not feel me; then am I thrust out of doors, though you prof-
fer me house and lands. No services are of any value, but only
likeness. When I have attempted to join myself to others by
services, it proved an intellectual trick — no more. They eat
your service like apples, and leave you out. But love them, and
they feel you and delight in you all the time.

JOHN HENRY NEWMAN

[1801–1890]

WHAT IS A UNIVERSITY?[1]

If I were asked to describe as briefly and popularly as I could what a university was, I should draw my answer from its ancient designation of a *Studium Generale*, or "School of Universal Learning." This description implies the assemblage of strangers from all parts in one spot — *from all parts*; else how will you find professors and students for every department of knowledge? and *in one spot*; else how can there be any school at all? Accordingly, in its simple and rudimental form, it is a school of knowledge of every kind, consisting of teachers and learners from every quarter. Many things are requisite to complete and satisfy the idea embodied in this description; but such as this a university seems to be in its essence — a place for the communication and circulation of thought, by means of personal intercourse, through a wide extent of country.

There is nothing far-fetched or unreasonable in the idea thus presented to us; and if this be a university, then a university does but contemplate a necessity of our nature and is but one specimen in a particular medium, out of many which might be adduced in others, of a provision for that necessity. Mutual education, in a large sense of the word, is one of the great and incessant occupations of human society, carried on partly with set purpose, and partly not. One generation forms another; and the existing generation is ever acting and reacting upon itself in the persons of its individual members. Now, in this

[1] From "Historical Sketches," Vol. III. Originally published with other papers in the *Catholic University Gazette* (Dublin, 1854).

John Henry Newman

process, books, I need scarcely say, that is, the *litera scripta,*[1] are one special instrument. It is true; and emphatically so in this age. Considering the prodigious powers of the press, and how they are developed at this time in the never-intermitting issue of periodicals, tracts, pamphlets, works in series, and light literature, we must allow there never was a time which promised fairer for dispensing with every other means of information and instruction. What can we want more, you will say, for the intellectual education of the whole man, and for every man, than so exuberant and diversified and persistent a promulgation of all kinds of knowledge? Why, you will ask, need we go up to knowledge, when knowledge comes down to us? The Sibyl wrote her prophecies upon the leaves of the forest, and wasted them; but here such careless profusion might be prudently indulged, for it can be afforded without loss, in consequence of the almost fabulous fecundity of the instrument which these latter ages have invented. We have sermons in stones, and books in the running brooks; works larger and more comprehensive than those which have gained for ancients an immortality issue forth every morning and are projected onward to the ends of the earth at the rate of hundreds of miles a day. Our seats are strewed, our pavements are powdered, with swarms of little tracts; and the very bricks of our city walls preach wisdom by informing us by their placards where we can at once cheaply purchase it.

I allow all this, and much more; such certainly is our popular education, and its effects are remarkable. Nevertheless, after all, even in this age, whenever men are really serious about getting what, in the language of trade, is called "a good article," when they aim at something precise, something refined, something really luminous, something really large, something choice, they go to another market; they avail themselves, in some shape or other, of the rival method, the ancient method, of oral instruction, of present communication between man and man,

[1] "the written letter" (as distinct from oral teaching or tradition).

The Formal Essay

of teachers instead of learning, of the personal influence of a master and the humble initiation of a disciple, and, in consequence, of great centers of pilgrimage and throng, which such a method of education necessarily involves. This, I think, will be found to hold good in all those departments or aspects of society which possess an interest sufficient to bind men together, or to constitute what is called "a world." It holds in the political world, and in the high world, and in the religious world; and it holds also in the literary and scientific world.

If the actions of men may be taken as any test of their convictions, then we have reason for saying this; namely, that the province and the inestimable benefit of the *litera scripta* is that of being a record of truth, and an authority of appeal, and an instrument of teaching in the hands of a teacher; but that if we wish to become exact and fully furnished in any branch of knowledge which is diversified and complicated, we must consult the living man and listen to his living voice. I am not bound to investigate the cause of this, and anything I may say will, I am conscious, be short of its full analysis; perhaps we may suggest that no books can get through the number of minute questions which it is possible to ask on any extended subject, or can hit upon the very difficulties which are severally felt by each reader in succession. Or, again, that no book can convey the special spirit and delicate peculiarities of its subject with that rapidity and certainty which attend on the sympathy of mind with mind, through the eyes, the look, the accent, and the manner, in casual expressions thrown off at the moment, and the unstudied turns of familiar conversation. But I am already dwelling too long on what is but an incidental portion of my main subject. Whatever be the cause, the fact is undeniable. The general principles of any study you may learn by books at home; but the detail, the color, the tone, the air, the life which makes it live in us, you must catch all these from those in whom it lives already. You must imitate the student in French or German, who is not content with his grammar, but goes to

John Henry Newman

Paris or Dresden; you must take example from the young artist, who aspires to visit the great masters in Florence and in Rome. Till we have discovered some intellectual daguerreotype, which takes off the course of thought and the form, lineaments, and features of truth as completely and minutely as the optical instrument reproduces the sensible object, we must come to the teachers of wisdom to learn wisdom; we must repair to the fountain, and drink there. Portions of it may go from thence to the ends of the earth by means of books, but the fullness is in one place alone. It is in such assemblages and congregations of intellect that books themselves, the masterpieces of human genius, are written, or at least originated.

The principle on which I have been insisting is so obvious, and instances in point are so ready, that I should think it tiresome to proceed with the subject, except that one or two illustrations may serve to explain my own language about it, which may not have done justice to the doctrine which it has been intended to enforce.

For instance, the polished manners and high-bred bearing which are so difficult of attainment and so strictly personal when attained, — which are so much admired in society, from society are acquired. All that goes to constitute a gentleman, — the carriage, gait, address, gestures, voice; the ease, the self-possession, the courtesy, the power of conversing, the talent of not offending; the lofty principle, the delicacy of thought, the happiness of expression, the taste and propriety, the generosity and forbearance, the candor and consideration, the openness of hand, — these qualities, some of them come by nature, some of them may be found in any rank, some of them are a direct precept of Christianity; but the full assemblage of them, bound up in the unity of an individual character, do we expect they can be learned from books? are they not necessarily acquired, where they are to be found, in high society? The very nature of the case leads us to say so; you cannot fence without an antagonist, nor challenge all comers in disputation before you

The Formal Essay

have supported a thesis; and in like manner, it stands to reason, you cannot learn to converse till you have the world to converse with; you cannot unlearn your natural bashfulness, or awkwardness, or stiffness, or other besetting deformity till you serve your time in some school of manners. Well, and is it not so in matter of fact? The metropolis, the court, the great houses of the land, are the centers to which at stated times the country comes up, as to shrines of refinement and good taste; and then in due time the country goes back again home enriched with a portion of the social accomplishments which those very visits serve to call out and heighten in the gracious dispensers of them. We are unable to conceive how the "gentlemanlike" can otherwise be maintained; and maintained in this way it is.

And now a second instance: and here too I am going to speak without personal experience of the subject I am introducing. I admit I have not been in Parliament, any more than I have figured in the *beau monde*[1]; yet I cannot but think that statesmanship, as well as high breeding, is learned not by books, but in certain centers of education. If it be not presumption to say so, Parliament puts a clever man *au courant*[2] with politics and affairs of state in a way surprising to himself. A member of the legislature, if tolerably observant, begins to see things with new eyes, even though his views undergo no change. Words have a meaning now, and ideas a reality, such as they had not before. He hears a vast deal in public speeches and private conversation which is never put into print. The bearings of measures and events, the action of parties, and the persons of friends and enemies are brought out to the man who is in the midst of them with a distinctness which the most diligent perusal of newspapers will fail to impart to them. It is access to the fountainheads of political wisdom and experience, it is daily intercourse of one kind or another with the multitude who go up to them, it is familiarity with business, it is access

[1] "fashionable society."
[2] "in the current " (in thorough familiarity).

John Henry Newman

to the contributions of fact and opinion thrown together by
many witnesses from many quarters, which does this for him.
However, I need not account for a fact, to which it is sufficient
to appeal — that the Houses of Parliament and the atmosphere
around them are a sort of university of politics.

As regards the world of science, we find a remarkable instance of the principle which I am illustrating, in the periodical
meetings for its advance which have arisen in the course of the
last twenty years, such as the British Association. Such gather-
ings would to many persons appear at first sight simply preposterous. Above all subjects of study, science is conveyed, is
propagated, by books or by private teaching; experiments and
investigations are conducted in silence; discoveries are made in
solitude. What have philosophers to do with festive celebrities,
and panegyrical solemnities with mathematical and physical
truth? Yet on a closer attention to the subject, it is found that
not even scientific thought can dispense with the suggestions,
the instruction, the stimulus, the sympathy, the intercourse
with mankind on a large scale, which such meetings secure. A
fine time of year is chosen, when days are long, skies are bright,
the earth smiles, and all nature rejoices; a city or town is taken
by turns, of ancient name or modern opulence, where buildings
are spacious and hospitality hearty. The novelty of place and
circumstance, the excitement of strange or the refreshment of
well-known faces, the majesty of rank or of genius, the amiable
charities of men pleased both with themselves and with each
other, the elevated spirits, the circulation of thought, the
curiosity; the morning sections, the outdoor exercise, the well-
furnished, well-earned board, the not ungraceful hilarity, the evening circle; the brilliant lecture, the discussions or collisions
or guesses of great men one with another, the narratives
of scientific processes, of hopes, disappointments, conflicts,
and successes, the splendid eulogistic orations, — these and
the like constituents of the annual celebration are considered to do something real and substantial for the advance

[261]

The Formal Essay

of knowledge which can be done in no other way. Of course they can but be occasional: they answer to the annual act, or commencement, or commemoration of a university, not to its ordinary condition; but they are of a university nature, and I can well believe in their utility. They issue in the promotion of a certain living and, as it were, bodily communication of knowledge from one to another, of a general interchange of ideas, and a comparison and adjustment of science with science; of an enlargement of mind, intellectual and social; of an ardent love of the particular study which may be chosen by each individual, and a noble devotion to its interests.

Such meetings, I repeat, are but periodical, and only partially represent the idea of a university. The bustle and whirl which are their usual concomitants are in ill keeping with the order and gravity of earnest intellectual education. We desiderate means of instruction which involve no interruption of our ordinary habits; nor need we seek it long, for the natural course of things brings it about while we debate over it. In every great country the metropolis itself becomes a sort of necessary university, whether we will or no. As the chief city is the seat of the court, of high society, of politics, and of law, so, as a matter of course, is it the seat of letters also; and at this time, for a long term of years, London and Paris are in fact and in operation universities, though in Paris its famous university is no more, and in London a university scarcely exists except as a board of administration. The newspapers, magazines, reviews, journals, and periodicals of all kinds, the publishing trade, the libraries, museums, and academies there found, the learned and scientific societies, necessarily invest it with the functions of a university; and that atmosphere of intellect, which in a former age hung over Oxford or Bologna or Salamanca, has, with the change of times, moved away to the center of civil government. Thither come up youths from all parts of the country — the students of law, medicine, and the fine arts, and the *employés* and *attachés* of literature. There they live, as chance determines; and they

[262]

John Henry Newman

are satisfied with their temporary home, for they find in it all
that was promised to them there. They have not come in vain,
as far as their own object in coming is concerned. They have
not learned any particular religion, but they have learned their
own particular profession well. They have, moreover, become
acquainted with the habits, manners, and opinions of their
place of sojourn, and done their part in maintaining the tradition of them. We cannot then be without virtual universities;
a metropolis is such; the simple question is, whether the education sought and given should be based on principle, formed upon
rule, directed to the highest ends, or left to the random succession of masters and schools, one after another, with a melancholy
waste of thought and an extreme hazard of truth.

Religious teaching itself affords us an illustration of our subject to a certain point. It does not, indeed, seat itself merely
in centers of the world; this is impossible from the nature of the
case. It is intended for the many, not the few; its subject
matter is truth necessary for us, not truth recondite and rare;
but it concurs in the principle of a university so far as this, that
its great instrument, or rather organ, has ever been that which
nature prescribes in all education, the personal presence of a
teacher, or, in theological language, oral tradition. It is the
living voice, the breathing form, the expressive countenance,
which preaches, which catechizes. Truth, a subtle, invisible,
manifold spirit, is poured into the mind of the scholar by his
eyes and ears, through his affections, imagination, and reason;
it is poured into his mind and is sealed up there in perpetuity by
propounding and repeating it, by questioning and requestion-
ing, by correcting and explaining, by progressing and then re-
curring to first principles, by all those ways which are implied in
the word "catechizing." In the first ages it was a work of long
time; months, sometimes years, were devoted to the arduous
task of disabusing the mind of the incipient Christian of its
pagan errors and of molding it upon the Christian faith. The
Scriptures indeed were at hand for the study of those who could

avail themselves of them; but St. Irenæus does not hesitate to speak of whole races who had been converted to Christianity without being able to read them. To be unable to read or write was in those times no evidence of want of learning: the hermits of the deserts were, in this sense of the word, illiterate; yet the great St. Anthony, though he knew not letters, was a match in disputation for the learned philosophers who came to try him. Didymus, again, the great Alexandrian theologian, was blind. The ancient discipline, called the "Disciplina Arcani," involved the same principle. The more sacred doctrines of Revelation were not committed to books, but passed on by successive tradition. The teaching on the Blessed Trinity and the Eucharist appears to have been so handed down for some hundred years; and when at length reduced to writing, it has filled many folios, yet has not been exhausted.

But I have said more than enough in illustration; I end as I began — a university is a place of concourse, whither students come from every quarter for every kind of knowledge. You cannot have the best of every kind everywhere; you must go to some great city or emporium for it. There you have all the choicest productions of nature and art all together, which you find each in its own separate place elsewhere. All the riches of the land and of the earth are carried up thither; there are the best markets, and there the best workmen. It is the center of trade, the supreme court of fashion, the umpire of rival talents, and the standard of things rare and precious. It is the place for seeing galleries of first-rate pictures and for hearing wonderful voices and performers of transcendent skill. It is the place for great preachers, great orators, great nobles, great statesmen. In the nature of things greatness and unity go together; excellence implies a center. And such, for the third or fourth time, is a university; I hope I do not weary out the reader by repeating it. It is the place to which a thousand schools make contributions; in which the intellect may safely range and speculate, sure to find its equal in some antagonist activity, and its judge

[264]

in the tribunal of truth. It is a place where inquiry is pushed forward, and discoveries verified and perfected, and rashness rendered innocuous, and error exposed, by the collision of mind with mind and knowledge with knowledge. It is the place where the professor becomes eloquent, and is a missionary and a preacher, displaying his science in its most complete and most winning form, pouring it forth with the zeal of enthusiasm, and lighting up his own love of it in the breasts of his hearers. It is the place where the catechist makes good his ground as he goes, treading in the truth day by day into the ready memory and wedging and tightening it into the expanding reason. It is a place which wins the admiration of the young by its celebrity, kindles the affections of the middle-aged by its beauty, and rivets the fidelity of the old by its associations. It is a seat of wisdom, a light of the world, a minister of the faith, an Alma Mater of the rising generation. It is this and a great deal more, and demands a somewhat better head and hand than mine to describe it well.

Such is a university in its idea and in its purpose; such in good measure has it before now been in fact. Shall it ever be again? We are going forward in the strength of the Cross, under the patronage of the Blessed Virgin, in the name of St. Patrick, to attempt it.

IRVING BABBITT

[1865–   ]

PRESIDENT ELIOT AND LIBERAL EDUCATION IN AMERICA

[This brilliant essay is perhaps the clearest presentation of the "new humanism." For an able statement of the philosophy attacked here, the student should read James Harvey Robinson's article on "Civilization" in the fourteenth edition of the "Encyclopædia Britannica" (1929).]

It would be reassuring if one could establish a connection between President Eliot's educational theory and his character and personality. His character and personality would seem, however, to derive from the Puritan tradition at its best, whereas his theory at the essential point marks an extreme recoil from Puritanism. This essential point is his attitude toward the problem of evil. The genuine Puritan had a lively and even exaggerated sense of the "Old Adam"; President Eliot, for his part, scarcely allows at all for a law of the members. The current mode is to disparage Puritanism because of its undue repressiveness and at the same time to overlook how much it repressed that actually needs repression. One may maintain, indeed, that it would not have been easy for President Eliot to take so idyllic a view of human nature if Puritanism had done its work less

[266]

Irving Babbitt

effectively. There is in general a danger that one may take to be a spontaneous emanation of the natural man what is in reality the result of generations of religious or humanistic discipline. The illusion of a President Eliot is that of a man who, himself born to great riches, deems it "natural" that everyone should have cash in the bank.

This illusion is, to be sure, one that he shared with many others. It is markedly present in no less a thinker than Emerson. Emerson, however, transcended his time in important particulars, whereas President Eliot did little more than reflect the time in its main tendency. For forty years he pushed American education in the direction in which it was already leaning. His whole career, indeed, illustrates the advantages of going with one's age quite apart from the question whither it is going.

If, however, one is finally to be accounted a great and wise leader, it is not enough thus to be the faithful servant of the wisdom of an age: one must also be true to the wisdom of the ages. The question whether President Eliot deserves this latter praise should, if it is to be discussed in a way worthy of him, be lifted above the petty and the personal into the region of ideas: this means practically to consider the value of the naturalistic philosophy that he and other leaders of the nineteenth century espoused so heartily.

This philosophy culminates in a doctrine of progress that would seem to be in serious conflict with the wisdom of the ages; for it is plain that there can be no such wisdom without the assumption in some form of a core of normal human experience that is set above the shifting tides of circumstance. The progress proclaimed by the naturalists, on the contrary, is to be achieved not by transcending the phenomenal flux but by a surrender to it. As Tennyson exclaimed in his most Victorian moment:

> Forward, forward let us range!
> Let the great world spin forever down the ringing grooves of change.

The Formal Essay

The belief in progress in its most naïve form is still held by multitudes, especially in America. It may be doubted, however, whether in the future anyone of a distinction comparable to that of President Eliot will be able to hold it with the same bland confidence. It has been receiving the most formidable of refutations — that of the facts. The contrast between the whole conception of a "far-off divine event" and incidents like the Great War is too flagrant.

The humanitarian idealism based on the faith in progress will be found on analysis to be either utilitarian or sentimental. Practically, in education as elsewhere, a utilitarian and sentimental movement has been displacing traditions that are either religious or humanistic. President Eliot deserves to rank as our chief humanitarian idealist in the educational field, not because of any novelty in his views, but because of the consistency and unwavering conviction with which he applied them. As a matter of fact, his views are anticipated on the utilitarian side by a writer like Locke in his "Thoughts on Education," and on both the utilitarian and the sentimental side by Rousseau, whose "Émile" has become, if not in its specific recommendations, at least in its general spirit, the Bible of the modern educator.

Superficially at least, humanitarianism is even more triumphant today than it was during the lifetime of President Eliot. Humanitarians are at present shaping our educational policy from the elementary grades to the university. One should, however, note in passing a curious circumstance: the most thoroughgoing humanitarians — for example, our professors of pedagogy and sociology — are held in almost universal suspicion in academic circles and are not infrequently looked upon by their colleagues as downright charlatans.

What would seem especially desirable in dealing with the whole situation is a critical clarification — in other words, an attempt to penetrate beneath its surface to first principles. For example, President Eliot's attack in the name of the elective

Irving Babbitt

system on the traditional college curriculum will be found, when thus probed to the bottom, to involve a clash between a familiar type of naturalistic philosophy and the wisdom of the ages; for nothing is more certain than that this wisdom has been neither utilitarian nor sentimental, but either religious or humanistic. In exhibiting the nature of this clash it would seem well to avoid, as far as possible, dogmatic affirmation and to proceed positively, and in the sound sense of the word, psychologically. What a survey of the past actually reveals is that considerable groups of men have at various times and in various places got together on certain fundamentals — have, in short, worked out conventions. These conventions have constituted the spiritual climate, as it were, of whole historical periods. Most men in these periods no more thought of questioning the convention under which they lived than they did the very air they breathed.

Those who assert that there is no permanent core of human experience set above mere historical processes would have a stronger case if it could be shown that the main conventions that have prevailed in the past are hopelessly at odds with one another. These conventions are, to be sure, all very much implicated in the local and the relative. Yet if one considers them from the point of view of the fruits at which they aimed in life and conduct, one cannot help being struck by certain important agreements. One may illustrate almost at random from the two chief religious conventions that have obtained respectively in the East and the West — the Buddhist and the Christian.

About the middle of the third century before Christ, Asoka, the Buddhist ruler of India, had carved on rocks and pillars at various points throughout his vast empire recommendations to practice certain virtues. These virtues will be found to be nearly or quite identical with those enumerated by Saint Paul as the fruits of religion: "Love, joy, long-suffering, kindness, goodness, faith, mildness, self-control." Chinese, again, who know the Confucian books — the main source of the humanism of the

The Formal Essay

Far East — are struck at once by the substantial accord between these books and the "Ethics" of Aristotle, perhaps the most authoritative single document in the humanistic tradition of the Occident.

Moreover, one may discover an important agreement not only between different forms of humanism but between humanism and religion — the assumption, namely, that man needs to be disciplined in his natural self to some standard; that he needs, in short, in the almost literal sense of the term to undergo conversion. Though conversion always involves a facing about or turning away from the natural man, it may be conceived very differently. The Augustinian Christian, for example, conceives of it somewhat melodramatically as brought about by a sudden irruption of divine grace. For the Aristotelian, on the other hand, it is to be accomplished rather by the gradual formation from childhood of right habits. In all its forms, however, conversion implies an opposition in the heart of the individual between the expansive desires and a principle of control.

The exercise of this principle of control requires the putting forth of a special quality of effort or will. What I have termed "the wisdom of the ages" is, in short, primarily concerned with the problems of the inner life, and in its attitude toward these problems it is dualistic. The activity that it promotes is on the religious level summed up in the word "meditation." Genuine meditation involves a subordination of the natural man to a higher will — humility, in short, a word that in the present naturalistic era has almost lost its true meaning. The subordination to the higher will may, as in the more austere forms of Christianity, amount to a renunciation of the desires of the natural man. The humanist, on the other hand, is satisfied with imposing on these desires a law of measure or decorum. His program may be summed up in the word "mediation."

Religion and humanism not only come together in the idea of conversion, but one must add that if the humanist is not to run the risk of sinking to the naturalistic level, his mediation

Irving Babbitt

needs to have a certain background in meditation. One is forced finally to agree, if only on psychological grounds, with Burke that "humility is the low but deep foundation of all true virtue." It does not follow that one must accept the thesis developed by Mr. T. S. Eliot in a recent issue of *The Forum* that humanism is something precarious and parasitical and that, for Occidental man in particular, it is doomed to speedy collapse unless it has the support of dogmatic and revealed religion. The most important manifestation of humanism that the world has yet seen — that in ancient Greece — did not have any such support.

One cannot admit, however, that humanism must necessarily derive from Greece any more than one can admit that Christianity has had a monopoly of religion. In these days of universal and facile communication and of an ever-increasing closeness of material contact, it is important to do justice to the achievements — religious and humanistic — of the Far East. The tendency of M. Henri Massis, for example, in his "Defense of the West," to discover no effective source of humanistic or religious wisdom outside of the Roman Catholic Church is due in part to sectarian narrowness, in part to sheer ignorance of the facts. The reasons why the Occidental should normally associate his humanism and religion with the traditions that go back to Rome and Greece and Judea, though extremely cogent, are a matter of expediency rather than of first principles. In direct proportion as one develops the critical temper, one is forced to base one's convictions, not primarily on any tradition, but on the immediate data of consciousness.

Let us inquire, as far as possible in this critical fashion, why the religious and humanistic teachers of the past have been so concerned with the exercise of the principle of control and in general with the problems of the inner life. Perhaps one may best reply to this query by bringing together three sentences of Aristotle, a thinker who will be found to be more completely experimental than many moderns who profess to found their

[271]

The Formal Essay

whole philosophy on experiment. The three sentences are as follows: "The end is the chief thing of all"; "The end of ends is happiness"; "Happiness is a kind of working."

Aristotle has himself admonished us to give heed to the sayings of the wise men of old only in so far as they are found to coincide with the facts. If, therefore, we attach weight to Aristotle, it should not be primarily because of his traditional authority, but because Aristotle turns out to be only another name for inspired good sense.

It would seem, indeed, that if a man deals honestly with himself he must grant that no concern can be nearer to him than that of his own happiness. Aristotle's treatment of happiness is especially relevant to our present topic because of the close connection he establishes between it and his scheme of education. An education, he says, deserves to be accounted liberal only in so far as it culminates in the idea of leisure. This idea requires that all partial aims and special disciplines should be subordinated to the specifically human form of effort, or "energy,"— the source of true felicity — that is put forth in mediation and finally in the contemplative life or life of vision.

With this background in mind one should be able to grasp the nature of the conflict between the wisdom of the ages and the humanitarian "idealism" of President Eliot. Like the religious and humanistic teachers of the past, President Eliot was very much and rightly preoccupied with the problem of happiness. Like these teachers, again, he held that to be happy one needs to be active and energetic. But in his notion of the kind of activity that tends to happiness he plainly diverged from these teachers widely. According to a French authority "happiness is not an easy matter: it is difficult to find it in ourselves and impossible to find it elsewhere." President Eliot must be numbered among those who hoped to find it "elsewhere." In the addresses given on the occasion of his ninetieth birthday, he advised his hearers to avoid introspection, to "look out and not in" (one gathers from the context that he identified introspec-

Irving Babbitt

tion with the morbid brooding of the introvert). The counsel he proceeds to give seems superficially the same as that carved on stone many centuries ago by the Buddhist Asoka: "Let all joy be in effort." "Let small and great exert themselves."

The effort that President Eliot recommends, however, is outer effort — effort of the utilitarian type. The primary concern of Asoka, on the other hand, was with inner effort — the kind that is put forth in meditation. President Eliot has, of course, here as elsewhere, the merit of being highly representative. The main effort of the Occident was in his day, and still remains in ours, utilitarian. If anyone thinks that utilitarian effort is going to lead to the fruits that Asoka and Saint Paul associate with religion, he would seem to have, even more than the English country curate to whom this trait has been attributed, "a large and easy swallow."

We are here, at all events, at the parting of the ways. If one is convinced of the essential rightness of President Eliot's idea of effort, one may continue to believe that we are now moving in America toward some glorious consummation of the kind postulated by the nineteenth-century doctrine of progress. Otherwise one may rather incline to believe that we are ripening for Nemesis; for Nemesis is the penalty visited upon spiritual blindness. Blindness to the need of a form of effort radically different from that of the utilitarian would seem to be rather serious.

The crucial assumption of President Eliot appears to be that the material efficiency promoted by utilitarian effort will be used altruistically. For the traditional attempt to train for culture and character he sought to substitute, in his own phrase, "training for service and power." Power is in itself desirable provided it be employed to some adequate end. The whole issue is whether service in the humanitarian sense can supply this end. Most Americans are convinced that it not only can but does. Service has been made the basis of the gospel of Rotary and may therefore be termed our Rotarian convention.

The Formal Essay

However thoroughly we may be persuaded of the admirableness of this convention, it is well for us to keep in mind that it has been accepted only to a very limited extent by the rest of the world. In general, foreigners incline to see in our idealism, so far as it is of the humanitarian type, either hypocrisy or self-deception — usually the former. The opinion is almost universal abroad that, in our relations with other countries in particular, we are altruistic in our feelings about ourselves and imperialistic in our practice. An increasing minority of Americans are also beginning to question the "religion of service," to maintain that it is only a varnish for commercialism, and that the varnish is wearing thin.

The word "service," it should be noted, has changed its meaning in the transition from Christianity to humanitarianism. In general, the representatives of the utilitarian-sentimental movement have tended, by a tampering with general terms, to dissimulate from others and perhaps from themselves the wideness of the gap between the new dispensation and the old. I choose almost at random as an example of the tendency the following advertisement of one of our life-insurance companies: "Buddha, who was born a prince, gave up his name, succession, and his heritage to attain security. But we do not have to give up the world; we have only to see a life-insurance agent who can sell us security for the future, the most direct step to serenity of mind." The issue raised by this advertisement touches Christianity at least as closely as it does Buddhism. The "serenity" and "security" at which both religions aim are scarcely of the kind that we may purchase from the agent of a life-insurance company. The net result of this transfer of the language of religion to an entirely different order has been, from the point of view of the wisdom of the ages, to encourage an extraordinarily complacent materialism.

The alteration in the meaning of the word "service" in particular — the substitution of the service of man for the traditional service of God — has been important in its influence on

[274]

Irving Babbitt

education, because it has meant practically a more or less complete elimination of the idea of conversion. The Christian had based this idea on the dogma of original sin. The form given to this dogma by Puritans like Jonathan Edwards is no doubt highly objectionable. Unfortunately President Eliot and the humanitarians have, in their rejection of the dogma, laid themselves open to the suspicion of pouring out the baby with the bath. Not merely Puritanism but every doctrine that asserts the dual nature of man must be felt, in its relation to man's natural self, as more or less repressive.

For this repression President Eliot wished to substitute full and free expression. The elective system, which he sponsored, tends to identify the ideal needs of the individual with the mere unfolding of his temperament and idiosyncrasy. Every youth, it is assumed, has some innate gift — a gift which is treated with almost religious seriousness, and is therefore to suffer no contradiction. The effort that he puts forth along the lines of his temperamental bias will make for his own happiness and finally be pressed into the service of humanity. Aristotle evidently had in mind a different type of effort based on a different conception of happiness when he declared :

> We ought also to take into consideration our own natural bias, which varies in each man's case, and will be ascertained from the pleasure and pain arising in us. Furthermore, we should force ourselves off in the contrary direction, because we shall find ourselves in the mean after we have removed ourselves far from the wrong side, exactly as men do in straightening out a crooked stick.

What proof is there, after all, that so purely temperamental a person as President Eliot's theory tends to produce will be altruistic? The humanitarian is finally forced to fall back on some theory of man's natural goodness of the kind that is commonly associated with Rousseau, but which was anticipated in England by the third Earl of Shaftesbury. According to Shaftesbury the unconverted man is not egoistic, as religion

E   [275]

The Formal Essay

has traditionally maintained. On the contrary, he has an instinctive affection for his fellows — a will to service, as one may say.

The theory has undergone surprisingly little modification from Shaftesbury's day to this. For example, Professor John Dewey, who has probably had more influence than any other living American on education, not merely in this country but in the new China, writes that "the child is born with a *natural* desire to give out, to do, to *serve*" (my italics). Let anyone who has growing children observe them closely and decide for himself whether they exude spontaneously this eagerness for service. Let him then supplement this observation by a survey of the working of the theory on the larger scale for several generations past. He may conclude that the amount of instinctive goodness released by the decline of religious and humanistic control has been somewhat exaggerated. He may fail to find evidence that a human nature that is neither meditative nor again mediatory, that has in short dispensed with humility and decorum, is likely to prove idyllic.

The unduly idyllic hopes of the humanitarian throw light on the quality of his imagination — an important point to determine in anyone's outlook on life. President Eliot was much preoccupied with the whole question. "The training of the imagination," he says rightly, "is far the most important part of education." It can be shown not only that the quality of his own imagination was idyllic rather than ethical, but that this fact accounts for his attitude toward the problem of evil of which I spoke at the outset. He asks us to discriminate between two forms of imagination — the constructive and the receptive. He further subdivides the constructive imagination according as its constructiveness is operative in literature or in physical science. He proceeds to contrast the imaginative construction of a Dante or a Zola, where everything is gloom and disharmony, with the imaginative construction of the man of science, as displayed, for instance, in a modern power plant, where everything

Irving Babbitt

is accurate, orderly, and beneficent. President Eliot evidently regarded those writers who are concerned with the element of evil in man as morose theorists rather than as hard-headed observers of the facts. One may also note in passing that he seems unaware of the incommensurable gap separating Dante's treatment of evil from Zola's.

As examples of the receptive imagination he paints a picture of a young woman poring unprofitably over the scenes in which Thackeray portrays the "malign motives and unclean soul of Becky Sharp," and then opposes to this picture that of another young woman who spends her time observing "two robins who have established their home and family in a notch of a maple near her window" and in learning from their ways with their young lessons of unselfishness and affection. One scarcely need insist on the idyllic and sentimental view of both nature and human nature that is implied in such a contrast.

President Eliot's whole treatment of the imagination — for example, his assertion that Darwin and Pasteur have by their imaginative activity done as much to satisfy the "spiritual needs" of man as Dante, Goethe, or Shakespeare — is already "dated." As the nineteenth century, with its own special atmosphere, recedes still further into the background, the "idealism" that he and other men of his time sought to erect on naturalistic foundations is likely to appear positively fantastic. What becomes of the beneficence of the control over the forces of nature that has been secured with the aid of the scientific imagination, should it turn out that in the unconverted man — the man whose impulses are free to overflow — the will to power overflows even more freely than the will to service? The Great War has enlightened us on this point.

Once grant that the humanitarian hypothesis has broken down at the center, and the alternative would seem to be to revive in some form the dualistic conception; to reaffirm once more that the individual needs in the interest of his own happiness to submit to some sound discipline of his outgoing

The Formal Essay

desires, to put aside, in the phrase of Buddha, the ignoble for the noble craving. "The universal thirst for the enjoyments of life," says President Eliot, "grows hotter and hotter and is not assuaged." In that case, one might suppose, it is urgent that this thirst be moderated with reference to some correct scale of values. On the contrary, President Eliot makes his observation part of a plea for the putting of political economy on a level with the traditional humanities.

Political economy, for its part, will be found in all its forms — orthodox and unorthodox — to have accepted the humanitarian substitutes for the principle of control. As a result of this substitution it is still under the suspicion of being the "dismal science." The political economist looks askance at any limitation of desires on the part of the individual, envisaged primarily as a consumer, lest such a limitation should lead to a slowing down of production. Production is apparently to expand indefinitely — a program that has been summed up in the formula "Pigs for more pigs for more pigs." One is reminded of this program by the articles Henry Ford recently contributed to *The Forum*. One may be sure that he would not have set forth his philosophy of industry so confidently — one is tempted to add so naïvely — were it not for the presence in the background of really dignified figures, like President Eliot, who are at one with him on certain underlying postulates.

The discrediting of the principle of control in favor of a sheer expansiveness is in general dubious. In the educational field it is not only dubious, but, so far as it leads to a primary emphasis on innate gifts and their supposed right to expand freely, it is also utopian. Anyone whose business it has been to advise college undergraduates will testify that as a rule they are not conscious of having any such gifts. They are determined most frequently in the choice of their life work by chance or necessity, and then become interested in this work in the very process of performing it. To be sure, an occasional student has, or seems to have, some inborn aptitude. It goes without saying that the

[278]

Irving Babbitt

humanist does not seek to thwart such aptitudes. He does, however, insist that its possessor needs supplementary training if he is not to become a lopsided specialist.

On his initial assumption that most students have instinctive bents that they are eager to follow, President Eliot bases the further assumption that effort does not need to be stimulated, as it was in the older education, by competition. His assertion that "lazy students are more likely to get roused from their lethargy under an elective system than under a required" is not confirmed by realistic observation. If the average student today is more interested in football than in things of the mind, one reason may be that football, unlike the college as it has become under the new education, has a definite goal and is frankly competitive with reference to it.

It is estimated that about three quarters of a million students are now enrolled in our institutions of higher learning, — more than in all other countries combined. At the same time the very idea of liberal education is in danger of perishing in America in the midst of a great bewilderment. It would not be fair to make President Eliot alone responsible for this confusion. His exaltation of the variable over the constant elements in human nature, has, however, been a contributing factor. "Every youth of eighteen is," he says, "an infinitely complex organization the duplicate of which neither does nor ever will exist." This dangerous half-truth, when made the foundation of a system of education, is simply incompatible with the survival of religious and humanistic standards.

We seem to be witnessing today the consequences of a weakening of standards. According to M. André Siegfried we are making a ruthless sacrifice of the higher cultural values to mass production and material efficiency. According to Mr. Charles Merz, in his good-natured satire, "The Great American Band Wagon," the spectacle offered by contemporary America is that of a multitude of essentially trivial people rushing restlessly from one inconsequential fad to another. Such pictures

The Formal Essay

are no doubt one-sided, but that there is in America a drift toward standardized mediocrity is indubitable. It is also indubitable that our education as a whole is not supplying the proper corrective.

How many of our college graduates, for example, are capable of leisure in the Aristotelian sense? It is notorious that the psychology of these graduates in their moments of release from merely vocational activity is indistinguishable from that of the tired business man; nay more, the psychology of college and university teachers themselves, including teachers of the traditional humanities, is, when they are not working as specialists, likely to be that of the tired business man. In the absence of humane purpose what has triumphed is the purpose of the utilitarian. A multitude of specialties, all viewed very much on the same level, has taken the place not only of the selection of studies in the old curriculum but of the selective principle itself. Education has become increasingly miscellaneous and encyclopedic.

The momentous nature of the change from the old to the new has been dissimulated under the blanket degree. This dissimulation has amounted at times to virtual dishonesty. A man wishes to enjoy the prestige of the traditional A.B. while dodging the discipline that this degree has traditionally represented. He wishes, for example, to elect a course on "The killing, trussing, and marketing of fowl" (I quote from the catalogue of one of our state institutions) and at the same time to pass as liberally educated.

Comparatively few Americans are likely to share the doubts I have been expressing about the humanitarian revolution in the theory and practice of education. The idea of service proclaimed by President Eliot and put at the basis of our Rotarian convention has not as yet been seriously shaken. Nevertheless there are signs that the utilitarian-sentimental movement has passed its crest even in America. An increasing number of persons are feeling disquiet at the sapping of the sense of moral

[280]

Irving Babbitt

responsibility by the sentimentalists. Others still more numerous are beginning to see that the utilitarian idea of effort is one-sided and that, as a result of this one-sidedness, modern life is in danger of degenerating into a wild rush one knows not whither. The complaint is, in fact, growing fairly common that "things are in the saddle," that we are being mechanized both outwardly in our acts and inwardly in our minds — that we are, in short, in a way to become "robots." Even a Sherwood Anderson has enough wit to perceive that all is not well with the present standardized America.

Unfortunately laments about the evils of standardization are not, unless supported by a sound constructive program, of much avail. If all that is needed is to scoff at the Rotarian convention and the "religion of service," writers like Mr. Mencken and Mr. Sinclair Lewis would seem to meet every requirement. These writers can be shown, however, to be a part of the very malady they are assailing. This malady may be defined as a refusal to recognize any norm or human law that acts restrictively on the free expansion of temperament.

Anyone who has made a study of the modern movement from the eighteenth century down will finally become convinced of the futility of a merely temperamental insurrection against convention. Whether the temperamentalist be of the soft or sentimental variety, or, like Mr. Mencken and his followers, of the hard or Nietzschean brand, is comparatively immaterial. The objection to the Rotarian convention is not that it is a convention — that is rather its strength — but that a dubious element has been built into its foundations; namely, an idea of service that does not seem a sufficient counterpoise to the "lusts" of the natural man. In the language of religion the Rotarian hopes to achieve salvation without conversion.

The effective opposition to the Rotarian is likely to come not from Bohemians, each flying off on his own temperamental tangent, but from persons who are getting together on an entirely different basis, who see that the pathway of escape from

The Formal Essay

standardization is not through ideals as currently conceived, but through standards, and that to get standards one will need to insist on the specifically human elements in man that have been eliminated by the naturalists. How complete this elimination has been may be seen in practically all forms of recent psychology. The behaviorists in particular, with Mr. J. B. Watson at their head, are in this matter sinking to depths previously unplumbed.

The person who refuses to accept pseudo-science or any other substitute for standards still has to decide whether he is to secure his standards in a critical or a purely traditional way. The Roman Catholic, for example, gets his standards in this latter way. If anyone desires to proceed more critically, he will then be confronted with what is known in Platonic language as the problem of the One and the Many. He will, in other words, have to choose between a surrender to the naturalistic flux and the assertion of a something in man that transcends it.

Periods of more or less complete emancipation from the past, which therefore have to get their standards, if at all, in terms of the One and the Many, have always proved crucial. There is evidence that we have already reached this crucial stage in our own development, and that we are taking the wrong turning. Pragmatism — the philosophy with which America has come to be associated in the eyes of the world — is from either a religious or humanistic point of view, raw and uncivilized. The difficulty with the pragmatist is not his preference for what works, but his one-sided notion of working — his failure to take account of the form of working that is, according to Aristotle, necessary if one is to achieve happiness. The reason why this one-sidedness should prevail in America more than elsewhere is obvious. The utilitarian form of effort has been especially needful in our conquest of a continent. Having developed in fullest measure the virtues of the pioneer, we are now in danger of becoming the victims of them.

Irving Babbitt

We should, however, be careful not to exaggerate the gap in this respect between America and other countries. Other countries are now lamenting the evils of "Americanism" and at the same time getting themselves Americanized as fast as they conveniently can. It may be that if there is to be any effective reaction from Americanism it will have to come from America itself. We cannot allege as an excuse for the utilitarian excess, as various other countries can with some plausibility, the pressure of economic necessity. So far as economic conditions are concerned, we are free to develop the idea of leisure as something distinct from either idleness or recreation; to show ourselves the "people of action" in a sense quite different from that given to the phrase by the utilitarians. The idea of leisure is in itself so important that if we did develop it adequately we might be in a position to assume the cultural leadership of the world. It is depressing that we are showing so little grasp of the situation, that our higher education, in particular, so far from aiming to produce the man of leisure, is being more and more completely dominated by the "ideals" of the humanitarian.

I have said that if one is to achieve standards in opposition to these ideals, — at least in a modern and critical fashion, — one will have to face finally the philosophical problem of the One and the Many. It should be added, however, that quite apart from the solution of this difficult problem, common sense will go far in uncovering the defects of the new education and in devising a remedy. There is probably even now a minority of shrewd observers who are ready to get together on a basis different from that of the reigning educational convention, to give adequate support to at least a few institutions of learning that are in their underlying spirit humanistic rather than humanitarian. It is just at this point that it may be possible to resist successfully the stupid drift toward standardization.

The question should be of special interest to the smaller colleges. With these colleges sound educational practice may be

The Formal Essay

found to coincide with self-interest. The new education requires an enormously elaborate and expensive apparatus. This elaborateness is encouraged by the prime emphasis of the utilitarian on the progress of humanity through the coöperation of a multitude of specialists, as well as by the prime emphasis of the sentimentalist on innate gifts and their right to gratification. The small college that accepts the department-store conception of education is at once put at a hopeless disadvantage. The humanistic college, on the other hand, even though its needs can no longer be fitly symbolized by Mark Hopkins at the end of the traditional log, may hope to flourish with a much more modest equipment.

Most of the heads of our institutions of learning, great and small, have been content for a generation and more to follow in the wake of President Eliot. The present need seems to be for educational leaders whose first aim is quality: quality in the teaching body; quality in the students; above all, quality in the subjects taught. The college must substitute selection for encyclopedic inclusiveness if it is to have a definite goal and concomitantly to witness a wholesome revival of the spirit of emulation. It is not to be supposed, however, that the reasons why certain subjects deserve to be preferred to others in a scheme of liberal training are arbitrary in the sense that the rules of football are more or less arbitrary. These reasons are, on the contrary, deeply rooted in the facts of history and human nature.

At the bottom of the whole educational debate, as I have been trying to show, is the opposition between a religious-humanistic and a utilitarian-sentimental philosophy. This opposition, involving as it does first principles, is not subject to compromise or mediation. Those who attempt such mediation are not humanists but Laodiceans. Many persons who deem themselves moderate are, in fact, only muddled. Hence the need I have already pointed out of critical clarification. The dis-

Irving Babbitt

criminations I have been attempting will not be in vain if even a few are led thereby to abandon the Laodicean attitude and to take sides on issues that involve finally the future of American civilization. It will be found to be no small matter whether our higher education is to have enshrined at its center the idea of leisure in Aristotle's sense or the idea of service in the sense given to the word by President Eliot and the humanitarians.

DANIEL DEFOE

[1659?–1731]

THE INSTABILITY OF HUMAN GLORY[1]

Sir, I have employed myself of late pretty much in the study of history, and have been reading the stories of the great men of past ages, Alexander the Great, Julius Cæsar, the great Augustus, and many more down, down, down, to the still greater Louis XIV, and even to the still greatest John, Duke of Marlborough. In my way I met with Tamerlane the Scythian, Tomornbejus the Egyptian, Solyman the Magnificent, and others of the Mahometan or Ottoman race; and after all the great things they have done I find it said of them all, one after another, AND THEN HE DIED, all dead, dead, dead! *Hic jacet*[2] is the finishing part of their history. Some lie in the bed of honor, and some in honor's truckle bed; some were bravely slain in battle on the field of honor, some in the storm of a counterscarp and died in the ditch of honor; some here, some there; the bones of the bold and the brave, the cowardly and the base, the hero and the scoundrel, are heaped up together; there they lie in oblivion, and under the ruins of the earth, undistinguished from one another, nay, even from the common earth.

> Huddled in dirt the blust'ring engine lies,
> That was so great, and thought himself so wise.

How many hundreds of thousands of the bravest fellows then in the world lie on heaps in the ground, whose bones are to this

---

[1] This editorial essay, addressed as a letter to the editor, appeared in *Applebee's Journal*, July 21, 1722, shortly after the death of the famous English general, the Duke of Marlborough.

[2] "Here [he] lies" (a common inscription on old tombs).

Daniel Defoe

day plowed up by the rustics or dug up by the laborer, and the earth their more noble vital parts are converted to has been perhaps applied to the meanest uses!

How have we screened the ashes of heroes to make our mortar, and mingled the remains of a Roman general to build a hogsty! Where are the ashes of a Cæsar, and the remains of a Pompey, a Scipio, or a Hannibal? All are vanished, they and their very monuments are moldered into earth, their dust is lost, and their place knows them no more. They live only in the immortal writings of their historians and poets, the renowned flatterers of the age they lived in, and who have made us think of the persons, not as they really were, but as they were pleased to represent them.

As the greatest men, so even the longest lived. The Methuselahs of the antediluvian world, the accounts of them all end with the same. Methuselah lived nine hundred sixty and nine years and begat sons and daughters—and what then? AND THEN HE DIED.

> Death like an overflowing stream
> Sweeps us away; our life's a dream.

We are now solemnizing the obsequies of the great Marlborough; all his victories, all his glories, his great projected schemes of war, his uninterrupted series of conquests, which are called his, as if he alone had fought and conquered by his arm what so many men obtained for him with their blood — all is ended, where other men, and, indeed, where all men ended: HE IS DEAD!

Not all his immense wealth, the spoils and trophies of his enemies, the bounty of his grateful mistress, and the treasure amassed in war and peace, not all that mighty bulk of gold — which some suggest is such, and so great, as I care not to mention — could either give him life or continue it one moment, but he is dead; and some say the great treasure he was possessed of here had one strange particular quality attending it, which might have been very dissatisfying to him if he had considered much on it; namely, that he could not carry much of it with him.

The Formal Essay

We have now nothing left us of this great man that we can converse with but his monument and his history. He is now numbered among things past. The funeral as well as the battles of the Duke of Marlborough are like to adorn our houses in sculpture as things equally gay and to be looked on with pleasure. Such is the end of human glory, and so little is the world able to do for the greatest men that come into it, and for the greatest merit those men can arrive to.

What then is the work of life? What the business of great men, that pass the stage of the world in seeming triumph as these men we call heroes have done? Is it to grow great in the mouth of fame and take up many pages in history? Alas! that is no more than making a tale for the reading of posterity till it turns into fable and romance. Is it to furnish subject to the poets, and live in their immortal rimes, as they call them? That is, in short, no more than to be hereafter turned into ballad and song and be sung by old women to quiet children, or at the corner of a street to gather crowds in aid of the pickpocket and the [poor]. Or is their business rather to add virtue and piety to their glory, which alone will pass them into eternity and make them truly immortal? What is glory without virtue? A great man without religion is no more than a great beast without a soul. What is honor without merit? And what can be called true merit but that which makes a person be a good man as well as a great man?

If we believe in a future state of life, a place for the rewards of good men and for the punishment of the haters of virtue, how [many] heroes and famous men crowd in among the last! How few crowned heads wear the crowns of immortal felicity!

Let no man envy the great and glorious men, as we call them! Could we see them now, how many of them would move our pity rather than call for our congratulations! These few thoughts, sir, I send to prepare your readers' minds when they go to see the magnificent funeral of the late Duke of Marlborough.

WILLIAM ALLEN WHITE

[1868-   ]

TO AN ANXIOUS FRIEND[1]

You tell me that law is above freedom of utterance. And I reply that you can have no wise laws nor free enforcement of wise laws unless there is free expression of the wisdom of the people — and, alas, their folly with it. But if there is freedom, folly will die of its own poison, and the wisdom will survive. That is the history of the race. It is the proof of man's kinship with God. You say that freedom of utterance is not for time of stress, and I reply with the sad truth that only in time of stress is freedom of utterance in danger. No one questions it in calm days, because it is not needed. And the reverse is true also; only when free utterance is suppressed is it needed, and when it is needed, it is most vital to justice. Peace is good. But if you are interested in peace through force and without free discussion — that is to say, free utterance decently and in order — your interest in justice is slight. And peace without justice is tyranny, no matter how you may sugar-coat it with expediency. This state today is in more danger from suppression than from violence, because in the end suppression leads to violence.

[1] From White's "The Editor and his People." Copyright, 1924, by The Macmillan Company. Reprinted by permission. First published in the *Emporia Gazette*, July 27, 1922, when the author's intimate friend, Governor Henry Allen of Kansas, had caused him to be arrested for allowing striking workers to put a card in the *Gazette* window, stating their position, in violation of the Industrial Court law. The case against White was dropped and the law repealed.

Similarly, it was in prison that Defoe (see page 286) wrote "A Hymn to the Pillory," an impassioned plea for freedom of speech.

The Formal Essay

Violence, indeed, is the child of suppression. Whoever pleads for justice helps to keep the peace; and whoever tramples upon the plea for justice temperately made in the name of peace only outrages peace and kills something fine in the heart of man which God put there when he got our manhood. When that is killed, brute meets brute on each side of the line.

So, dear friend, put fear out of your heart. This nation will survive, this state will prosper, the orderly business of life will go forward if only men can speak in whatever way given them to utter what their hearts hold — by voice, by posted card, by letter, or by press. Reason never has failed men. Only force and repression have made the wrecks in the world.

Bibliography

The essay has received much less attention as a type of literature than either the drama or the novel; consequently it will be found most satisfactory in many instances, especially in studying the formal essayists of the nineteenth century, to make use of the collected writings of individual authors and general works on the literature of the period.

In the list which follows some books which contain helpful bibliographies are starred. No attempt has been made to give a complete list of all the more recent collections of essays, especially of those by contemporary writers.

GENERAL WORKS OF REFERENCE

*Cambridge History of American Literature (4 vols.). Putnam, 1917–1921.

*Cambridge History of English Literature (15 vols.). Putnam, 1907–1927.

Catalogue of the British Museum.

Catalogue of the Library of Congress.

*CUNLIFFE, J. W. English Literature during the Last Half-Century (Revised Edition). Macmillan, 1923.

Dictionary of National Biography (with supplements, 70 vols.). Oxford University Press, 1885–1921.

*Encyclopædia Britannica (Fourteenth Edition). 1929.

*LEISY, E. E. American Literature, an Interpretative Survey. Crowell, 1929.

*MANLY, J. M., and RICKERT, E. Contemporary American Literature (revised by F. B. Millett). Harcourt, Brace, 1929.

*MANLY, J. M., and RICKERT, E. Contemporary British Literature (Revised Edition). Harcourt, Brace, 1928.

*PATTEE, F. L. A History of American Literature since 1870. Century, 1915.

Reader's Guide to Periodical Literature.

*SHERAN, W. H. Handbook of Literary Criticism. Noble, 1905.

Bibliography

VAN DOREN, C., and VAN DOREN, M. American and British Literature since 1890. Century, 1925.
Who's Who.
Who's Who in America.

GENERAL WORKS ON THE ESSAY

BINKLEY, H. C. Essays and Letter-Writing (in *Publications of the Modern Language Association of America*, Vol. XLI). 1926.
*CONWAY, A. M. The Essay in American Literature. New York University Press, 1914.
*CROTHERS, S. M. The Modern Essay. American Library Association, Chicago, 1926.
*GRAHAM, B. Essays and Letters (in her "Bookman's Manual," third edition). Bowker, 1929.
*HORTON, M. L. Viewpoints in Essays. American Library Association, Chicago, 1922.
MABIE, H. W. Essay and Criticism (in "Counsel upon the Reading of Books," by H. M. Stephens and others). Houghton Mifflin, 1900.
MARY ELEANORE, SISTER. The Literary Essay in English. Ginn, 1923.
MOULTON, R. G. Literary Organs of Personality: Essays and Lyrics (in his "World Literature and its Place in General Culture"). Macmillan, 1911.
SMITH, A. On the Writing of Essays (in his "Dreamthorp"). Edinburgh, 1863.
*UPHAM, A. H. The Typical Forms of English Literature. Oxford University Press, 1917.
WALKER, H. The English Essay and Essayists. Dutton, 1915.
WHITMORE, C. A. The Field of the Essay (in *Publications of the Modern Language Association of America*, Vol. XXXVI). 1921.
WILLIAMS, O. The Essay. Doran, 1914.
WINCHESTER, C. T. A Group of English Essayists of the Early Nineteenth Century. Macmillan, 1910.
WYLIE, L. J. Social Studies in English Literature. Houghton Mifflin, 1916.

GENERAL COLLECTIONS OF ESSAYS

Adventures in Essay Reading. Selected by Members of the Department of Rhetoric and Journalism of the University of Michigan. Harcourt, Brace, 1924.
ALDEN, R. W. (Editor). Essays, English and American (revised by Robert M. Smith). Scott, Foresman, 1927.

[292]

Bibliography

BREWER, D. J. (Editor). Crowned Masterpieces of Literature that have advanced Civilization, as preserved in the World's Best Essays, from the Earliest Period to the Present Time (10 vols.). F. P. Kaiser, St. Louis, 1908.

BROWN, S. (Editor). Essays of Our Times. Scott, Foresman, 1928.

CHAMBERLAIN, E. (Editor). Essays Old and New. Harcourt, Brace, 1926.

CODY, S. (Editor). A Selection of the Best English Essays illustrative of the History of English Prose Style. McClurg (no date).

DICKINSON, T. H., and ROE, F. W. (Editors). Nineteenth Century English Prose. American Book Co., 1908.

ELIOT, C. W. (Editor). English Essays from Sir Philip Sidney to Macaulay, Harvard Classics, Vol. XXVII. Collier, about 1910.

FUESS, C. M. (Editor). Selected Essays. Houghton Mifflin, 1914.

HALE, E. E. (Editor). American Essays. World Book Co. (no date).

HALE, E. E. (Editor). English Essays. World Book Co. (no date).

*HASTINGS, W. W., and MASON, K. O. (Editors). Essays from Five Centuries. Houghton Mifflin, 1929.

HEYDRICK, B. A. (Editor). Types of the Essay. Scribner, 1921.

LAW, F. H. (Editor). Modern Essays and Stories. Century, 1922.

LOBBAN, J. H. (Editor). English Essays. Scribner, 1909.

LODGE, H. C. (Editor). The Best of the World's Classics (10 vols.). Funk and Wagnalls, about 1909.

MAKOWER, S. V., and BLACKWELL, B. H. (Editors). A Book of English Essays (1600–1900). Oxford University Press, 1924.

MANCHESTER, F. A., and GIESE, W. F. (Editors). Harper's Anthology: Prose. Harper, 1926.

MATTHEWS, B. (Editor). The Oxford Book of American Essays. Oxford University Press, 1914.

MORLEY, C. (Editor). Modern Essays (First and Second Series). Harcourt, Brace, 1921, 1924.

PEACOCK, W. (Editor). Selected English Essays. Oxford University Press, 1903.

PEACOCK, W., and WHEELER, C. B. (Editors). English Essays, Bacon to Stevenson. Oxford University Press (no date).

*PENCE, R. W. (Editor). Essays by Present-Day Writers. Macmillan, 1924.

POTTINGER, D. T. (Editor). English Essays. Macmillan, 1917.

PRITCHARD, F. H. (Editor). Essays of Today. Little, Brown, 1924.

PRITCHARD, F. H. (Editor). From Confucius to Mencken; the Trend of the World's Best Thought as expressed by Famous Writers of All Time. Harper, 1929.

Bibliography

Prose Masterpieces from Modern Essayists (3 vols.). Putnam, 1915.
KEILLY, J. J. (Editor). Masters of Nineteenth Century Prose. Ginn, 1930.
RHYS, E. (Editor). Modern English Essays (5 vols.). Dutton, 1922.
RHYS, E., and VAUGHAN, L. (Editors). A Century of English Essays. Everyman's Library No. 653, Dutton (no date).
Selected Modern Essays. Oxford University Press, 1925.
SHEPARD, O. (Editor). Essays of 1925. E. V. Mitchell, Hartford, Connecticut, 1926.
STARKWEATHER, C. C. (Editor). Essays of American Essayists.
STARKWEATHER, C. C. (Editor). Essays of British Essayists (2 vols.).
STARKWEATHER, C. C. (Editor). Essays of French, German, and Italian Essayists (All in "The World's Greatest Literature"). Collier, 1900.
TAYLOR, W. (Editor). Essays of the Past and Present. Harper, 1927.
TAYLOR, W. (Editor). Representative English Essays. Harper, 1923.
*WANN, L. (Editor). Century Readings in the English Essay. Century, 1926.
WINCHESTER, C. T. (Editor). Book of English Essays. Holt, 1914.

THE APHORISTIC ESSAY; THE CHARACTERS

ALDINGTON, R. (Editor). A Book of Characters. Dutton, 1924.
BALDWIN, E. C. The Relation of the English "Character" to its Greek Prototype (in *Publications of the Modern Language Association of America*, Vol. XVIII). 1903.
BALDWIN, E. C. The Relation of the Seventeenth-Century Character to the Periodical Essay (in *Publications of the Modern Language Association of America*, Vol. XIX). 1904.
BALDWIN, E. C. Marivaux's Place in the Development of Character Portrayal (in *Publications of the Modern Language Association of America*, Vol. XXVII). 1912.
BALDWIN, E. C. The "Character" in Restoration Comedy (in *Publications of the Modern Language Association of America*, Vol. XXX). 1915.
MACDONALD, W. L. Beginnings of the English Essay. University of Toronto Studies, 1914.
MORLEY, H. Character Writings of the Seventeenth Century. The Carisbrooke Library, London, 1891.
THOMPSON, E. N. S. The Seventeenth-Century English Essay. University of Iowa Humanistic Series, Vol. III, No. 3, 1926.
*ZEITLIN, J. (Editor). Seventeenth Century Essays, from Bacon to Clarendon. Scribner, about 1926.

Bibliography

THE PERIODICAL ESSAY

CHALMERS, A. (Editor). The British Essayists (45 vols.). (The most important single collection of periodical essays.) London, 1803 and subsequent editions.

*CRANE, R. S., and KAYE, F. B. A Census of British Newspapers and Periodicals, 1620–1800 (in *Studies in Philology*, University of North Carolina, Vol. XXIV). 1927.

DOBSON, A. (Editor). Eighteenth Century Essays. Appleton (no date).

DOBSON, A. (Editor). Steele: Selections from the *Tatler, Spectator*, and *Guardian* (Second Edition). Oxford University Press, 1896.

GRAHAM, W. (Editor). Selections from the *Tatler*, the *Spectator*, and their Successors. Nelson, 1928.

HAZLITT, W. On the Periodical Essayists (in his "Lectures on the English Comic Writers"). London, 1819.

LEWIS, L. The Advertisements of the *Spectator*. Houghton Mifflin, 1909.

MARR, G. S. The Periodical Essayists of the Eighteenth Century. Appleton, 1924.

The Spectator. Edited by G. A. Aitken; in 8 vols. Nimmo, London, 1898.

The Spectator. Edited by G. G. Smith; in 8 vols. Dent, London, 1897–1898.

The Tatler. Edited by G. A. Aitken; in 4 vols. Duckworth, London, 1898–1899.

WENDELL, B., and GREENOUGH, C. N. (Editors). Selections from the Writings of Joseph Addison. Ginn, 1905.

THE FAMILIAR ESSAY

[The familiar essay is more fully represented in the sections on General Works on the Essay and General Collections of Essays.]

Atlantic Classics (First and Second Series). (Essays reprinted from the *Atlantic Monthly*.) Little, Brown (no date).

BRYAN, W. F., and CRANE, R. S. (Editors). The English Familiar Essay. Ginn, 1916.

CHASE, M. E., and MACGREGOR, M. E. (Editors). The Writing of Informal Essays. Holt, 1928.

HICKS, P. M. The Development of the Natural History Essay in American Literature. University of Pennsylvania thesis, 1924.

SHELLEY, P. VAN D. The Familiar Essay (in University of Pennsylvania Lectures, Vol. IV). 1917.

TANNER, W. M. (Editor). Essays and Essay-Writing. Little, Brown, 1917.

TANNER, W. M., and TANNER, D. B. (Editors). Modern Familiar Essays. Little, Brown, 1927.

[295]

Bibliography

THE FORMAL ESSAY

ALDEN, R. M. (Editor). Critical Essays of the Early Nineteenth Century. Scribner, 1921.

CAMPBELL, O. J., and GINGERICH, S. F. (Editors). Critical Essays on Poetry, Drama, and Fiction. Wahr (Ann Arbor), 1924.

COLLINS, J. C. (Editor). Critical Essays and Literary Fragments. (From Arber's "English Garner.") Dutton (no date).

DURHAM, W. H. Critical Essays of the Eighteenth Century, 1700-1725. Yale University Press, 1915.

FOERSTER, N., MANCHESTER, F. A., and YOUNG, K. Essays for College Men (First and Second Series). Holt, 1913, 1915.

JONES, E. D. English Critical Essays (Nineteenth Century). Oxford University Press, 1916.

KURTZ, B. P., and Others. Essays in Exposition. Ginn, 1914.

McLAUGHLIN, E. T. Literary Criticism for Students, selected from English Essays. Holt, 1893.

ROE, F. W. (Editor). Nineteenth Century English Prose: Early Essayists. Harcourt, Brace, 1923.

SAMPSON, G. Nineteenth Century Essays. Macmillan (no date).

SMITH, C. A. Essays on Current Themes. Ginn, 1923.

SMITH, G. G. Elizabethan Critical Essays (2 vols.). Oxford University Press (no date).

SPINGARN, J. E. Critical Essays of the Seventeenth Century (3 vols.). Oxford University Press (no date).

STEEVES, H. R., and RISTINE, F. H. Representative Essays in Modern Thought. American Book Co., 1913.

Transactions of the Royal Society of Literature of the United Kingdom, London, 1829 to date. (Since 1921 issued with the title "Essays by Divers Hands" etc.)

Index of Authors, Titles, and Types

Index of Authors, Titles, and Types